读易应用型本科系列教材

国际贸易实务双语教程

A Bilingual Textbook of Import and Export

主　编　王小娟
副主编　刘　伟
编　委　杨　越　刘　旻　李改梅
插　图　陈　思

对外经济贸易大学出版社
中国·北京

图书在版编目（CIP）数据

国际贸易实务双语教程：汉英对照 / 王小娟主编.
—北京：对外经济贸易大学出版社，2023.3
读易应用型本科系列教材
ISBN 978-7-5663-2406-1

Ⅰ.①国… Ⅱ.①王… Ⅲ.①国际贸易–贸易实务–双语教学–高等学校–教材 Ⅳ.①F740.4

中国版本图书馆 CIP 数据核字（2022）第 112010 号

国际贸易实务双语教程
A Bilingual Textbook of Import and Export

王小娟　主编
责任编辑：谭利彬

出版发行：对外经济贸易大学出版社	邮政编码：100029
社　　址：北京市朝阳区惠新东街 10 号	邮购电话：010－64492338
网　　址：www.uibep.com	发行部电话：010－64492342
资源网址：www.uibepresources.com	E-mail：uibep@126.com

成品尺寸：185mm×260mm	印　　刷：北京市泰锐印刷有限责任公司
印　　张：18	版　　次：2023 年 3 月北京第 1 版
字　　数：404 千字	印　　次：2023 年 3 月第 1 次印刷
ISBN 978-7-5663-2406-1	定　　价：59.00 元

前　言

笔者担任商务英语学科多门课程的教学 17 年，发现国际贸易双语教材较为缺乏，在使用过程中发现以下问题：

第一，一本国际贸易双语教材应该了解国际惯例和术语，但国内外对“国际贸易”概念的理解不同。我国业界和高校课程中所称的“国际贸易”，有时指国际贸易理论研究，有时指国际贸易实务操作。而受我国经济发展阶段及产业政策的影响，人们口中的“国际贸易实务”往往只是对国际贸易的一种狭义理解，即进出口实务，而且是货物贸易的进出口实务，没有过多关注服务贸易。实际上，国际贸易既包括理论研究也包括实务操作，既包括货物贸易，也包括服务贸易。英语文献中“international trade”主题下的教材，主要研究国际贸易理论，而我国所关注的“国际贸易实务”领域在英文文献或教材中似乎并不置于“international trade”主题之下，而置于“import and export”主题之下，且因实务活动的综合性，甚至散落于“international logistics”“international payments”和“international law”等主题之下。因此，应注意国内外关于“国际贸易”概念理解方面的差异给我们学习和研究造成的影响。

第二，由于贸易商们须在不同国家间按统一的规则进行交易，国际贸易实务中几乎每个阶段都受到国内外法律、法规、惯例、公约或条约的约束，可以说它们指导着进出口的每一个环节。因此有的教材直接采取“拿来主义”，将法律条文直接用作教材语言，这种做法容易造成教材枯燥，可读性和趣味性较低。此外，法律条文都是在司法实践基础上的成文条例，从实践到法律，存在由因到果的逻辑关系。而直接采用法律条文语言撰写教材的后果是颠倒了学习者由因到果的自然认知顺序，使得学生只知法律如此规定，但却不知为何如此规定，知其然而不知其所以然。对于商务英语专业学生而言尤其如此，因为他们并不具有国际贸易领域的许多先导性知识。对于如此编写的教材，学生理解效率不高，不利于培养学生灵活应变、举一反三的能力。

第三，国际贸易实务中许多时候需要同时掌握中英文术语和表述。因此，单一的汉语或英文教材都不能达到此要求，这呼唤着双语教材的诞生。双语教材如何编写和呈现，需要考虑学习者认知心理等多方面的问题。例如，仅以教材的排版为例，这是一个多媒体问题，因为教材也是一种多媒体呈现，因此需要掌握多媒体学习理论，这属于认知心理学的分支。

本教材主要以认知心理学中的认知负荷理论为指导进行编写。认知负荷理论认为，人的记忆可分为工作记忆和长时记忆。工作记忆是将新知识、新信息向长时记忆转化时的暂存通道，可类比电脑的内存。工作记忆的特殊性是其容量是有限的，一定时间内信息量过多，工作记忆认知负荷过重，就无法有效学习了，正如电脑打开的程序过多，就会死机。认知负荷理论将人脑在学习时承担的负荷分为三种：内在认知负荷、外在认知负荷和关联认知负荷。内在认知负荷是学习对象本身所包含的负荷，本身无法改变，而且学习对象要素越多，要素之间的关系越复杂，内在认知负荷越高。外在认知负荷是由学习材料的呈现方式带来的工作记忆负荷，可以通过改善呈现方式而减小。而关联认知负荷是指人脑为了在长时记忆中建立永久图式而做出努力时所承受的认知负荷，在工作记忆总负荷不超载的情况下，增加一些关联认知负荷是有利于学习的。在认知负荷理论基础上发展起来的多媒体学习理论认为，知识或新信息可以以语词或画面的方式呈现，语词和画面相邻呈现会有助于学习。如果相隔较远呈现，则人脑就需要在工作记忆中一边暂存语词，一边耗费工作记忆的容量去寻求语词和画面之间的匹配。例如，将这一理论应用在双语教材的排版方面，会发现以英文为正文以中文为附录的排版方式由于中英双语相隔较远，而本课程中的许多术语或表达，学习者又必须同时掌握中英双语，这就容易造成学习者短时间内耗费大量脑力不断在英文与中文之间进行搜寻和匹配，从而对工作记忆造成较大负荷，降低学习效率。那么英汉逐段对照如何呢？这种方式似乎也没有必要，因为对于我国大学生而言，绝大部分学生不可能每一句英文都看不懂，多数情况下，他们只是部分词汇或句子看不懂。过多的中文反而会干扰阅读英文的学习效率。这一点也为认知负荷理论所证实。认知负荷理论研究证实，某些信息能够提高新手的学习效率，而对熟练者却会起到干扰作用，实际构成冗余信息。因此本教材在清晰定位目标读者的前提下，采用了部分双语的形式，仅对可能造成目标读者阅读障碍的重点词汇、术语或表达进行了中文标注。

此外，本教材也以文学创作中的叙事视角理论为指导，降低认知负荷，提高教材的“读者友好性”。国际贸易实务环节涉及角色众多，包括出口商、进口商、政府部门、物流公司和银行等角色。大多数教材同时讲述进口和出口，实际上无意识下采用了全局视角，在如此众多角色参与的情况下，时而讲述出口商的责任、义务，时而又讲述进口商的责任、义务，很容易造成学习者混淆自己的立场，产生“我到底需要干什么”的困惑。本教材摒弃全局视角，采用第二人称作为主人称视角，首先仅从出口商角度探讨，通过第 1 到第 13 章内容讲解出口流程，之后再仅从进口商角度通过一章内容（第 14 章）简要介绍进口流程，使得学习者立场明确，思路清晰。最后在第 15 章跨境电商一章综合了进出口双方立场，结束教材。由于第二人称天然地存在于对话中，因此，教材呈现的是一种与读者对话的口吻，通过主人称“you”与附属人称“I”和“we”与读者实现对话，给学习者一种友好的体验——“读者友好性”。此外，第二人称下假设读者是一位出口商或进口商，可以增强知识点的情景带入感。认知心理学研究也发现，当让读者设身处地去感受学习对象时，学习效果较好。

此外，这本教材还努力做到以下几点：

1. 沟通学术与实务，努力从实务界汲取知识，争取解决某些理论到实践的“最后一公里问题”，使学生学了就可以上手。本教材编写团队有三名教师具有外贸企业或外资企业工作经验，其中一名教师具有 10 年以上大型外贸企业工作经验。

2. 语言尽量做到通俗化，在不失准确性的前提下尽量避免法律性枯燥语言直接进入教材，尽量采用日常语言。

3. 在讲述知识点时，注重因果关系的阐释，使学生知其然知其所以然，提高学生的理解效率和举一反三的能力。

4. 教材从始至终，用一个大案例贯穿，避免知识点零散化，实现学习者对一笔交易的整体认知。

5. 关注 *Incoterms 2020* 对 *Incoterms 2010* 的变化，在教材及练习中都涉及相关知识点。

6. 关注新型冠状病毒感染疫情对国际贸易的影响，如检验、不可抗力，增强学生学以致用的能力。

7. 练习丰富新颖，题型包括判断、选择、案例、计算、实践。针对重点难点精心设计，使学生在思考中充分巩固重点难点。全部练习基于 *Incoterms 2020* 进行设计。（a）本书配套 PPT 课件。课后客观题同时制作成雨课堂试卷，可实现自动批阅，方便教师核算学生平时成绩。如有需要，请扫二维码观看使用说明进行操作。另外，本书配有包含案例和计算的小型题集，请登录出版社资源网（http://www.uibepresources.com）下载。（b）练习注重合作学习，使学生在合作学习中实现深度思考，同时帮助教师减轻批阅大量作业的繁重负担。（c）案例情景化，有助于联想。（d）关注产业升级换代，提高学生学习兴趣。（e）关注内陆地区外贸实践，启发学生关注内陆地区外贸前景，增强内陆地区学生服务家乡的能力。

需要说明的是，教材和练习中所有企业名称均为虚构，如有雷同，纯属巧合。

党的二十大报告指出，要“开辟发展新领域新赛道，不断塑造发展新动能新优势”，在对外开放领域，要“推进高水平对外开放……，加快建设贸易强国，推动共建‘一带一路’高质量发展，维护多元稳定的国际经济格局和经贸关系”。报告体现了创新发展、高质量发展的核心要求，这也为高等教育人才培养提出了同样的要求。在这一背景下，我们真心希望能为老师、同学们编写一本好读、好用、更加人性化的国际贸易双语教材，助力同学们成为时代发展需要的善于思考、开拓创新、实践能力一流的优秀人才，在服务国家和时代的要求中实现个人价值。

本教材可供高校商务英语或国际贸易专业本科或研究生使用，也可供职场人士自学使用。感谢与笔者一起合作完成本教材的几位老师。本书第 1 章到第 13 章由王小娟老师编写，第 14 章由刘伟老师编写，第 15 章由刘旻老师编写。全书案例和练习由杨越、王小娟、刘伟和李改梅老师共同编写。插图由陈思同学绘制。此外，杨越老师制作了配套小型案例集，王小娟、刘伟和李改梅老师制作了课件。全书由王小娟老师完成统稿和审稿。最后，感谢索金梅老师的宝贵意见；感谢逄承国老师的认真审读和宝贵意见；感谢对外经济贸易大学出版社，特别是谭利彬编辑的帮助；感谢家人的大力支持。但由于作者水平有限，本书在编写过程中差错难免，诚请读者批评指正或提出改进建议。您可发邮件至：153822058@qq.com.

王小娟
2022 年 12 月
于天津

Contents

Chapter 1 An Overview of the Export Process

第一章 出口流程概述 …… 1

1.1 Three Ways to Get Going 开启出口的三种方式 …… 1

1.2 Basic Process of Export 出口基本流程 …… 3

1.3 Two Stages of Export 出口的两个步骤 …… 4

1.4 Fulfilling an International Order 履行国际订单 …… 5

1.5 Case Study: Your Routine Work 案例研究：你的日常工作 …… 9

Exercises 练习 …… 11

Chapter 2 International Market Research and Development

第二章 国际市场调研和开发 …… 15

2.1 International Market Research 国际市场调研 …… 15

2.2 Watching for Export Risks 注意出口风险 …… 18

2.3 Sourcing International Trade Leads 寻找国际买家 …… 20

2.4 Establishing Business Relations 建立商业联系 …… 28

Exercises 练习 …… 29

Chapter 3 Business Negotiations and Signing the Contract

第三章 商务磋商和签订合同 …… 33

3.1 Contents and Forms of Business Negotiations 商务磋商的内容和形式 …… 33

3.2 General Procedures of Business Negotiations 商务磋商的一般程序 …… 34

3.3 Signing Business Contract 签订商业合同 …… 40

Exercises 练习 …… 44

Chapter 4 Description of Commodities

第四章 产品描述 …… 49

4.1 Measuring Quantities 衡量数量 …… 49

4.2 Measuring Quality 衡量质量 …… 55

4.3 Packaging for Export 出口包装 …… 60

Exercises 练习 …… 63

Chapter 5 International Commerce Terms and Export Prices and Earnings
第五章 国际商业条款及出口价格和利润 ······ 67
5.1 International Commerce Terms 国际商业条款 ······ 67
5.2 *Incoterms 2020* Rules in 4 Groups 分成四组的《2020 通则》术语 ······ 71
5.3 How to Use *Incoterms 2020*？如何使用《2020 通则》？ ······ 77
5.4 Export Costs, Prices and Earnings 出口成本、价格和利润 ······ 81
Exercises 练习 ······ 85

Chapter 6 International Cargo Transport
第六章 国际货物运输 ······ 89
6.1 Ocean Transport 海上运输 ······ 89
6.2 Air Transport 航空运输 ······ 94
6.3 Land Transport 陆路运输 ······ 96
6.4 Multi-Modal Transport 多式联运 ······ 98
6.5 Container Transport 集装箱运输 ······ 99
Exercises 练习 ······ 103

Chapter 7 Transport Documents
第七章 运输单据 ······ 107
7.1 Bill of Lading 海运提单 ······ 107
7.2 Other Transport Documents 其他运输单据 ······ 117
7.3 Multi-Modal Bill of Lading & Through Bill of Lading
多式联运提单和直达提单 ······ 122
Exercises 练习 ······ 122

Chapter 8 International Cargo Transport Insurance
第八章 国际货物运输保险 ······ 127
8.1 Marine Cargo Transport Insurance 海上货物运输保险 ······ 128
8.2 Insurance Under Other Modes of Transport 其他运输方式下的保险 ······ 134
8.3 Institute Cargo Clauses 协会货物保险条款 ······ 135
8.4 Procedures in Purchasing Insurance 投保的程序 ······ 135
8.5 Procedures for Filing a Claim 提出索赔的程序 ······ 138
8.6 Principles of Indemnification 保险赔偿的原则 ······ 139
Exercises 练习 ······ 140

Chapter 9 Methods of Payment (1)
第九章 支付方式（1）…… 145
9.1 Cash in Advance and Open Account 预付货款和赊账 …… 146
9.2 Documentary Collection 跟单托收 …… 147
Exercises 练习 …… 152

Chapter 10 Instrument of Payment
第十章 付款工具 …… 155
10.1 Bill of Exchange 汇票 …… 155
10.2 Promissory Note 本票 …… 166
10.3 Cheque 支票 …… 168
10.4 Bill of Exchange, Promissory Note and Cheque Compared
汇票、本票和支票比较 …… 169
Exercises 练习 …… 170

Chapter 11 Methods of Payment (2)—Letter of Credit
第十一章 支付方式（2）——信用证 …… 173
11.1 An Introduction to Letter of Credit 信用证简介 …… 174
11.2 Definition in *UCP 600*《跟单信用证统一惯例》中的概念 …… 175
11.3 Participants and Flowchart 参与方和流程图 …… 175
11.4 Characteristics of a Letter of Credit 信用证的特征 …… 179
11.5 Sample of a Letter of Credit 信用证样本 …… 180
11.6 Exporter's Tasks Under a Letter of Credit 信用证下的出口商任务 …… 182
11.7 Types of Letter of Credit 信用证的类型 …… 187
Exercises 练习 …… 190

Chapter 12 Inspection, Claim, *Force Majeure* and Dispute Resolution
第十二章 检验、索赔、不可抗力和争议解决 …… 195
12.1 Inspection 检验 …… 196
12.2 Claim 索赔 …… 197
12.3 *Force Majeure* 不可抗力 …… 198
12.4 Dispute Resolution 争议解决 …… 199
Exercises 练习 …… 203

Chapter 13 Documentation
第十三章 制单 …… 207
13.1 Major Documents in the Export Process 出口中的主要单证 …… 207
13.2 Notes on Documentation 制单中的注意事项 …… 239
Exercises 练习 …… 240

Chapter 14 An Overview of the Import Process
第十四章 进口流程概述 …… 243
14.1 Overview 概述 …… 244
14.2 The Import Process 进口流程 …… 246
Exercises 练习 …… 250

Chapter 15 Cross-Border E-Commerce
第十五章 跨境电商 …… 255
15.1 Overview 概述 …… 256
15.2 Cross-Border E-Commerce for Import 进口跨境电商 …… 259
15.3 Cross-Border E-Commerce for Export 出口跨境电商 …… 262
15.4 Conclusion 结论 …… 267
Exercises 练习 …… 267

附录 1：国际贸易相关机构 …… 271
附录 2：国际贸易法律法规、惯例和公约 …… 274
参考文献 …… 277

Chapter 1 An Overview of the Export Process

第一章 出口流程概述

Learning Objectives:

◆ Three ways to start export
◆ Basic process and two stages of export
◆ How to fulfill an international order

Export is to sell products or services produced within one country or customs border to another. This may sound **intuitive**, but how? Some perceive the export transaction process as an obstacle, but please don't let that **deter** you. The truth is that anyone can **grasp** the **nuts and bolts** of international trade. The bridge from producers to buyers has existed for many years, and it has been tested and retested. By investing some time and money in yourself, you can easily learn this process.

凭直觉的

阻碍 理解 基本要点

1.1 Three Ways to Get Going 开启出口的三种方式

In China, to export, you need to obtain **the right for import and export** before you can do so in your firm's own name. It is so required by the Foreign Trade Law and other governing laws and regulations of China. For most categories of goods, getting this right is not complicated today, which is supervised by the Department of Foreign Trade, **Ministry of**

进出口经营权

商务部

对外贸易经营者备案登记表

Commerce. Whether you are a manufacturer or a merchant, just register with the department of your provincial government that deals with international trade by filling out a critical document called **the Form for Registration as a Foreign Trade Dealer** (see Figure 1-1), and completing other related procedures.

对外贸易经营者备案登记表

备案登记表编号：　　　　　　　　进出口企业代码：

经营者中文名称			
经营者英文名称			
组织机构代码		经营者类型 （由备案登记机关填写）	
住　所			
经营场所（中文）			
经营场所（英文）			
联系电话		联系传真	
邮政编码		电子邮箱	
工商登记注册日期		工商登记注册号	

依法办理工商登记的企业还须填写以下内容

企业法定代表人姓名		有效证件号	
注册资金		（折美元）	

依法办理工商登记的外国（地区）企业或个体工商户（独资经营者）还须填写以下内容

企业法定代表人/ 个体工商负责人姓名		有效证件号	
企业资产/个人财产		（折美元）	

备注：	

填表前请认真阅读背面的条款，并由企业法定代表人或个体工商负责人签字、盖章。

备案登记机关

签章

Figure 1-1　The Form for Registration as a Foreign Trade Dealer

Right here, you may ask, “What if I don’t have this qualification?” or “When I just have occasional orders from foreign buyers, can I export?” For Sure! You can export through “someone else”—another company with such a qualification. This company, likewise, could be a manufacturer or a merchant (a trading company), which effectively assumes the role of an agency for you. In either case, all **formalities** are completed by this company and export is done in its name.

手续

The third option **is more geared to** small exporters, such as those self-employed individuals. As an individual, you can set up your SOHO (small office and home office) mode for export by **tapping** your existing social networks or cross-border e-commerce platforms such as Alibaba, **AliExpress** or **Amazon**. You may earn big but less frequent orders as an individual, but to run a successful cross-border e-business, you probably need a team instead of working alone.

更适合

利用

阿里速卖通 亚马逊

In this textbook, let's suppose you have just started to work for a trading company called Tianjin Binhai Import and Export Co., Ltd.—one that has obtained the right for import and export, so that you can import or export in the name of your company. You may both import and export, but let's first navigate the export process from Chapter 1 through Chapter 13 from an exporter's perspective. When that is done, hopefully, you may have gained a good understanding of export. After that, the import process will be no problem, either, which shall be discussed briefly in Chapter 14, from an importer's perspective. And in Chapter 15, the last chapter, you'll get acquainted with the basics about cross-border e-commerce from both an importer's and an exporter's perspective.

1.2 Basic Process of Export 出口基本流程

For beginners like you, a brief overview of the export process may help your work ahead (see Figure 1-2).

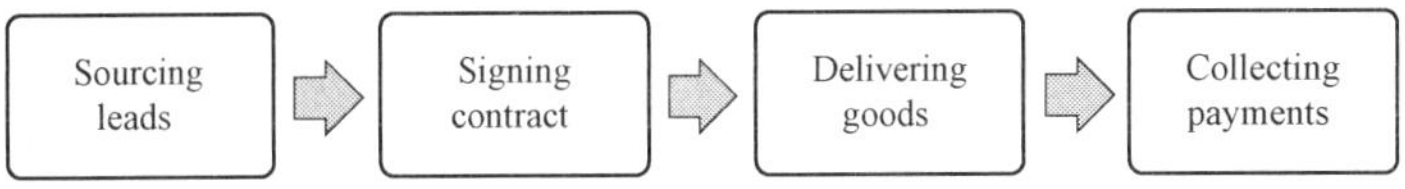

Figure 1-2 Basic Process for Export

Like domestic trade, export also goes through the basic process of **sourcing trade leads**, signing contract, delivering goods and collecting payments. In practice, however, variations from domestic trade do exist, including different ways to obtain and fulfill an order, different authorities to deal with, different formalities to complete, etc.

寻找贸易线索，寻找客户

1.3 Two Stages of Export 出口的两个步骤

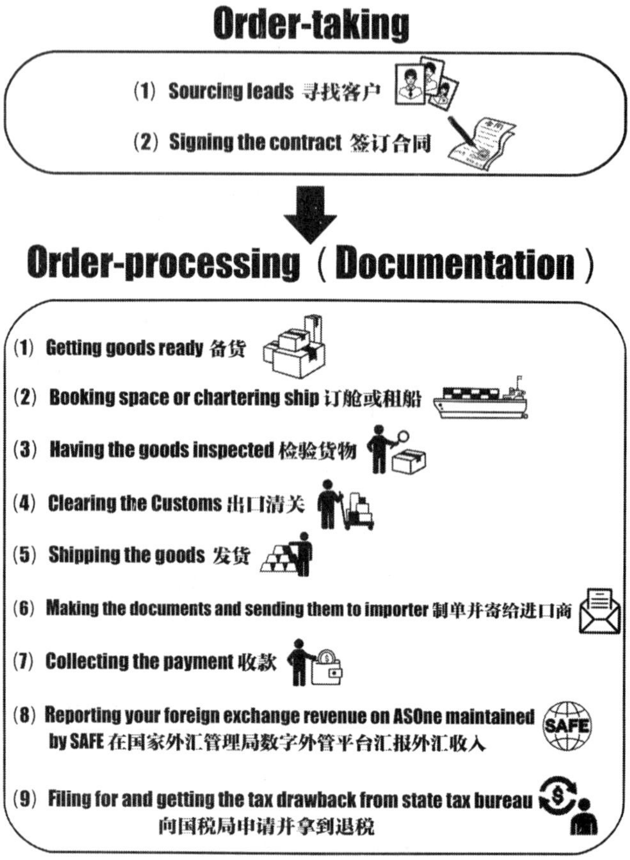

Figure 1-3 Two Stages of Export

The above basic process can be classified roughly into two stages: **order-taking** and **order-processing** (see Figure 1-3). Order-taking involves a lot of **strenuous** work aiming at developing the market to generate trade leads and sign the contract. Order-processing, involves fulfilling the order in accordance with the contract and trade practices. Order-taking and order-processing, therefore, make up the main body of your routines. Obviously, taking an order **hinges** more on your marketing skills, capability and experience, while processing an order, on the other hand, is more of a routine job which requires patience and **meticulousness**.

订单获取或称“接单”
订单处理或称“跟单”
艰苦的
取决于，依赖
细心

These are merely principles. In practice, however, you don't need to shoulder all the responsibilities listed above, particularly those involved in order-processing. For example, you can **authorize** the **freight forwarder** or a **customs broker** to **clear customs** and **delegate** your accountant to report the foreign exchange revenue and **file for tax refund**. If your company is not exporting in its own name, but commissioning a trading company as your agency, all the work after contracting and manufacturing is left with the trading company. Once you ship the goods and the trading company receives the payment, it pays you in RMB. Exporting through a trading company, therefore, is no different from a domestic transaction. It is to be noted, however, many procedures now can be completed on the Internet, such as on **China E-port**.

授权 货运代理
报关行 清关 委托
申请退税
中国电子口岸

1.4 Fulfilling an International Order 履行国际订单

Though essentially the same with domestic trade, some major differences in fulfilling the order should be highlighted here. Overall, international trade is more complicated and of higher risk than domestic trade. It is more open and spreads farther around the globe, reaching highly diversified markets with much more complex business environment. Elements like different languages, cultures, currencies, laws, regulations and trade conventions, long distances and riskier logistics process, as well as difficulties in market research, all make contributions to the complexities and ultimately translate into the following major differences in the procedures for export.

1.4.1 Acquiring Trade Leads 获取销售线索

While domestic traders enjoy the advantage of acquiring trade leads face to face in many cases, in addition to a number of other means such as by fax, phone and the Internet, international buyers and sellers, probably contrary to your **intuition,** seldom meet, unless necessary. They contact each other mainly via the Internet, fax or phone. The most heavily used tool for sourcing trade leads is search engines, which help you collect emails of prospective customers for

直觉

社交媒体平台
视频会议应用
无限性

direct email marketing. Latest techniques like **social media platforms** and **video-conferencing apps** are also employed for sourcing trade leads and conducting business negotiations. Thanks to their **infinity** in time and space, they have become essential and powerful tools in a trader's routine work, enhancing work efficiency dramatically over their counterparts in the history. However, when they do meet, they do so mostly at trade fairs or the exporter's premise, which, though costly, is very effective for concluding a deal.

1.4.2 Obtaining License and Quotas 获取许可证和配额

配额

Some importing countries require an import license or import **quota** for goods to be imported, which is mainly for the purpose of limiting the import of certain categories of goods. A quota is the limited quantity of something that is officially allowed for import or export. You need to confirm with the importer to make sure he/she has obtained the required document(s) before you sign the contract. Otherwise, the contract, signed though, is invalid. Some products are also subject to an export quota or even an export license, which is often for a similar purpose of limiting export, particularly if you are dealing with certain scarce resources. Likewise, make sure you have obtained the required document(s) before you sign the contract.

1.4.3 Inspection and Clearing the Customs 检验和报关

海关
走私　编纂
中国海关总署
法定的

The customs is a government body and important player in the process of import and export. Its functions relating to import and export include: supervising the movement of goods across national or customs borders, collecting import and export duties and other taxes, preventing **smuggling** and **compiling** business statistics, etc. Without its permission, you cannot move the goods across the national or customs border. One of the functions now under **the General Administration of Customs of China** is commodity inspection. Most products for export have to pass an inspection as required by the contract, the exporting country or the importing country. Some of them are of a **statutory** nature, which means, that the merchandise cannot be exported without passing the required inspection. Some importing country also requires a **certificate of origin** from the importer to determine the import duty, which can be issued by the inspection authority under the Customs of China or other recognized institutions. 原产地证书

1.4.4 Documentation and Presentation 制单和交单

As exporter, you need to make a set of documents **as per** the contract and in line with the industry format. This is known as documentation. The documents may include commercial documents, such as the invoice, financial documents such as the **letter of credit** and **draft**, shipping documents such as the **bill of lading** and the packing list, insurance documents such as the **insurance policy**, etc. An inspection certificate may also be required by the importer, the exporting country or the importing country. These documents are important to both you and the importer—you need them for collecting the payment while the importer needs them for **taking delivery**. They are also needed by other parties involved in the transaction, such as certain government authorities, banks, the shipping company, the insurance company, etc.

依据
信用证
汇票 提单
保险单
提货

1.4.5 Shipping the Cargo 发送货物

Cargoes are mostly shipped via ocean shipping, even though air shipping and railway shipping volumes are on the rise. You normally authorize this task to a **freight forwarder**. On behalf of you, the forwarder books the shipping space on a **vessel** or charters a ship if you need the space of an entire ship. Once your cargo is loaded, the **carrier** or its agent issues you a document as proof of its receipt of the cargo and **contract of carriage**, which could be a "bill of lading" or other transport documents that is forwarded to you by the forwarder. And you send it, via other parties when necessary, to the **consignee** for him/her to take delivery.

货运代理
船
承运人
运输合同
收货人

1.4.6 Collecting the Payment 收取货款

将款项打入某人账户
外汇 国家外汇管理局
真实性

Payment is normally **credited into** your bank account in **foreign exchanges**. **The State Administration of Foreign Exchange (SAFE)** supervises exporters' bank account for receipt of this revenue as it is tasked to verify the **authenticity** of the deal and source of the foreign money. For that purpose, you must register with the Administration beforehand. Figure 1-4 is the platform maintained by the SAFE for exporters to report their exchange revenues.

提交 国家外汇管理局
数字外管平台
国家税务总局 申请
数据库
符合条件的 公平公正地
骗税

Once you have cleared customs, shipped the goods and received the payment in foreign exchange, you report your exchange earnings to the SAFE by **filing** this information on **ASOne**①, a specific online platform maintained by SAFE. Then you may go to **the State Taxation Administration (STA)** to **file for** your tax refund. As the Customs, the SAFE and the STA collaborate on verifying the authenticity of the transaction and receipt of payment by integrating their **databases** for import and export, you will rightly get your refund if your category of products is **eligible** and you are doing business **fair and square**, without **defrauding on the refund**.

Figure 1-4 ASOne Maintained by SAFE

① http://zwfw.safe.gov.cn/asone/WelcomeServlet?code=90000&flag=false

1.4.7 Getting Tax Refund 获得出口退税

Once your transaction is verified by the Customs and the revenue is reported to SAFE, the State Taxation Administration refunds a certain amount of the **value-added tax (VAT)** that you have already paid if your category of product is eligible. This refund is known as the **tax refund/tax rebate/tax drawback** for export, which exists to avoid **international double taxation** and is allowed by WTO as per **General Agreement on Tariffs and Trade (GATT)** as long as the amount of refund does not exceed the VAT that the exporter has paid.① Once you have shipped the cargo, collected the payment, and reported your exchange revenue on ASOne, you go to STA to file for this refund. After a while, this money will be credited to your bank account. For specific refund rate, you need to know **the Harmonized System Code (HS code)** of your product category. The Harmonized System is a unified coding system for goods and services developed by **the World Customs Organization** to facilitate import and export. Participating countries are required to use this code when describing their **tariff schedules**. Nearly all international trade occurs under the Harmonized System.

增值税
退税
国际双重征税
关贸总协定
协调系统代码
世界海关组织
关税表

1.5 Case Study: Your Routine Work 案例研究：你的日常工作

Let's examine your routine work through a case.

Case: A US outdoor retailer has ordered 1,000 tents and required shipment be made before Oct. 20th from the Port of Qingdao to the **Port of Long Beach**.

美国长滩港

- **If you are an independent exporter with the right for import and export, your routines include tasks as follows:**

1. Around Oct. 10th, you phone/fax the freight forwarder to book the shipping space and get your goods to the designated location (warehouse) as required by the forwarder.

---

① Article 6.4, GATT.

2. Prepare a set of invoices and packing lists and send them to the freight forwarder together with a letter or authorization for inspection and customs clearance, authorizing which to the forwarder. However, you may also complete inspection and customs clearance on your own.
3. Get the bill of lading from the forwarder once the latter receives the goods and completes the customs formalities; prepare another set of invoices and packing lists as well as other documents required by the importer.
4. Notify the importer of the shipment of goods and ask for payment; send the whole set of documents to the importer, often through the banking system.
5. Around 10 days after shipment, you receive the copy of customs clearance form for tax refund returned by the Customs (transferred by the forwarder) and you give it to the accountant for filing for tax refund.
6. Work done.

♦ **If you are collaborating with a trading agency, your routines are as follows:**

1. Notify the agency of the order.
2. Around Oct. 10th, notify the agency that "the goods are ready".
3. Get the goods to the designated location (warehouse) as required by the agency.
4. Work done. Payment, once received from the importer, will be converted to RMB and credited into your bank account by the agency. This is the case when no inspection or quota is required, otherwise, inspection has to be completed and quota obtained before Oct. 10th. Now you may have got an overview of the export procedures.

Exercises 练习

I. True or False

1. If you are not familiar with international trade procedures, you can choose an import and export trading company to handle some procedures. ( )
2. The export process can be divided into two stages: taking orders and processing orders. The former is more important than the latter. ( )
3. Nowadays, many trade procedures are completed on the platform of China E-Port. ( )
4. Individuals cannot engage in export. ( )
5. Quotas can be an export quota or an import quota. ( )
6. You have to clear customs for whatever you export. ( )
7. You can apply for a tax refund on any category of merchandise that you have exported. ( )
8. In China, the Department of Foreign Trade under the Ministry of Commerce is in charge of import and export. ( )
9. The specific refund rate for an exported product depends on its category that is determined by the Harmonized System Code. ( )
10. Every product for export must go through a statutory inspection. ( )

II. Multiple Choice Questions

This section contains both questions with one correct answer and questions that might have more than one correct answer. The latter type of questions is marked with a "*". This also applies to other chapters of this book.

1. What is true about international trade compared with domestic trade? ( )

   [A] International trade and domestic trade are no different.

   [B] International trade is more profitable.

   [C] International trade involves more procedures.

   [D] International trade has smaller risk than domestic trade.

2. The functions of the Customs include ( ). *

   [A] monitoring the movement of goods across borders

   [B] collecting tariff and other taxes

[C] preventing smuggling

[D] compiling customs statistics

3. Which of the following is(are) (a) non-governmental organization(s)? (　　) *

[A] State Administration of Foreign Exchange.

[B] China International Economic and Trade Arbitration Commission.

[C] China Council for the Promotion of International Trade.

[D] Department of Commodity Inspection under General Administration of Customs of China.

4. Which of the following government body is charged with overseeing your foreign exchange revenue as an exporter? (　　)

[A] State Administration of Foreign Exchange.

[B] General Administration of Customs of China.

[C] State Taxation Administration.

[D] Department of Foreign Trade, Ministry of Commerce.

5. Which one of the following statements is CORRECT about jurisdiction over international trade ? (　　)

[A] Domestic laws and regulations cannot be applied to international transactions.

[B] International treaties are binding on traders from different countries.

[C] International trade conventions cannot be binding on traders from different countries.

[D] International treaties are binding on traders of signatory countries.

6. When we export, (　　).

[A] we always need an export quota, export license, import quota or import license

[B] we never need an export quota, export license, import quota or import license

[C] we may need an export quota, export license, import quota or import license, depending on the category of commodity we export

[D] we can sign the contract before or after we apply for the export quota, export license, import quota or import license, depending on the category of commodity we export

7. An inspection of the commodity for export may be needed due to requirement from ( ).*
   [A] the importer
   [B] the importer's country
   [C] the exporter
   [D] the exporter's country
8. Tax refund ( ).
   [A] is sure to result in dumping in the importing country
   [B] may be a source of profit for exporting some categories of product
   [C] can be claimed even if we don't export any commodity
   [D] can be claimed even if we don't receive revenue in foreign exchanges
9. Which of the following organizations is a government body? ( )
   [A] China Council for the Promotion of International Trade.
   [B] China Maritime Arbitration Commission.
   [C] Department of Animal and Plant Quarantine.
   [D] China Certification & Inspection Group.
10. A number of documents are needed for export because ( ).*
   [A] the importer needs those documents to clear customs for import
   [B] the exporter needs those documents to clear customs for export
   [C] the banks need those documents for payment or assisting you with collecting payment
   [D] the shipping and insurance companies need those documents for performing their respective obligations.

III. Group Work

1. Find out the ***Foreign Trade Law***, the ***Customs Law***, ***Law on Import and Export Commodity Inspection*** and its ***Regulations for Implementation***, ***Regulations on Foreign Exchange System*** of China, go over them quickly and find out the articles that relate to import and export, and discuss with your team member what you have learned from these laws and regulations.

   《对外贸易法》
   《海关法》
   《进出口商品检验法》及《实施条例》
   《外汇管理条例》

2. Decide on a product that you want to export within a group of 4 or 5 people, follow the procedures introduced in this chapter, discuss what you need to do for exporting it, and write a summary as group work.

Chapter 2 International Market Research and Development

第二章 国际市场调研和开发

Learning Objectives:

- Necessity of international market research
- Major sources of risks involved in export
- Ways to find out foreign customers
- How to establish business relations

For beginners like you, the international market may seem fascinating enough, as it opens up new opportunities for business. However, it is challenging as well. Obstacles must be cleared to reap the reward of that market. In this chapter, the **nuts and bolts** of international market research and market development will be introduced. 基本要点

2.1 International Market Research 国际市场调研

When you are doing business across borders, researching your target market is **imperative**. To do that, you need to set clear goals and master a few common methods, which shall help you avoid some unnecessary setbacks. 必要的

2.1.1 Goals of International Market Research 国际市场调研的目标

To explore an unknown or untapped market, locating your customer is critical. When you **set about** that, two issues surface that make international market research necessary. First, international business is generally riskier than domestic business due to its higher uncertainties. A thorough understanding of your market and **prospects** would improve your decision by controlling those uncertainties. Second, you normally need to start off by sending emails to trade leads; if you come up with the same information to all leads, chances are—you will never get a single reply. So, the **gist** of market development is to research your leads as thoroughly as possible, followed by a tailored marketing endeavor. Successful businesses have extensive and profound knowledge of their market, customers and competitors and continuously upgrade this knowledge. Such an analysis leads you to two preliminary goals for international market research: controlling risk and locating your target customers.

着手

潜在客户

要点

You may conduct the research at two levels—a macro-environment research of your target market and a micro-environment research of your target customer. For the former, you can make a PEST analysis—political, economic, social and technological analysis. For the latter, consider investigating your target customer's size, positioning, expected annual purchase quantity, financial standing, market prospect, price sensitivity, geographic distribution of its customers, competitors, suppliers, media coverage, etc. for a thorough understanding of the customer.

2.1.2 Methods of International Market Research 国际市场调研的方法

To begin with, it is essential to set clearly-defined goals for the research, including what you want to know and why. Then, set off gathering data for the goal. Depending on your budget, time available and experience, research at different levels of **sophistication** is possible. Simple researches can be accomplished totally on your own,

复杂度

such as a study of **demographic data** of your target market or creating a short **questionnaire** on purchase preferences of prospects. Complex ones may require assistance from professional market research firms. Regardless of various **constraints**, a certain type of market research is always possible—be it a macro level or a micro level research, a **desktop research (sometimes called a secondary research)**, a **field research (sometimes called a primary research)** or a combination of the two.

人口统计数据
调查问卷
限制因素
案头调研，或称二手调研
实地调研，或称一手调研

♦ **Desktop research 案头调研**

Desktop research exploits existing resources for the issues in question, which could be company records, government statistics, publications, and studies by research institutions like libraries, universities, international organizations, industry associations and consulting firms. A big plus of these resources is that they are readily available and cost-effective. Customer information from your past records of transaction is the most convenient place to start out. Try sales invoices, receipts and/or customers' complaining letters. Oftentimes desktop research **sheds light on** just the same issue you try to resolve through field research. Therefore, you are highly recommended to consider these resources before conducting a field research. This is particularly cost-effective for international business.

揭示

Admittedly, however, desktop research is less targeted than field research. The statistics or studies may not tailor to your specific needs and some statistics are too expensive to purchase. Whichever the case, it still **yields** valuable information and answers questions that are not suited to address through field research, such as assessing macro-economic conditions or asking questions that may make **respondents** feel uncomfortable, such as questions about age and income levels.

产生
被调查者

♦ **Field research 实地调研**

Field research gathers first-hand information for a specific question or a series of questions. This is often difficult for international market research if you rely on your own. So, a market research firm can be hired. Information for a field research could normally be gathered through surveys, observations, or experiments. The pros of a field research lie in that you can specifically target your desired groups (such as your prospects or a geographic area for your business) and tailor the research to specific issues, which helps you better understand the market. The **downside** is that it can be time-consuming and expensive, and the results are not readily available, particularly when you need to hire a research firm. However, some cost for international research can be greatly reduced by using online survey services. Like in China, online survey services are popular in many countries. There are both free and paid services online. Try one called "easyquest" at "https://www.easyquest.com/en/". It is free and handy, like **Wenjuanxing** in China.

不利的一面

问卷星

2.2 Watching for Export Risks 注意出口风险

As export is more complicated than domestic trade, we must watch for their differences in practice and their potential risks. Major risks in export include: political risk, legal risk, commercial and credit risk, cargo risk, foreign exchange risk, etc.

2.2.1 Political Risk 政治风险

China is blessed with a stable macro environment, which should be cherished by all Chinese citizens. However, this is not to be expected from every economy in the world. Globally, cases occur when governments are toppled and industries disturbed by regional wars, rebellions, strikes, commotions, or civil wars, etc. The conflict between Russia and Ukraine starting in 2022 has hiked up prices for many products, such as natural gas and sunflower seed oil. And these are not unique to emerging or underdeveloped economies. Developed countries also experience social unrest occasionally. As most democratic countries today have a ruling party and one or more opposition parties, when a new government takes office, policies of the former government might be **annulled**. For example, the Trump administration did away with Obama's health care package, withdrew from the North America Free Trade Agreement, initiated trade wars with China, etc. Therefore, it is necessary for you to keep a close watch on the political climate of your target region.

宣告无效，取消

2.2.2 Legal Risk 法律风险

Every economy has its commercial laws and regulations, and legal proceedings may be different. Foreign or domestic laws may change, which sows the seed of legal risks. When disputes arise between traders from different economies, whose law shall have **jurisdiction**? The fact is, international trade is a field of a long history. A large body of rules and customs have been formed over the years to harmonize trade practices globally. These **institutions** cover each stage of a transaction from business negotiations, making delivery, collecting payment, to settling disputes. They generally fall into three categories: international **treaties** and **conventions**, international trade customs and domestic laws. International treaties and conventions are **binding** as long as a country or region is a **signatory** of the treaty or convention, such as the ***United Nations Convention on Contracts for the International Sale of Goods (CISG)***. International trade customs and domestic laws are not binding unless both exporter and importer mutually agree to adopt them in their contract. However, as some important international trade customs are commonly recognized by both international treaties and domestic laws, sometimes they are used as **default** criteria for settling international disputes, such as ***Incoterms*** and ***UCP 600***. For beginners, a working knowledge of international business law shall help you clear obstacles and smooth your work down the road.

司法权
制度
条约　公约
有约束力的
签字者，签字国
《联合国国际货物销售合同公约》
默认的
《国际贸易术语解释通则》
《跟单信用证统一惯例》

2.2.3 Commercial and Credit Risk 商业和信用风险

People around the world speak different languages and have different cultures, which often breed unique demands in a region. Commercial risks exist mainly because there is a lack of knowledge of the foreign market and your product lacks adaptability. There is also the possibility of the goods being rejected by the importer due to a delay in transit that prevents him/her from **fulfilling his/her commitment** to his/her customers. Changes in the international market may cause the importer to ask for **amendment** or cancellation of the order, posing difficulties or incurring a loss to you. And globally, as at home,

履行承诺
修改

competitors may enter the market or turn to local production, which brings down the price. What's more, if you are negligent in investigating the importer's **credit standing**, you may have higher credit risks—the importer may **default** when market changes or when he/she is **insolvent**. Worst of all, the importer may even be a **fraud**.

资信状况
违约
资不抵债 骗子

2.2.4 Cargo Risk 货物风险

The list for cargo risks is long. If you ship by sea, there might be risks particular to the ship's state at sea. For instance, the ship can run into **natural calamities**, such as storms, lightning, **tsunamis**, etc.; it can sink, be **stranded** or **collide** with icebergs or other objects in a storm. There might also be risks which have no direct relevance with its state at sea, but equally **hazardous**. For example, the cargo can be stolen, **damped, contaminated**, etc.; delivery might be **impeded** by wars, strikes, or the importer's refusal to take delivery. If you ship by air, it's safer, but the flight could be canceled or delayed due to bad weather. On extreme occasions, the airplane can **crash**. If you ship by land, infrastructure of the importing country, particularly those politically high-risk countries should be taken into consideration.

自然灾害 海啸
搁浅 碰撞
危险的
受潮 污染的 阻碍
坠毁

2.2.5 Foreign Exchange Risk 外汇风险

Fluctuation of foreign exchange influences how much you realize in **sales proceeds**. In most cases, you sign the contract at a time but get paid some time later. This lag in collecting payment is vulnerable to fluctuation of exchange rate between a foreign currency and RMB. For example, If USD **depreciates** against RMB after you sign the contract, you cannot expect to realize as much revenue as in the contract once you convert Dollar to RMB.

销售收入
贬值

2.3 Sourcing International Trade Leads 寻找国际买家

Once you have decided on your target market and customers, you can set off sourcing your trade leads. Every exporter has his/her own way of doing the job. This section definitely cannot **exhaust** all the methods or techniques, but shall only touch on the most common **avenues** or techniques at a decreasing order of convenience or availability.

穷尽
途径

2.3.1 Company Websites 企业网站

With the Internet getting **prevalent** and penetrating deeper in our life, marketing tends to find its way online, too. This is more so for international marketing. Therefore, setting up your company website should be a priority. A well-built website with product details makes your company **credible** and respected in the eyes of international buyers, as they normally turn to the Internet for sourcing suppliers when they **procure** from overseas. So, make sure you set up your website and maintain it at a regular basis. Providing pictures of your manufacturing facilities helps demonstrate your strength and add to your credibility. **Search Engine Optimization (SEO)** plays a vital role in searching the content **tags** of your product details by anyone looking for a supplier of product similar to yours.

普遍的
可信的
采购
搜索引擎优化
标签

2.3.2 B2B Platforms B2B 平台

Cross-border B2B platforms are great facilitators to global trade. Once you set up your company websites, you may further register with a B2B platform and upload your product information to increase exposure. If you are a new or small business without enough finance or manpower to maintain an independent company website, use the existing B2B or B2C platforms. Well known platforms include Alibaba, Global Sources, Made-in-China, Kompass, Amazon, eBay, etc. (see Table 2-1), with different strength for different regions or categories of commodities. Driven by the general trend of **Big Data** in all sectors of our life, these platforms are increasingly powerful in data collection and analysis. They generate business opportunities for traders by processing large amount of information. However, they are not only **portals** to international business, but also helpful in improving order-processing efficiency by providing diversified functions on the entire supply chain.

大数据
门户

Table 2-1 A List of Popular B2B or B2C Platforms

Alibaba.com, Aliexpress.com, Amazon.com, Global Sources.com, Made-In-China. com, Ec21.com
ECplaza.net, DIY Trade.com, Busytrade.com, Buyer Zone.com, Taiwan Commerce. com, Eceurope.com, Kompass.com

2.3.3 Search Engines 搜索引擎

A study by Google and Millward Brown[①] shows, 42% of international buyers take search engines as their first choice for sourcing suppliers. 11% of them source products from a suppliers' website, 10% by **word of mouth** and 7% through B2B platforms. To exporters, search engines rank the most important avenue to prospects, as almost every company engaged in international business maintains a website, a blog, a **social media account**, or any other kind of **company profile** that contains their contact information. To get this information, you may start with searching the Internet with one or a combination of key words, mostly your product name plus additional information, which may yield websites of trading companies for import and export, distributors or retailers. Most websites contain an email address or other sorts of contact information, from which you can write emails or make contacts by other means to establish business relationship. Don't forget to try some sophisticated searching techniques, such as searching for prospects in a certain country by using the key word of the product together with the **suffix** of the **domain name** unique to that country. For instance, if you want to search for dealers of tents in Germany, you can type in "Zelt .de" in the search box of the search engine as "Zelt" is the translation of "tent" in German. You may also integrate search engine with other techniques, such as starting with a search for trade associations, trade fairs or online yellow pages instead of individual businesses. And be aware that certain countries or regions may have their own preferred search engines, such as Yandex for Russia, East Europe and West Asian.

口碑

社交媒体账户

公司简介

后缀 域名

① Millward Brown is a global company focused on brands, media and communications. It is part of Kantar, the insights arm of WPP plc, and the world's second largest market research organization after Nielsen Company.

2.3.4 Trade Associations 行业协会

A trade association, also called a trade group, business association, sector association or industry body, is an organization founded by businesses that operate in a specific industry. Many associations are non-profit organizations governed by laws and directed by officers from member companies. Trade associations in developed economies play a bigger role for businesses than those in China. With a focus on collaboration between companies, they offer services ranging from education, advertising, information, holding conferences to publishing journals to members. Their classification is more detailed, too. For instance, instead of a general "Building Material Association", they may have an "Association of the Wall and Ceiling Industry" or a "Ceramic Tiles Distribution Association". Most trade associations have their websites, some of which publish names of member companies on the site. However, when you search for trade associations using a search engine, it's better to know that they are not necessarily called an "association". "Alliance" "bureau" "council" "institute" "society" or even "guide" are alternative words that refer to organizations of a similar nature. You may want to have a try on these key words. Why not? Go ahead! Table 2-2 gives a list of some trade associations.

Table 2-2 Some Trade Associations

1. American Association of Exporters and Importers
2. North American Importers Association
3. GlobalTrade.net
4. GlobeTrade.com
5. Import-Export International Business Help Center
6. Port Import-Export Reporting Service
7. Small Business Exporters Association
8. The Federation of International Trade Associations (FITA)

2.3.5 Yellow Pages 黄页

Figure 2-1 Yellow Pages of Auckland 2004

Yellow pages are telephone directories of businesses organized by category of product or industry. The directories, originated in North America more than 100 years ago, were originally printed on yellow paper, as opposed to white paper for non-commercial listings, hence the name. Figure 2-1 shows us a 2004 version of Auckland's yellow pages. Like trade associations, yellow pages in developed economies are also highly detailed in classifications, covering a broad **spectrum** from comprehensive ones to those for specific industries or category of goods. Some of them even advertise within other yellow pages. Normally you can buy one or get one for free at hotels, post offices, trade associations, trade fairs, or special bookstores.

范围

The traditional yellow pages also turn to the Internet, resulting in the emergence of online directories of businesses, known as Internet yellow pages (or IYP). Statistics shows that "yellow pages" is one of the most-searched terms on the Internet. Experian/Hitwise reported in January 2011 that "yellow pages" was one of the top 50 searched terms across all search engines and all searched terms (among millions of search terms). It was also among the top 5 highest revenue generators of all searched terms in Google's **Ad Words platform** in 2010.①

广告词平台

2.3.6 Trade Fairs 贸易博览会

A Trade fair (trade shows, trade exhibitions or expos) is an exhibition for businesses to showcase their latest products or services. Attending a trade fair is often the most effective means to make contacts

① 李博婵. 新编国际贸易实务双语教程［M］. 北京：中国人民大学出版社，2016.

and learn about products, markets, competition, potential customers and distributors. Europe, particularly Germany, is a center of trade fairs for many industries. It organizes a majority of the 100 top trade fairs in the world each year. China Import and Export Fair, or Guangzhou fair, is the largest trade fair in China and a comprehensive event of international importance. It is held in spring and autumn each year since 1957 in Guangzhou (Canton), China, hence the name. Figure 2-2 is a picture of its exhibition complex. China also initiated the first China International Import Expo in 2018, which ever since has boosted China's import a great deal and won **acclaim** in the international community. 赞赏

Figure 2-2 The Canton Fair Complex

Trade fairs are more and more in line with demands of the Internet age, such as providing online ordering of **stands** or online exhibitions. 展位 If you have an interest in a particular industry, keep an eye for important trade fairs in that industry. Even if you don't attend a trade fair, it helps you accumulate business names and contact information in your interested industry.

2.3.7 Chinese Embassies and Foreign Embassies 中国大使馆和外国大使馆

In sourcing trade leads, don't forget we have Motherland behind us. Logging onto the website of the Ministry of Commerce, you'll find China has set up 215 **economic and commercial counselor's offices** 经济商务参赞处

around the world under her embassies.① Probably no business is capable of **weaving** such a vast and widespread net around the world. And one of their most important functions is to serve economy and trading between Chinese businesses and **the host country**. Many websites of Counselor's Offices maintain a column for posting local business information, such as local **procurement** needs or **calls for bid**. You can contact them for more information, have your products registered with them or even send a pamphlet of your products to the counselor's office, which not only increase the exposure of your products but also help the counselors' work.

编织

东道国

采购 招标

By the same token, many countries may send state-sponsored or controlled import agents in other countries for buying **in bulk**. They actively look for suppliers, like you. They may publish the information through their embassies in the target countries. Once you have identified your target countries for export, contact local embassies of those countries in China to get a list of these agents. Some of them are pretty **proactive**.

大量

积极主动的

2.3.8 Social Media Platforms 社交媒体平台

When you **browse** a foreign company's website, normally you'll find links to its social media accounts, mostly Facebook, Twitter, LinkedIn or YouTube. Individual traders, too, publish their social media links online. Nowadays, almost every foreign business or individual owns a social media account of some sort. Social media is so **pervasive** that you just can't ignore them in your marketing endeavor. Compared with email direct marketing, social media marketing is mainly featured by its **timeliness** and **interactivity**. For international trade, social media platforms can be used in two ways: for brand-building or for sourcing trade leads. Social media has changed broadcasting, a prominent feature of traditional media, into a two-way communication. For brand-building, you need to select the right platform, identify **key influencers** and **post engaging contents** to create word-of-mouth online. For sourcing trade leads, you can establish business relations

浏览

渗透的，无处不在的

及时性 互动性

关键影响者

发布吸引人的内容

① 张劲松. 金牌外贸业务员找客户［M］. 北京：中国海关出版社，2016.

by **adding connections**, joining interest groups, sharing a posting, commenting on others' postings or creating and sharing your own postings. 添加联系人

2.3.9 Customs Databases and Commercial Databases 海关数据库和商业数据库

Conducting international marketing relying on databases may not have come into your mind, but it surely gives you an **edge** in this era driven by Big Data almost in all sectors of our life. 优势

As all import and export transactions are subject to supervision by the customs of both the exporting and the importing country, information from the customs is important and reliable sources of trading intelligence. This information is normally in the form of a customs database, for which the customs mostly charges a fee. Some countries, like Canada, provide this service for free. It is reliable in that it provides the same information as a bill of lading does, such as the shipper, consignee, notify party and details of the merchandise.

Some B2B platforms also provide databases of business contacts for a fee, such as Kompass, Thomas, Zoominfo, Dun & Bradstreet, etc. These definitely are of a higher quality than information that is free of charge, but some of them also offer free service on certain conditions, such as a "**One for One**" service, which means that you give them one piece of contact information, and they will give you one piece for exchange. 以一换一

2.3.10 Other Sources of Trade Leads 其他潜在客户信息渠道

Information about trade leads can also be obtained from the following sources:

- Websites of inspection institutions—some of them post names of their clients on their websites;
- Forums of import and export such as **FOB Business Forum** at "https://bbs.fobshanghai.com/" and many regional forums home and abroad; 福步外贸论坛

• Books, magazines or journals—news or advertisement therein might either be a direct source of business intelligence or spark your interest in a particular field;

推荐

• **Referrals** from business partners—this is more reliable;

• Competitors—finding out what and how your competitors are doing may give you inspirations. However, I would not suggest you compete with domestic peer companies.

锻炼你的技能

This list definitely cannot exhaust all the techniques for international market development. No matter which strategy or technique you apply for sourcing trade leads, you need always be creative and persistent. The export sector is increasingly competitive. When you have no direct control in production, as in the case of a trading company, information is critical. A prominent feature of this era is that information creates wealth. So, to obtain an edge over your rivals, you must keep improving your information literacy and **temper your skills**.

2.4 Establishing Business Relations 建立商业联系

电子邮件直接营销

Once you know who your prospects are, and what their contact information is, you may start off establishing business relationship. This can be achieved in a number of ways. You can write an email, add connections at a social media platform, send a fax, make an international phone call or attend a trade fair, etc. Mostly, however, exporters start by writing an email, as it is the most convenient and cost-effective way for establishing business relations, particularly for international business. This is often termed "**email direct marketing**". Sending a fax or making a phone call may come at a later stage or when necessary. When you make phone calls, remember to prepare a list of topics you want to talk on the phone, in case you forget. And when you attend a trade fair, selecting the right trade fair, preparing it well and following up timely are essential to the success of that endeavor. As email direct marketing is so prevalent in international business, I would like to introduce a few basic principles for an effective email as follows.

The Internet has greatly changed our way of communication. Emails and instant messaging have made our words shorter and shorter. So is our attention span. A survey of international buyers shows that they spend an average of 2 to 3 seconds on an email. Plus, cultures differ in their dependence on **contexts** for communication. Different from people from **high-context cultures**, people from a **low-context culture** are generally less dependent on the context for communication. They prefer straightforward to **roundabout** expressions, which requires us to use the fewest possible words to make our expression straightforward and **stick to point**. For an effective email, I'd like to offer the following basic principles: draft a short and attractive subject line; be short and concise with your main body; stress your strength briefly; use simple words in case the receiver is not a native speaker of English; and end your email with a call to action.

语境
高语境文化
低语境文化
迂回的
到位

Exercises 练习

I. True or False

1. For international market research, you should first conduct a micro-environment analysis. (　　)
2. A desktop research normally relies on primary data while a field research on secondary data. (　　)
3. A desktop research generally costs the same as a field research. (　　)
4. The outcomes of desktop research are generally not as targeted as field research. (　　)
5. The United States withdrew from the North American Free Trade Agreement (NAFTA) during the Obama administration. (　　)
6. China International Import Expo (CIIE), which started in 2018, has greatly boosted imports. (　　)
7. Canton Fair is the largest trade fair in China and an important international comprehensive exhibition. (　　)
8. We can search for potential customers in a certain country by using

domain name suffixes, such as ".cn " for China and ".de " for France. ( )

9. Yandex is a preferred search engine for Russia, East Europe and West Asian. ( )
10. In international trade, direct email marketing is heavily used because it is convenient and economical in establishing business relations. ( )

II. Multiple Choice Questions

1. A "PEST" analysis comprises of ( ) of the target market.*
   [A] political analysis
   [B] economic analysis
   [C] social analysis
   [D] technological analysis
2. When the market researcher starts the investigation, ( ).
   [A] he/she always collects secondary data before deciding whether to collect primary data
   [B] he/she only collects secondary data
   [C] he/she always collects primary data before deciding whether to collect secondary data
   [D] he/she only collects primary data
3. Foreign trade risks include ( ).*
   [A] commercial and credit risk
   [B] political and legal risks
   [C] cargo risk
   [D] exchange risk
4. Compared with primary data, advantages of secondary data include: ( ).*
   [A] being more informative
   [B] being readily available
   [C] being more targeted
   [D] being cost-effective
5. Generally speaking, a devaluation of RMB tend to ( ).*
   [A] reduce China's import
   [B] reduce China's export

[C] promote China's import
[D] promote China's export

6. When RMB devalues after you sign the contract with the importer in USD, you will (　　).
[A] have more revenue in RMB
[B] have less revenue in RMB
[C] have the same revenue in RMB
[D] have the same profit in RMB

7. Through customs databases, you expect to learn about (　　) of a transaction.*
[A] the shipper
[B] the consignee
[C] the notify party
[D] details of the merchandise

8. Which is NOT an appropriate way of writing the first email to a prospective customer? (　　)
[A] Drafting an appealing subject line.
[B] Being short and concise with your main body.
[C] Elaborating on your strengths.
[D] Using simple words.

9. Which of the followings is (are) (a) sources of secondary statistics? (　　)*
[A] Websites of government departments.
[B] Websites of international organizations.
[C] Websites of trade associations.
[D] Databases of public or college libraries.

10. Which of the following statements is NOT true about social media marketing? (　　)
[A] Social media marketing still relies on broadcasting.
[B] Exporters should identify key influencers for brand-building.
[C] Exporters should post engaging contents to audience for brand-building.
[D] Exporters could add connections for establishing business relationships.

III. Web Page Clipping

1. Please log onto the B2B platforms mentioned in this chapter, browse, choose one you like and clip one of its web pages. Select one company you like from the platform. Find out its homepage and the web page for company profile, which, for your reference, is mostly under the menu of "About" or "About Us".
2. Search on the Internet and find top 10 foreign distributors or retailers in a certain country and clip two of their web pages.
3. Find a product category you are interested in, search the Internet for any trade fair in the category, find out its homepage and clip a web page.

IV. Group Tasks

1. A company exported 200 metric tons of meat ducks to Iran. On arrival at the Iranian customs, they were rejected, because the slaughter method of ducks did not comply with Islamic regulations. However, a watch company developed a watch with unique functions for the Middle East market. No matter where you are in the world, the watch can convert local time into Muslim time, and automatically remind you of the time for prayers. And a "compass" on the watch always points to **Mecca** (麦加). Once the watch was launched on the market, it became an instant success. Discuss in groups about reasons for the failure of one exporter and the success of another and comment on the two cases.
2. Write a market research plan for a certain product for export. Then conduct the research and write a report. The research report should include: the product, the research goal, the research plan, the research methods and major findings. You should complete all the tasks in a group, including handing in one research report as a group.

Chapter 3 Business Negotiations and Signing the Contract

第三章 商务磋商和签订合同

Learning Objectives:

- Contents and forms of business negotiations
- General procedures of business negotiations
- Formats of international sales contracts
- How to sign international sales contracts

Identifying your target customers is just the first step in developing new markets. After that, business negotiations follow. Negotiations deal with major issues for concluding a deal: product, price, quality, quantity, time and place of delivery, terms of payment, resolving disputes, etc. A successful negotiation ends with a contract.

3.1 Contents and Forms of Business Negotiations 商务磋商的内容和形式

International negotiations can be conducted orally, in writing or indicated by acts. For example, an oral negotiation can be a face-to-face talk at your place, the importer's place or at a trade fair; or a talk on the phone or via a video conferencing platform. Oral negotiations are normally suitable for complex transactions that involve many issues,

电子数据交换
商品交易所

such as transactions of large equipment. A negotiation in writing includes correspondence through letters, **electronic data interchange (EDI)**, faxes, emails, instant messages, etc. Sometimes, traders also conclude a deal by performing an act, which occurs more at an auction house or a **commodity exchange**.

《联合国国际货物销售合同公约》
多边的
截止到　批准

The ***United Nations Convention on Contracts for the International Sale of Goods*** (*CISG*) is an important international convention that governs the majority of international sales of goods. Sometimes known as the Vienna Convention, it is a **multilateral** convention that establishes a uniform framework for international merchandise trade. **As of** 2020, it has been **ratified** by 94 countries, representing two thirds of world trade. As China is a signatory of this convention, we are bound by it in our international business of merchandise trade. However, important non-signatories include the United Kingdom, India, many nations in the Middle East, South Africa, and many other African nations, which should be noted when you negotiate a contract.

3.2 General Procedures of Business Negotiations 商务磋商的一般程序

询盘，发盘，还盘和接受
必不可少的

Generally speaking, you go through four stages in a typical business negotiation—**enquiry, offer, counter-offer, and acceptance**, though some stages might be skipped or repeated under certain circumstances. Among the four stages, only "offer" and "acceptance" are **indispensable**. If your negotiations turn out well, hopefully, you'll make a deal. According to *CISG*, a deal is concluded the moment an acceptance of an offer becomes effective. In what follows, let's examine the key points for each stage from your perspective as an exporter, but as each stage can be initiated by both you and the importer, rules or suggestions in each stage for you also apply to the importer.

3.2.1 Enquiry 询盘（询价/邀请发盘）

When you enter a clothing store, you may ask the shop owner, "Do you have jackets?" or "How much is this jacket?" This is an enquiry in a domestic context. An enquiry in an international negotiation, also called an invitation to offer, is an action initiated by the importer or exporter, but mostly the importer, to ask the other party about price and other terms of sale for certain products. Either party, for importing or exporting something, can enquire about one or more terms of sale, such as prices, catalogs, samples, quality and quantity, time and place of delivery, terms of payment, etc. It can be made orally or in writing with no fixed format. Nor is it binding on either you or the importer. It is not an indispensable stage for a negotiation, either. Regular business partners may skip it and go straight to making offers. An importer's enquiry may read: "Please **quote** the price of CIF London for Chinese **Rosin**, June shipment." An exporter's enquiry may be: "Can supply Chinese cotton, October shipment. If interested, please fax or email."

报价
松香

Figure 3-1 below is a detailed enquiry sent by a Singapore trading company to your company inquiring about a type of swimming suits.

SINGAPORE WONKA TRADING COMPANY LTD
67 ANG MO KIO AVENUE 8 SINGAPORE 560250

Enquiry Sheet

No. SWTC-SO-03
Date: April 09, 2022

Messrs.: TIANJIN BINHAI IMPORT & EXPORT CO., LTD.
NO. 188 HAIHE ROAD, BINHAI DISTRICT, TIANJIN, P. R. CHINA

1	Subject	Purchase of 3,000 pcs of swimming suits
2	Description	Men & Women swimming suits
3	Quantity	3,000 pcs in total
4	Specification	Men & Women suits in sizes X, XL, XXL
5	Size & Quantity Assortments	X 500 pcs; XL 500 pcs; XXL 500 pcs for both Men & Women
6	Delivery	May 31, 2022
7	Price	CIF Singapore

Figure 3-1 Enquiry from an Importer

3.2.2 Offer 发盘（报盘/报价/要约）

In the above store-shopping example, the shop owner may respond to your enquiry by showing you the jacket and telling you its price—"It's 200 yuan." This makes a **quotation** in a domestic negotiation. A quotation is part of an offer. You may bargain, for sure, but if you like the jacket and

报价

accept the price, a deal is concluded and the shop owner must sell you the jacket under this price. Similarly, in an international negotiation, an offer is a business **proposal** made by the exporter or importer to express his/her wish to sell or buy particular goods under stated terms. An exporter can make a "selling offer", and an importer a "buying offer", or a "**bid**". Figure 3-2 below is a possible selling offer you can make for the above case of selling swimming suits. If the same terms in the case were proposed by the importer for procurement, that would make it a buying offer.

商业提议

递盘

TIANJIN BINHAI IMPORT & EXPORT CO., LTD.
NO.188 HAIHE ROAD, BINHAI DISTRICT, TIANJIN, P R. CHINA
TEL No.: 0086-22-8835097X FAX No.: 0086-22-8835099X
WEB: www.tjbhix.com MAIL: trade@tjbhix.com

PRICE LIST -OFFER SHEET

Date: April 12, 2022
No. TBIM - SWTC - 09

Atten: SINGAPORE WONKA TRADING COMPANY LTD
67 ANG MO KIO AVENUE 8 SINGAPORE 560250

Item	Description	Quantity	Unit Price	Amount
Swimming suits	spandex 80%, polyamide 20%		CIF Singapore Incoterms 2020	
	Men's suits			
	Size X	500 pcs	USD75 per pc	USD37,500. –
	Size XL	500 pcs	USD85 per pc	USD42,500. –
	Size XXL	500 pcs	USD95 per pc	USD47,500. –
	Women's suits			
	Size X	500 pcs	USD80 per pc	USD40,000. –
	Size XL	500 pcs	USD90 per pc	USD45,000. –
	Size XXL	500 pcs	USD100 per pc	USD50,000. –
Total		3,000 pcs		USD262,500. –

Terms of Payment: By L/C available by draft at sight

Packing: To be packed in transparent poly bag, one pc per bag, 100 pcs to one carton

Date of Shipment: June 15, 2022

Port of Loading: Tianjin, China

Port of Destination: Singapore

Insurance: To be covered by the Seller for 110% of the invoice value against All Risks & War Risk

Offer Valid By: April 18, 2022.

Special Requirement: L/C to be opened and shall reach the Seller 30 days before date of shipment

Figure 3-2 Offer Made by an Exporter

Offers in international negotiations mostly contain more terms and are more formal (including price, quantity, time of shipment, terms of payment, etc.) An offer, defined by *CISG*, is **legally binding on** the **offeror**—he/she has to execute the deal under his/her proposed terms. See the above offer for swimming suits sent by the exporter.

法律上有约束力的

发盘人

According to *CISG*, not all business proposals can be interpreted as "offers". A business proposal has to meet certain qualifications to be an "offer", otherwise, it's just an **invitation to make offers,** or the so-called "non-firm offers" or "indefinite offcrs" in practicc. Mistaking an invitation to make offers for an offer may cause you troubles. For example, sometimes, the proposal is sent without a specific audience, seeming to be addressing the general public. Don't rush acting on it—possibly, it's just an ad. At other times, you, as the **"offeree"**, feel that the "offeror" is rather **vague** about his/her intention or readiness to execute the deal under his/her proposed terms. Don't rush acting, either—the "offeror" may just want to **sound out** the market by giving you general instead of specific information. At still other times, the "offeror" may want to reserve the right to modify his/her proposed terms by stating "for your reference" or "subject to our final confirmation." These proposals are **indefinite**. That's why they are also referred to as **"indefinite offers"** or **"non-firm offers"** as opposed to the so-called **"definite offers"** or **"firm offers"**, but essentially, these proposals are not offers, because they don't have specific audience, nor are they sufficiently definite or clear in their intention to execute the deal under proposed terms. They are just invitation to make offers by nature.

邀请发盘

受盘人

含糊不清

试探

不确定的

虚盘

实盘

Then, what kind of business proposals qualify for an "offer"? *CISG* states in Article 14(1) that "A proposal for concluding a contract addressed to one or more specific persons constitutes an offer if it is sufficiently definite and indicates the intention of the offeror to be bound in case of acceptance", and in Article 14(2) that "A proposal other than one addressed to one or more specific persons is to be considered merely as an invitation to make offers, unless the contrary is clearly indicated by the person making the offer". According to this definition, two criteria can be used to make the judgement: First, does it have a specific audience? You cannot address a general public in your proposal, like in an ad or a pamphlet, unless otherwise indicated. You

"缔结一项针对一个或多个特定人的合同的提议，如果足够明确，并表明发盘人在接受时有受约束的意图，则构成发盘。"

"非向一个或一个以上特定的人提出的建议，仅应视为邀请做出发盘，除非提出建议的人明确表示相反的意向。"

have to address a specific audience by stating the name of the audience, such as the name of an individual or a business. Second, your proposal has to be "sufficiently definite and indicate your intention to be bound" in case the offeree accepts your proposal.

But how to interpret "definite"? Unfortunately, traders around the world have different understandings regarding this. *CISG* states in Article 14(1) that "a proposal is sufficiently definite if it indicates the goods and expressly or implicitly fixes or makes provision for determining the quantity and the price". In other words, it considers a proposal definite as long as it has the name, quantity and price of the goods. However, this interpretation is rarely used in practice due to its difficulties in execution. A better solution remains the two criteria mentioned above—a specific audience and a clear intention and readiness to conclude the deal. Phrases like "subject to our final confirmation" or "for reference only" to indicate finality, if present, may also be used for reference. Without these phrases, however, you have to rely on yourself to figure out when you are bound by your offer and how you interpret offers made to you. You are highly suggested to ask the other party to clarify if you are not sure.

"如果一项报盘表明货物，并明确或含蓄地确定或规定确定货物的数量和价格，则构成实盘。"

An offer generally has to fix a **period for acceptance**. Please avoid making offers without fixing such a period. An offer takes effect when it reaches the offeree and his/her acceptance within that period is considered effective.

接受的有效期

Sometimes, you may want to **withdraw** your offer after you've made it. This often happens when you find an error in the offer or when the market has changed so much that executing the offer would bring you a great loss. Whether can an offer be withdrawn? It depends on the time it reaches the offeree. Article 15(1) of *CISG* states that "an offer becomes effective when it reaches the offeree." Therefore, it can be withdrawn "if the **withdrawal** reaches the offeree before or at the same time as the offer." (Article 15(2)). This implies that you need a faster means of communication to withdraw your offer, which is sort of like you chase a horse by driving a car. But these stipulations don't apply when a means of communication that reaches the offeree **instantly**, such as telephone calls, emails, instant messages, etc., is employed, which means, the offer cannot be withdrawn in these cases.

撤回

撤回通知

即刻地

What if the offer has already become effective? Can we **cancel** it? Article 16(1) of *CISG* states that "Until a contract is concluded, an offer may be revoked if the revocation reaches the offeree before he has dispatched an acceptance." But it cannot be revoked if the offer has fixed a period of time for acceptance, or has indicated by other means that it is irrevocable. Besides, if it is reasonable for the offeree to **rely on** the offer as being irrevocable and he/she has acted in reliance on the offer, it cannot be revoked, either. What's more, when a rejection reaches the offeror, the offer is **terminated**, even if it is irrevocable.

撤销

"在合同订立之前，发盘在受盘人发出接受通知之前可以撤销。"

信赖

终止

3.2.3 Counter-Offer 还盘（还价）

Again, in the store-shopping example, you may not like the price or other terms of the deal and offer your desired terms—"your price is too high. How about 150 yuan?" That is a bargain in a domestic negotiation. Counter-offers in an international negotiation is similar, which is a reply to an offer with additions, limitations or other modifications. Both the exporter and importer can counter-offer the other's offer or counter-offers and be further counter-offered by the other. So, counter-offers can go on and on for several rounds, but they can also be skipped altogether when the offer is accepted straight away. A counter-offer cancels the original offer and constitutes a new one. As a result, if you are counter-offered, your offer shall **lapse** and you will not be bound by that offer. The same is true for the importer.

失效

3.2.4 Acceptance 接受

Finally, in the store shopping example, after several rounds of negotiations, you or the shop owner may accept the terms offered by the other. That makes an acceptance in a domestic negotiation. Similarly, in an international negotiation, an acceptance is the final and definite expression of assent to the terms of an offer or a counter-offer, together with previously agreed upon terms. Both exporter and importer can make an acceptance, which should be in statement or indicated by an act, such as the importer's placing an order. Silence or **inactivity** dose not in itself **amounts to** an acceptance. Like an offer, an acceptance should also be addressed to a specific audience—

不行动 等于

individual(s) or business(es). If someone else learns about the terms of the negotiation and accepts, it is not considered an **eligible** acceptance.

合格的

到期，失效

An acceptance must be delivered before the offer **expires**. If you accept the offer beyond the expiry date, the acceptance is ineffective, unless the other party accepts your late "acceptance" by informing you orally or sending you a notice to say so without delay. But in case your means of communication, such as the courier, is solely responsible for the delay, your late acceptance is still regarded as effective, unless the other party thinks otherwise and timely informs you of his/her decision. An oral offer must be accepted immediately unless the circumstances indicate otherwise. An acceptance can be withdrawn before or at the same time it reaches the other party, but you need a faster means of communication for sending the withdrawal.

Sometimes, a tricky issue regarding acceptance is how to distinguish it from a counter-offer. Inexperienced traders tend to mistake some counter-offers for acceptances. For example, the importer may reply that he/she accepts the offer, but still wants to make minor alterations. You need to be alert to this type of reply—it could be an acceptance or a counter-offer, depending on which terms the importer wants to modify. According to *CISG*, if the modifications relate, among other things, to the price, payment, quality and quantity of the goods, place and time of delivery, extent of one party's liability to the other or the settlement of disputes, they are considered to **materially** alter the offer and therefore **constitute** a counter-offer in effect; otherwise, they may be considered non-material alterations and constitute an acceptance, unless the offeror, without **undue** delay, objects orally to the discrepancy or sends a notice to say so. To sum up, an acceptance must be in strict accordance with the offer. Any modification alters an offer. Material modifications turn it into a counter-offer, while non-material modifications keep it as an acceptance, unless the offeror objects to them without delay.

实质性地

构成

过分的

3.3 Signing Business Contract 签订商业合同

Once an acceptance, be it oral or in writing, reaches the other party, a deal is concluded. Different from those in domestic trade, international lawsuits are costly and time-consuming, so no one likes to get involved into any lawsuits. It is thus important that you negotiate with care so that when a deal is made, both of you reach common understanding of the terms of sale and know exactly and unmistakably what is expected of you.

However, owning to the inconveniences caused by the long distance between exporter and importer, international contracts tend to be more flexible than domestic ones in format, which could be a traditional contract or alternative formats such as a sales confirmation, a purchase confirmation, an agreement or a confirmed ***proforma* invoice**. A sales confirmation is normally drafted by the exporter and sent to the importer for confirmation, while a purchase confirmation is the other way round. A *proforma* invoice, as a "preview" of the final **commercial invoice**, can serve as an offer in negotiations, and a contract when confirmed by both parties. However, for large and complicated sales, a detailed contract is still needed and signed by both parties. The contract can be signed face to face, but this is rare in international businesses. Mostly you send two signed copies to the importer, asking him/her to sign and send one back **for file**. This practice is known as **counter-sign**. Faxed contracts are also acceptable at times of urgency.

形式发票

商业发票

存档　会签

An import or export contract is generally more detailed than a domestic one and may include the following terms (see Figure 3-3):

- Name and address of the exporter and importer
- Date and location of signing the contract
- The willingness and guarantee of both sides to signing the contract
- Product description: name, model, quality, quantity, packaging and marking, etc. of the goods.
- Unit price and **total amount**
- Terms of payment
- Time of shipment
- Port of loading and port of destination
- Insurance
- Inspection
- Documents required by the importer
- Complaint or Claim
- Dispute Resolution
- ***Force majeure***
- **Remarks**
- Signature

总金额

不可抗力

备注

TIANJIN BINHAI IMPORT & EXPORT CO., LTD.
NO.188 HAIHE ROAD, BINHAI DISTRICT, TIANJIN, P. R. CHINA
TEL No.: 0086 - 22 - 8835097X FAX No.: 0086 - 22 - 8835099X
WEB: www.tjbhix.com E-MAIL: trade@tjbhix.com

SALES CONTRACT

No.: TBIM-SWTC-09

Date: April 17, 2022

Signed at: Tianjin, China

SELLER

TIANJIN BINHAI IMPORT & EXPORT CO., LTD.
NO. 188 HAIHE ROAD, BINHAI DISTRICT, TIANJIN, P. R. CHINA

BUYER

SINGAPORE WONKA TRADING COMPANY LTD
67 ANG MO KIO AVENUE 8 SINGAPORE 560250

Item	Description	Quantity	Unit Price	Amount
	Swimming suits, polyamide 80%, spandex 20%		CIF Singapore Incoterms 2020	
	Men's Suits			
Swimming Suits	Size X	500 pcs	USD75 per pc	USD37,500. –
	Size XL	500 pcs	USD85 per pc	USD42,500. –
	Size XXL	500 pcs	USD95 per pc	USD47,500. –
	Women's suits			
	Size X	500 pcs	USD80 per pc	USD40,000. –
	Size XL	500 pcs	USD90 per pc	USD45,000. –
	Size XXL	500 pcs	USD100 per pc	USD50,000. –
Total		3,000 pcs		USD262,500. –
Total amount in words	SAY USD TWO HUNDRED AND SIXTY-TWO THOUSAND FIVE HUNDRED ONLY			

The seller agrees to sell and the buyer agrees to buy the undermentioned goods on the terms and conditions stated below:

Terms of Payment

By LC available by draft at sight to be opened and shall reach the Exporter 30 days before the date of shipment.

Packing

To be packed in transparent poly bag, one pc per bag, 100 pcs to one carton.

Shipping Marks

SWTC
SINGAPORE
NO.1-30
TBIM-SWTC-09

Delivery Time

June 15, 2022

Port of Loading

Tianjin, China

Port of Destination

Singapore

Partial Shipments

Not Allowed

Transshipment

Not Allowed

Insurance

To be covered by the Exporter for 110% of the invoicc value against All Risks and War Risk.

General Terms and Conditions

(1) The Importcr of this Salcs Contract shall open the Letter of Credit no later than the time stipulated by this Sales Contract, failing which the Exporter has the right to rescind without prior notice, or to take the whole or any part of this Sales Contract as non-fulfilled by the Importer, or to claim any losses sustained.

(2) For transactions concluded on CIF basis, this insurance coverage will be for 110% of the invoice value against the risks specified in this Sales Contract. If additional coverage is required by the Importer, the Importer must have the consent of the Exporter before shipment, and the additional premium is to be borne by the Importer.

(3) Quality/Quantity Discrepancy: In case of quality discrepancy, the Importer may, within 60 days after the arrival of goods at the Port of Destination, lodge a claim against the Exporter. In case of quantity discrepancy, the Importer may, within 15 days after the arrival of the goods at the Port of Destination, lodge a claim against the Exporter. The claim(s) should be supported by reports issued by a recognized public surveyor appointed by the Exporter, and the Exporter shall not be liable for any discrepancies attributable to the insurance company, shipping company, other transportation organization or post office.

(4) All disputes arising from the execution of this contract shall be settled through friendly negotiation. If no settlement can be reached through negotiation, the case shall be submitted to Hong Kong International Arbitration Centre for arbitration in accordance with its rules of procedure. The arbitral award is final and binding upon both parties.

(5) The Exporter shall not be held liable for failure or delay in the delivery of the entire lot or a portion of the goods under this Sales Contract in consequence of any Force Majeure incidents.

(6) The Importer is requested to quote the number of this Sales Contract in the Letter of Credit opened in favor of the Exporter.

(7) Upon receipt of this Sales Contract, the Importer is requested to sign and return one copy of the Contract immediately. Objection, if any, should be raised by the Importer within five days after the receipt of this Sales Contract, otherwise, it is assumed that the Importer has accepted all the terms and conditions of this Sales Contract.

(8) The above General Terms and Conditions of this Sales Contract are integral parts of this Sales Contract.

THE SELLER	THE BUYER
李明	Willy Worka
Authorized Representative	**Authorized Representative**

Figure 3-3 A Sample Sales Contract for Export

Exercises 练习

I. True or False

1. Business negotiation includes the steps of enquiry, offer, counter-offer and acceptance, each of which is indispensable. (　　)
2. A deal is concluded when an offer is accepted within the period of validity. (　　)
3. An enquiry in an international business negotiation generally contains as much information as a domestic negotiation. (　　)
4. No matter whether or not the importer and exporter are familiar with each other, the enquiry should not be skipped in a business negotiation. (　　)
5. According to *CISG*, an invitation to make offers is not an offer. (　　)
6. According to *CISG*, an offer containing the commodity name, quantity and price of the goods is a definite offer. (　　)
7. An offer usually requires a fixed period for acceptance. (　　)
8. Acceptance should be in the form of a statement or an act. Silence does not constitute an acceptance. (　　)
9. In international trade, contracts are seldom signed face to face. (　　)
10. The functions of *pro forma* invoice and commercial invoice are basically the same. (　　)

II. Multiple Choice Questions

1. According to *CISG*, (　　　) are indispensable elements for an offer.
   [A] commodity name, quality, quantity
   [B] commodity name, quantity, price
   [C] commodity name, quality, price
   [D] commodity name, price, payment
2. According to *CISG*, a deal is concluded (　　　).
   [A] when the buyer receives the offer
   [B] by the time of signing written contract
   [C] when the buyer accepts the offer
   [D] when the contract is approved by the superiors

3. Which of the following statements about the relationship between a withdrawal and a cancellation of an offer is TRUE? (　　)
   [A] Both occur after the offer takes effect.
   [B] The former occurs before the offer takes effect, while the latter occurs after the offer takes effect.
   [C] Both occur before the offer takes effect.
   [D] The former occurs after the offer takes effect, while the latter occurs before the offer takes effect.
4. The amendment to (　　) may not materially alter an offer.
   [A] means of dispute settlement
   [B] package of the goods
   [C] quantity and term of payment
   [D] time and place of delivery
5. Under what condition(s) cannot an offer be revoked? (　　)*
   [A] When it has fixed a period of time for acceptance.
   [B] When it has indicated by other means that it is irrevocable.
   [C] If it is reasonable for the offeree to rely on the offer as being irrevocable and he/she has acted in reliance on the offer.
   [D] When the rejection reaches the offeree so that the offer is terminated, even if it is irrevocable.
6. "We accept, but just prefer you to change the term of payment from D/P at sight to D/A." This is (　　).
   [A] a counter-offer
   [B] an indication of concluding a deal
   [C] a valid acceptance
   [D] a rejection of the offer
7. The main reason(s) leading to the termination of offer include: (　　).*
   [A] The offer is expired
   [B] The offeror has withdrawn the offer
   [C] The importer refuses the offer
   [D] A *force majeure* incident occurs to the exporter after the offer is made

8. Which of the following statements is TRUE about *CISG*? (　　)
   [A] *CISG* is binding on every exporter or importer in an international transaction.
   [B] According to *CISG*, an oral offer must be accepted immediately, unless otherwise indicated.
   [C] *CISG* is an international convention that is not binding unless made reference in the contract.
   [D] *CISG* governs both merchandise trade and service trade.
9. Which of the following statements is TRUE about the validity of an offer? (　　)
   [A] An offer cannot be withdrawn once it is sent to the offeree.
   [B] An offer cannot be canceled once it is sent to the offeree.
   [C] An offer cannot be withdrawn once it reaches the offeree.
   [D] An offer cannot be canceled once it reaches the offeree.
10. Which one of the following is NOT a precondition for a business proposal to constitute an offer? (　　)
   [A] It must have a clear audience.
   [B] It must be clear about its readiness to conclude the deal.
   [C] It is for reference only.
   [D] It must contain the commodity name, quantity and price.

III. Case Study

1. Sinomada Machinery Co., Ltd., a Chinese exporter of heavy industry machinery, made an offer of forklifts to a Japanese company Kishida Construction Co., Ltd., quoting: "We can sell you 50 forklifts at $ 12,000 CIF Tokyo. Shipment is to be made within two months after the contract is concluded. Payment is to be made by LC at sight. Please reply as soon as possible." Kishida Construction replied: " We accept your offer, but we need delivery be made within one month after the contract is entered into." Sinomada Machinery didn't respond but sold the forklifts to a French customer. Then Kishida sued Sinomada for breach of contract. Question: Is there a contract between the two parties? Why?
2. A buyer from Snugdomus Trading Co, Ltd., an Italian importer of furniture, visited the stall of a **Dongguan** based Chinese furniture manufacturer Okart Furniture Co., Ltd. at the Canton Fair and negotiated terms for a set of wardrobes. Okart made an offer orally to

东莞

the buyer, but he did not respond on the spot. However, in the afternoon, the buyer revisited the stall to express his willingness to accept the morning's offer. But during the day, Okart had learned that the price of this type of wardrobe had been on the rise. How do you think Okart should handle the matter? And why?

Chapter 4 Description of Commodities

第四章 产品描述

Learning Objectives:

- How to measure quantities in international sales contract
- How to measure quality in international sales contract
- How to package and mark products for export

When you give a price quotation to or draft a contract with the importer, you need to be aware that people around the world might use different **systems of measurement** or standards to describe product quantity and quality. So, before settling on anything, you need to achieve common understanding with the importer regarding quantity and quality in order to avoid possible misunderstandings or disputes in the subsequent transactions. Besides, you need also to get familiar with some common requirements for packaging in international trade. 度量衡

4.1 Measuring Quantities 衡量数量

Quantity is an indispensable term for concluding a contract. According to *CISG*, the quantity delivered should conform to what is required in the contract. Otherwise, the importer can reject the over-loaded quantity, or **make claims** for the under-loaded portion. 索赔

4.1.1 Measurement Systems in International Trade 国际贸易中的度量衡制度

In any contract, quantities of goods need to be measured in a unit, but this is where problems may arise in international sales, as people from the world use different **measurement systems** and may have different understandings even for the same unit. Though the world is progressing toward a uniformed system of measurement, **customary units** still hold in a few countries and result in confusions. For example, a ton has a different real weight depending on whether you are speaking of a so-called **metric ton**, a **short ton** or a **long ton** and that an **ounce** of sugar, of water and of gold have different real weights too. A U.S **gallon** is different from a British imperial gallon. Shocked? I'm not surprised if you say yes. In the above example, 1 metric ton ≈ 1.104 2 short ton ≈ 0.984 2 long ton and the same unit called "ounce" weighs differently for dry goods, fluids or precious metals in the U.S. as well as in the U.K. A U.S. gallon is equal to 3.875 liters while an imperial gallon to 4.564 liters. Even a local could be **baffled** by the peculiarities and complexities, let alone a foreigner. Therefore, when you draft a contract, you need to be explicit about the units of measurement used and the corresponding measurement system to avoid misunderstandings. Common measurement systems used in international trade include **the Metric System** (a system based on the unit of "meter"), **the British Imperial System**, **the U.S. Customary Measurement Systems** and **the International System of Units (SI)**, the last one being a development of the Metric System. The Metric System and the International System of Units have been gaining popularization around the world. Now most countries have **granted** an official status to SI, including the United Kingdom, Canada and the United States, although these three countries are among a handful of nations that, to various degrees, also keep using their customary systems. The UK and Canada adopt both the Metric System and the Imperial System, and the United States is still dominated by its customary unit systems, particularly in daily life. Therefore, confusions and misunderstandings regarding quantity may still exist and you need to keep an eye on it. In many cases, traders

度量衡制度
习惯单位
公吨 短吨 长吨 盎司
加仑
困惑的
公制
英制
美国习惯单位制
国际单位制
给予，授予

use "M/T" or "tonne" for weight in order to specifically refer to a ton in the Metric System and distinguish it from a long ton or a short ton. Besides, units like "**piece**" "**set**" "**dozen**", etc. are common in trade for counting numbers. Table 4-1 gives a list of the common units of measurement. Table 4-2 demonstrates how to convert between units of length and Table 4-3 between units of capacity. Figure 4-1 is an intuitive representation of the relationship between yard, foot and inch and Figure 4-2 one of the conversions between fluid units under the US customary units. 件 套 打

Table 4-1 Common Units of Measurement

	The Metric System Units	British Imperial and US Customary Units
Weight (重量)	gram (克), kilogram (千克), metric ton/tonne (公吨),	ounce (盎司), pound (磅) long ton (长吨), short ton (短吨)
Length (长度)	meter (米), centimeter (厘米),	inch (英寸), foot (英尺), yard (码), mile (英里)
Area (面积)	square meter (平方米), square centimeter (平方厘米)	square foot (平方英尺), square yard (平方码), square inch (平方英寸)
Volume (体积)	cubic-meter (立方米), cubic centimeter (立方厘米),	cubic foot (立方英尺), cubic yard (立方码), cubic inch (平方英寸)
Capacity (容积)	liter (公升), milliliter (毫升)	gallon (加仑), pint (品脱), quart (夸脱), bushel (蒲式耳)

Table 4-2 Conversion Between Units of Length

Metric System		British Imperial System/American Customary System		
meter	centimeter	yard	foot	inch
1	100	1.094	3.281	39.370
square meter	square centimeter	square yard	square foot	square inch
1	10,000	1.196	10.764	1,550
cubic meter	cubic centimeter	cubic yard	cubic foot	cubic inch
1	1,000,000	1.303	35.315	61,024

Table 4-3 Conversion Between Units of Capacity

Metric System	British Imperial System	American Customary System
liter	British gallon	American gallon
1	0.22	0.254
4.546	1	1.201
3.785	0.833	1

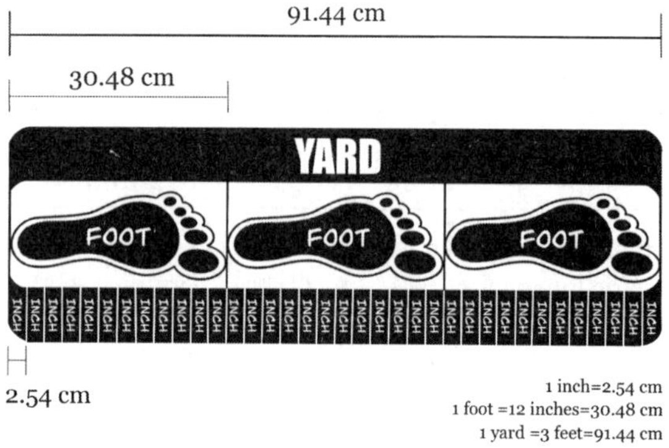

Figure 4-1 Conversion Between Yard, Foot, Inch and Centimeter

Figure 4-2 Conversion Between Fluid Units under the US Customary Units

4.1.2 Methods for Calculating Weight 计算重量的方法

Methods for calculating weight vary for different types of commodities.

♦ **Gross weight 毛重**

Gross weight is the total weight of the commodity plus the package weight.

♦ **Net weight 净重**

Net weight is the weight of commodity without the package. In international trade, if the commodities are sold by weight, net weight is often implied.

♦ **Conditioned weight 条件重量**

Conditioned weight is the weight derived by removing the moisture content of a commodity and adding a standardized amount of moisture. This method is applicable for cargoes of high economic value but unstable moisture content, such as wool, raw silk, etc. The formula for calculating the conditioned weight is:

conditioned weight = dried weight + standard moisture

条件重量=干燥重量+标准含水量

♦ **Theoretical weight 理论重量**

Commodities that have regular **specifications** and sizes, such as **galvanized iron, tin plate and armor plate**, are often eligible for theoretical weight. As long as the specifications and the sizes of such commodities are the same, their total theoretical weight can be calculated by adding up the number of the commodities.

规格

镀锌铁，锡板和装甲板

♦ **Legal weight 法定重量**

Legal weight is the weight of merchandise **per se** plus that of its **immediate wrapping** but not that of the shipping package. The immediate wrapping could be **cans**, small paper boxes, small bottles, etc. This method is mainly used in some Latin American countries for the purpose of assessing import duties.

本身

直接包装

罐

4.1.3 Quantity Tolerance 数量公差

For bulk cargoes like farm produce or mineral products such as corn, soybean, wheat, coal, out of various reasons, their quantity delivered often has a high possibility of not being exactly the same with the quantity contracted. Therefore, quantity tolerance terms are introduced into international sales contracts in order to avoid disputes. This is often achieved through a so-called "more or less" clause, which sets the limits the variance in quantity is allowed.

大宗散装货物，如农产品或矿产品，如玉米、大豆、小麦、煤炭，出于各种原因交付的数量不完全等同于合同数量的可能性很高。因此，为了避免争议，国际销售合同中引入数量公差条款，以避免争议。这通常通过所谓的"溢短装"条款来实现，该条款规定了允许的数量偏差的范围。

4.1.3.1 "More or less" clause 数量溢短装条款

A complete "more or less" clause should generally include three elements: First, the allowed range of variance in quantity, which is often expressed as a percentage of the total quantity. Second, the party who determines the quantity to be delivered, which is mostly the exporter in practice, but the importer may also determine for convenience if he/she charters the ship so that the quantity to be delivered is limited by the capacity of the ship. Third, the price used to calculate the value of the over-load or under-load portion of the merchandise. It is generally calculated based on the contract price, though sometimes market price at the time of loading or unloading is also applied to prevent an intentional overloading or under-loading by the party who determines the "more or less" quantity. The following is an example of a "more or less" clause: "Quantity: 100,000 M/T, 5% more or less, at exporter's option and at contract price."

以下是"溢短装"条款的一个示例：数量：100 000 公吨，可多交或少交 5%，由卖方选择，增减部分按合同价格计算。

4.1.3.2 Quantity tolerance in *UCP 600*《跟单信用证统一惯例》中的数量公差条款

However, when it comes to delivery under a letter of credit, you need to obtain a proper understanding of the **wording** about quantity tolerance **delineated** in the credit.

措辞　描述

For example, article 30a of *UCP 600* states that: "The words "about" or "approximately" used in connection with the amount of the credit or the quantity or the unit price stated in the credit are to be construed as allowing a tolerance not to exceed 10% more or 10% less than the amount, the quantity or the unit price to which they refer."

《跟单信用证统一惯例》第 30 条 a 款规定："约"或"大约"用于信用证金额或信用证规定的数量或单价时，应解释为允许有关金额或数量或单价有不超过 10%的增减幅度。

And article 30b of *UCP 600* states: "A tolerance not to exceed 5% more or 5% less than the quantity of the commodities is allowed, provided the credit does not state the quantity in terms of a stipulated number of packing units or individual items and the total amount of the drawings does not exceed the amount of the credit." This implies that a quantity tolerance does not apply when the credit states the quantity in terms of a stipulated number of packing units or individual items, for example, a certain number of laptop computers.

《跟单信用证统一惯例》第 30 条 b 款：在信用证未以包装单位件数或货物自身件数的方式规定货物数量时，货物数量允许有 5%的增减幅度，只要总支取金额不超过信用证金额。这意味着，当信用证以规定数量的包装单位或单个物品（例如，一定数量的笔记本电脑）说明数量时，数量公差不适用。

4.2 Measuring Quality 衡量质量

In international trade, you and your customers are in different countries. You cannot see the commodity as conveniently as in domestic trade. Then how can you describe product quality to achieve common understandings in this aspect? The following methods have been developed over the years by practitioners for such a purpose.

4.2.1 Methods for Measuring Quality 衡量质量的方法

Methods for measuring quality can be roughly divided into two broad categories: measuring quality by commodities per se or by descriptions of commodities.

4.2.1.1 Measuring quality by commodities per se 通过商品本身衡量质量

♦ **Measuring quality by inspection 凭检验衡量质量**

When quality is measured by inspection, the quality is determined by the **on-site** inspection staff of the importer or the importer's agents. It applies to non-standardized products, such as ornaments, craftwork, **agriculture commodities** and **heavy machinery** or, for occasions, of a **transaction on the spot**, a **consignment**, a trade fair, an auction or an exhibition.

现场

大宗农产品 重型机械

现场交易 寄售

♦ **Measuring quality by sample 凭样品衡量质量**

You may also measure quality by sample, which is a small quantity of products **randomly** taken out from **a whole lot**, or specifically designed and processed for a customer for reference or for confirmation before **mass production**. Depending on the party who provides the sample, a sample could be a seller's sample, a buyer's sample, or a **return sample**, which is the seller's copy of the buyer's sample for the buyer's confirmation. To prevent possible disputes about quality, the following tips need to be noted before you send samples to the importer: First, the sample should be of average quality, representing the whole lot. You don't want your

随机 一整批

批量生产

回样

公证人；封样；清楚地，明确地

sample to be too super or too poor in quality. Second, keep a copy of the sample with yourself and with an agreed-upon **notary** or inspection institution; alternatively, both you and the importer may keep some copies of the confirmed samples and seal them as **sealed samples**. Third, don't use sample together with another measurement of quality, such as specifications, which tends to cause disputes resulting from a double standard. If the importer does need a sample in addition to a quality term in the contract, you'd better state **explicitly** in the contract that "the sample provided is just for reference".

4.2.1.2 Measuring quality by commodity descriptions 通过商品描述衡量质量

♦ **Measuring quality by specifications 凭规格衡量质量**

成分　含量；歧义

A specification is a detailed standard of workmanship or materials required to produce a product. A specification may include the **composition**, **content**, purity, strength, size, etc., depending on category of the goods. The precise feature of a specification facilitates production, procurement, and taking delivery by reducing **ambiguities** and possible disputes. It is applicable for products whose specification information is available, such as most manufactured goods.

♦ **Measuring quality by grade 凭等级衡量质量**

精细化程度；纯粮率

Grade is a rank of quality representing a certain degree of **refinement** of materials or products, or level of features or functions. Grade is widely used for farm produce such as nuts, meat, fruits, vegetables, etc., and also for industrial goods. Chinese soybeans are classified into 5 grades based on their **pure grain rate**. And raw

Raw open shell pistachios　　Raw closed shell pistachios

Figure 4-3　Grades of Raw Pistachio

pistachios are generally classified into two grades: **open shell pistachio nuts** and **closed shell pistachio nuts** (see Figure 4-3). But a measurement of quality by grade alone normally does not provide enough information about quality. Specifications are often used as supplements. Here is a description of grades of **cocoa** delineated in ***the International Cocoa Standards***:

开心果 开壳开心果
闭壳开心果

可可
《国际可可标准》

"Cocoa shall be graded on the basis of the count of defective beans in the cut test. Defective beans shall not exceed the following limits:

Grade I -

(a) mouldy beans, maximum 3 per cent by count;

(b) slaty beans, maximum 3 per cent by count;

(c) insect-damaged, germinated, or flat beans, total maximum 3 per cent by count.

Grade II -

(a) mouldy beans, maximum 4 per cent by count;

(b) slaty beans, maximum 8 per cent by count;

(c) insect-damaged, germinated, or flat beans, total maximum 6 per cent by count.[①]

"可可应根据切割试验中有缺陷的可可豆的数量进行分级。有缺陷的豆子不得超过以下限制：

一级-

(a)霉变豆，按计数最多为3%；

(b)板豆，按计数最多为3%；

(c)虫害、发芽或扁豆，总数量最多为3%。

二级-

(a) 霉变豆，按计数最多为4%；

(b)板豆，按计数最多为8%；

(c)虫害、发芽或扁豆，总数最多为6%。"

♦ **Measuring quality by standard 凭标准衡量质量**

A standard is a set of unified specifications or grades issued by international organizations, domestic or foreign government authorities, trade associations or businesses per se, some of which are compulsory in a certain industry or market. Generally, meeting a standard enhances business image, particularly those internationally recognized standards. For instance, **The International Organization for Standardization (ISO)** is the world's largest developer of voluntary international standards and facilitates world trade by providing common standards between nations. Over twenty thousand standards have been set covering everything from manufactured products and technology to food safety, agriculture and healthcare.[②] Passing an ISO test enhances business image, customer confidence and saves inspection costs.

国际标准化组织

---

① https://onlinelibrary.wiley.com/doi/pdf/10.1002/9780470698983.app2

② https://encyclopedia.thefreedictionary.com/ISO

例如，出口到欧盟的化学品必须通过 REACH——化学品注册、评估、授权和限制条例——一项严格的化学品测试。进入美国、英国、德国、法国和日本的工具必须分别符合 ANSI、BS、DIN、NF 和 JIS 工具标准。

However, for certain industries, national standards have to be met before you can enter their market. For example, chemicals exported to the European Union have to pass *REACH—Regulation on Registration, Evaluation, Authorization and Restriction of Chemicals*—a rigorous test for chemicals. And tools entering the US, UK, Germany, France and Japan have to meet *ANSI*, *BS*, *DIN*, *NF* and *JIS* tool standards respectively.

Notably, however, standards can be modified or replaced by new ones. Consequently, if the quality of commodity is measured by standard, it is necessary to mention the version of the standards.

♦ **Measuring quality by trademark or brand 凭商标或品牌衡量质量**

A brand of a product is the version of a product made by one particular manufacturer. A brand holder generally wants to pose a certain image for its product, service or business in the minds of the public, in order to highlight its feature or quality and differentiate it from competing manufacturers. A brand thus constitutes identity of a specific product, service or business. The brand image can be expressed in many ways, including a name, a logo, a store decoration, a way of management or a business culture. A trademark is one of the physical representations of a brand that comprises of a name, symbol or design which cannot be used by anyone else. An officially registered trademark is legally protected and known as a registered trademark. Brands and trademarks are often reliable indicators of quality and are welcome in the international market, such as appliances made by Haier and telecommunications equipment made by Huawei.

♦ **Measuring quality by place of origin 凭产地衡量质量**

Some commodities are well known for their place of origin, which has become an indicator of recognized quality. Naturally the quality is measured by their places of origin. A case in point is **Shawo radish**, a well-known farm produce originated in the village of Shawo and surrounding villages of Tianjin. It has a unique sweet flavor instead of the **pungent** taste for radish grown in other places. For this reason, it is also referred to as Shawo fruit radish and granted the honor of

沙窝萝卜

辛辣的

"**National Product of Geographical Indication**". It has been planted for more than 600 years. Since the 1930s, the radish has been exported to Japan and Southeast Asian countries, and is well-known at home and abroad. Other examples include **French wine of champagne, Yunnan Pu-erh Tea, porcelain from Jingdezhen,** etc.

"国家地理标志产品"

法国香槟酒，云南普洱茶，景德镇瓷器等

♦ **Measuring quality by technical descriptions 凭技术描述衡量质量**

Technical description is often used for measuring qualities of large or whole sets of equipment with complex structures, which have high standards for material, design and technology. Therefore, technical manuals, booklets of directions, drawings or diagrams are used for describing quality.

4.2.2 Quality Tolerance 质量公差

For some categories of products, it's difficult or impossible for the quality delivered to be exactly the same as the quality contracted. This may be due to a number of reasons, such as **fair wear and tear**, inevitable loss in transit, limitations in the precision of the measuring tool used for manufacturing the product, or just due to the nature of the goods. For example, a watch may not go 100% right. Therefore, a quality tolerance is also needed for certain categories of goods to prevent the importer from rejecting the goods or making a claim on **pretext** of a minor non-conformity of quality to the contract.

正常磨损

借口

Quality tolerance is the allowed variance or departure from a specification or standard that is considered not affecting the proper functioning of the product. Generally, the tolerance is stipulated in terms of an allowed range or limit for the key indicators of quality, which could be a recognized one in the industry or, should no such recognized tolerance exist, be agreed-upon by both parties in the contract. For example, a specification for a certain type of **screw** may be: **diameter 0.8 cm, tolerance ±0. 001 mm**. In case the agreed-upon tolerance is recognized internationally or in the industry, the contract price shall not adjust if variance of the quality falls within the recognized range. The tolerance is often stipulated as an allowed **latitude** of specific quality indicators, such as in the following cases:

螺钉

直径0.7厘米，公差±0.001毫米

机动幅度

羊毛规格：水分含量 5%～10%
小麦规格：碎粒不超过 25%，杂质不超过 0.5%，水分不超过 15%。
羽绒服规格：羽绒含量 80%，上下不超过 1%

(1) specification of wool: moisture 5%～10%

(2) specifications of wheat: broken grains (Max) 25%, admixture (Max) 0.5%, moisture (Max) 15%

(3) specification of eiderdown coat: eiderdown 80%, 1% more or less.

4.3 Packaging for Export 出口包装

第三级的

Packages protect a commodity, promote sales, facilitate identification and accelerate importer's taking delivery. You need to package the merchandise in a way to meet the requirements for both international shipping and marketing. For this purpose, packaging strategies may be formulated at three levels: the primary level (for retailing), the secondary level (for wholesaling) and the **tertiary** level (for international shipping). And notably, marking your packages properly also plays a big role in achieving the above functions.

4.3.1 Packaging for Transportation 运输包装

板条箱　桶　大包
托盘
结实

Transportation packages protect merchandise in international shipping. You may use individual packages, such as cartons, wooden cases, **crates**, **barrels**, bags, cans, **bales**, bundles, etc. and collective packages, such as containers and **pallets** for transportation. They have to be **sturdy** enough. It should be noted that, poor packaging may result in the banker's refusal to make payment in the case of a payment method by letter of credit and that a claim for damage to or loss of goods due to the same reason will not be supported by the insurance company, either.

4.3.2 Packaging for Sales 销售包装

携带
有吸引力的

Sales packages help to sell products by providing product differentiation, brand awareness and convenience. The ever-changing demands of consumers will necessarily require increasing emphasis on the appearance and quality of retail packages. Some considerations for sales packaging include: The package should facilitate a retailer or wholesaler's handling and display, a consumer's identification, **taking along** and use, and it should also be artistically **appealing** in appearance. For example, the manuals or labels should be translated into the language of the importing country.

4.3.3 Markings 包装标记

Cargoes for international shipping often go for a longer and rougher journey and through people speaking different languages and of varied skills, experiences, educational levels and cultural backgrounds, which requires a clear, correct and complete marking on the packages of the cargo.

Marking in such a way helps to prevent incorrect handling or delivery, theft, customs fine and injury to workers. According to international standards, such as ISO 780 etc., a complete marking generally comprises the information mark, the handling mark and the shipping mark.

The information marks tell the country of origin, weight and dimension, which facilitate customs clearance, transportation and handing. The handling marks instruct workers to exert care with cargo

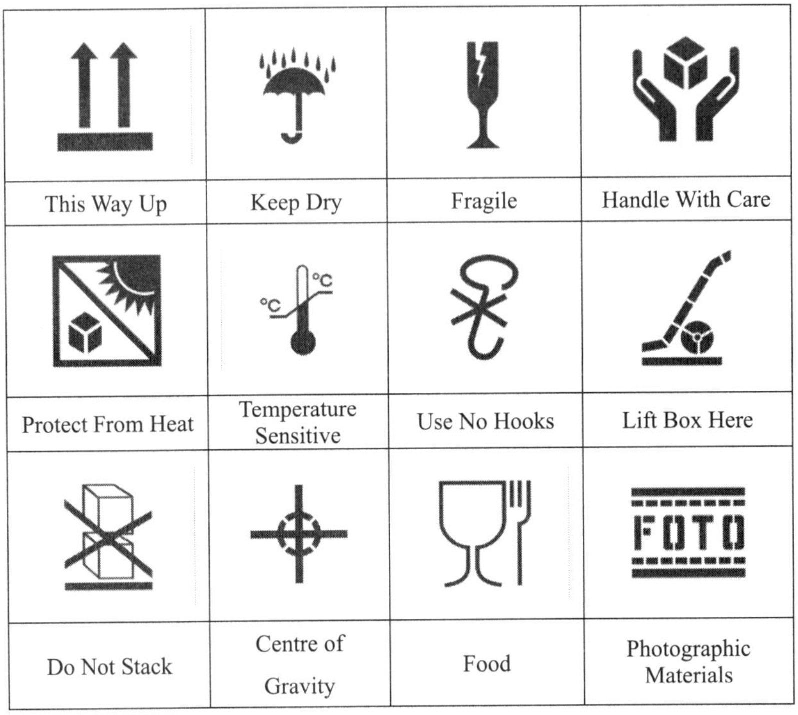

Figure 4-4 Common Handling Marks for International Shipping

handling and storage (see Figure 4-4). Pictorials are used to tell whether the package is at risk of breakage; whether it is sensitive to heat or moisture; where the top and bottom are and where the **center of gravity** is; where loading **tackle** may be **slung** and whether the cargo is dangerous such as **flammable** or explosive.

重心
吊钩　挂
易燃的

The shipping marks facilitates identification of the cargo and prevents mistakes in loading or unloading, particularly in the case of a less-than-container load, which is normally stuffed into a container with someone else's goods. Without a **conspicuous** and recognizable shipping mark on the outer package, **stevedores** or officers may have difficulties in identifying and sorting out your cargo from others' and additional sorting cost may be incurred. The shipping mark is also required on such documents as the invoice and the bill of lading. Thus, it is often essential to fix a shipping mark in the contract and keep it consistent through all documents that require it. A standard shipping mark recommended by the International Organization for Standardization includes initials or abbreviations of the consignee's name, a reference number which could be the contract number, order number or the credit number, the destination and the piece number (see Figure 4-5).

醒目的
装卸工人

SWTC	→	importer's initials
SINGAPORE	→	destination
NO.1-30	→	package serial number
TBIM-SWTC-09	→	contract number

Figure 4-5　A Shipping Mark

Exercises 练习

I. Complete the Conversion Between Units of Measurements

Conversion Between Units of Measurements

Weight	
Metric System	1 metric ton (MT)= ( ) kilograms= ( ) grams
British Imperial System	1 long ton= ( ) pounds = ( ) ounces
American Customary System	1 short ton= ( ) pounds = ( ) ounces
1 pound= ( ) ounces	
1 metric ton= ( ) long ton= ( ) short ton	
Length	
1 inch= ( ) cm, 1 foot= ( ) inch= ( ) cm	
1 yard= ( ) feet= ( ) inches= ( ) cm	
1 meter= ( ) yards= ( ) feet= ( ) inches	
1 mile= ( ) meters= ( ) yards= ( ) feet	
Area	
1 square meter= ( ) square yards= ( ) square feet	
Volume	
1 cubic meter= ( ) cubic yards= ( ) cubic feet= ( ) cubic inches	
Capacity	
1 liter= ( ) British gallon= ( ) American gallon	
1 American gallon= ( ) liters= ( ) British gallon	
1 British gallon= ( ) liters= ( ) American gallons	
1 American barrel= 31.5 American gallons= ( ) liters	
1 British barrel=36 British gallons= ( ) liters	
1 hogshead= ( ) American gallons= ( ) British gallons	
1 bushel= ( ) liters	

II. True or False

1. The quantity of the goods delivered should be the same as that stipulated in the contract. ( )
2. In international trade, if goods are sold by weight, gross weight is often applied. ( )
3. Conditioned weight is often used for weighing wool. ( )
4. For bulk goods, the contract usually contains a quantity tolerance clause. ( )
5. Brands and logos alone can be used as criteria of quality. ( )
6. Although some goods are known by their places of origin, places of origin cannot be used to describe quality. ( )
7. Under a quality tolerance clause in the contract, the contract price shall adjust according to variations in quality within the agreed range. ( )
8. Transport packages includes cartons, wooden cases, pallets and containers. ( )
9. Samples should always be used together with other quality indicators. ( )
10. Commodity quality can be measured on the spot or by description. ( )

III. Multiple Choice Questions

1. The current statutory measurement system in China is ( ).
   [A] the Metric System
   [B] the International System of Units
   [C] the British Imperial System
   [D] the American Customary System

龙口粉丝

2. The quality of **Longkou Vermicelli** is stated by ( ).
   [A] standard [B] specification
   [C] trademark [D] place of origin
3. Which of the following is (are) element(s) for a shipping mark recommended by the International Organization for Standardization ( ).*
   [A] consignee's initials or abbreviations
   [B] contract/order/credit number

[C] destination

[D] piece number

4. When you export **bulldozers**, ( ) is not a common method for measuring their quality. 推土机

[A] specification [B] instruction manuals

[C] place of origin [D] trademark

5. To which of the following product, does not a quantity tolerance clause in the contract normally apply? ( )

[A] Wheat. [B] Smartphones.

[C] Coffee beans. [D] Pistachios.

6. When the seller makes a copy of the sample provided by the buyer for the latter's confirmation, this sample for confirmation is called a ( ).

[A] **return sample** 回样

[B] **duplicate sample** 复样

[C] **reference sample** 参考样

[D] seller's sample

7. "About" in the *UCP 600* means that the amount, quantity and unit price shall not be increased or decreased by more than ( ).

[A] 9% [B]10%

[C] 11% [D] 8%

8. Which one of the following is NOT necessary for a term of quantity tolerance? ( )

[A] The allowed range of variance in quantity.

[B] The party who determines the tolerance.

[C] The price at which the overload or underload portion of goods is calculated.

[D] The Incoterms rule for the overload or underload portion of goods.

9. A shipping company normally measures the weight of a cargo by its ( ).

[A] **gross weight** 毛重

[B] **average tare weight** 平均皮重

[C] **net weight** 净重

[D] **customary tare** 习惯皮重

10. Which of the following organizations can publish a quality standard? (   )*
    [A] International organizations.
    [B] Government authorities.
    [C] Trade associations.
    [D] Businesses.

IV. Case Study

1. In Sept., 2019, Delicasa, a Chinese import and export trading company, entered a deal of exporting 1,000 electric cookers to Thailand, which prohibited partial shipment in line with the letter of credit. Unexpectedly, 10 cookers were found damaged and malfunctioning at the loading port just before shipment. As time was pressing, replacement was impossible. Luckily, it occurred to Stanly He, sales manager of Delicasa, that a 5% quantity tolerance was allowed by *UCP 600* and 10 units was far below this limit. So, 990 units were actually loaded and shipped in order to maintain the brand image. However, when they presented the documents for negotiation, the negotiating bank rejected it. Please discuss why the bank refused to pay.
2. An Italian garment trading company Vestimenta has ordered 2000 cartons of a silk pajama from a Chinese company Sleepcomfy for resale to its two retailers. The pajamas ordered were all under the same article number, loaded into a 20' container, but each retailer required two different styles. However, sales people of Sleepcomfy forgot to remind their factory of marking each carton with the piece number. Upon arrival at the port of discharge, workers of Vestimenta could not distinguish which carton was for which customer. It cost the company a lot of money and effort to sort them out. Vestimenta made a claim against Sleepcomfy, which **indemnified** the former for some of its losses, but the Italian company terminated its business relationship with the Chinese company once and for all. What can we learn from this case?

赔偿

Chapter 5 International Commerce Terms and Export Prices and Earnings

第五章 国际商业条款及出口价格和利润

Learning Objectives:

- How complexities of international logistics affect the terms of sale
- The commonly adopted trade terms in international sales—*Incoterms 2020*
- How to calculate export cost, price and earnings

Sales terms for export are more complex than domestic ones as they are affected by the complexities of international logistics. This chapter shall elaborate on international commerce rules—a summarization of common wisdom accumulated over the years in the industry to deal with such a tricky issue.

5.1 International Commerce Terms 国际商业条款

What are international commerce terms? How did they come into being? What functions do they achieve in international business? This section will help you answer these questions.

5.1.1 Complexities of International Logistics 国际物流的复杂性

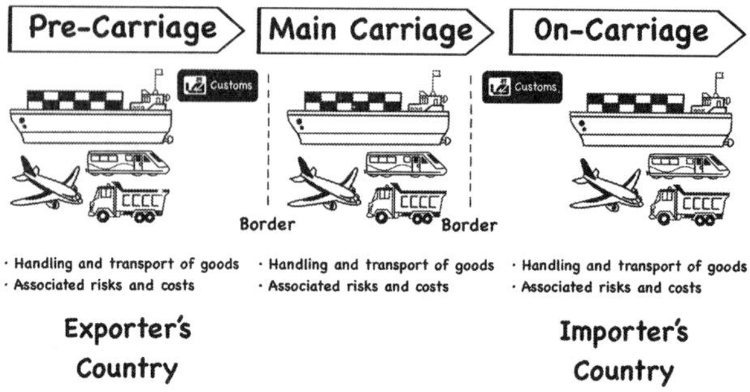

Figure 5-1 Pre-Carriage, Main Carriage and On-Carriage

Whenever you sell goods to a foreign market, be it directly or through a trading company, you need to go through many steps to get the goods to your customer, which is a complex process (see Figure 5-1):

出口清关 (1) The goods must be **cleared for export**.

(2) You must arrange the transport of the goods with the importer, often using several means of transport—including at least three distinct **legs** in that journey: 旅程的一段

- **Pre-carriage**, the transport that takes place in your country (country of export). 前程运输
- **Main carriage**, the international transport between your country and the country of import. 主程运输
- **On-carriage**, the transport that takes place in the country of import. 续程运输

进口清关 (3) The goods must be **cleared for import**

5.1.2 Solutions by *Incoterms 2020* Rules《2020 通则》提供的解决方案

Who will be responsible for which task? Given the complexity of this process, misunderstandings or disputes **are prone to occur** (容易发生) regarding the division of cost, risks and obligations between you and the importer. Fortunately, **the International Chamber of Commerce** (国际商会)

has created a set of standardized **terms of trade** in 1936, which have evolved into eleven ***International Commerce Terms Rules****, or* ***Incoterms*** for short and are illustrated in the publication of ***International Rules for the Interpretation of Trade Terms.*** The publication was revised in 1953, 1967, 1976, 1980, 1990, 2000, 2010 and most recently in 2020. For example, a *proforma* invoice would read: FCA 2300 industrial Parkway, Milwaukee, WI 53223, USA, *Incoterms 2020.*

贸易术语
《国际商业条款规则》
《通则》
《国际贸易术语解释通则》

If you and the importer agree to use an *Incoterms 2020* rule in your transaction, **making reference to** it in your sales contract helps to define clearly your respective obligations and reduce the possibilities of disputes because **ample** information is available and substantial **jurisprudence** has accumulated for each through the International Chamber of Commerce **arbitration system**. An *Incoterms 2020* rule defines five aspects of an international sale:

引用
充分的
大量判例
仲裁体系

- Which task will be performed by the exporter?
- Which task will be performed by the importer?
- Which activities will be paid by the exporter?
- Which activities will be paid by the importer?
- When the transfer of responsibility for the goods will take place?

In applying these rules, please be noted that a few key words used in these rules have a different meaning from their daily usage. For example, "**carrier**" refers to the party with whom carriage is contracted and who undertakes the obligation of transportation; "**delivery**" indicates the point where the risk of loss or damage to the goods passes from the exporter to the importer; and "**customs formalities**" are requirements to be met in order to comply with any applicable customs regulations and may include documentary, security, information or physical inspection obligations.

承运人
承运人是指与托运人订立合同，并承担运输义务的一方。
交货
交货用来表明在货物由卖方向买方转移的过程中毁损风险在何处转移。
报关手续
报关是指为了遵守海关条例而需要满足的一些要求，包括了单据、安全、信息或实体检验之义务。

5.1.3 11 *Incoterms 2020* Rules in Two Classes 分成两类的 11 条《2020 通则》术语

Incoterms 2020 has taken effect since January 1st, 2020. The changes over *Incoterms 2010* are summarized in Table 5-1:

Table 5-1 Changes of *Incoterms 2020* over *Incoterms 2010*

◆ The Incoterms FCA (Free Carrier) now provides the additional option to make an on-board notation on the Bill of Lading prior loading of the goods on a vessel. ◆ The costs now appear centralized in A9/B9 of each Incoterms rule. ◆ CIP now requires at least an insurance with the minimum cover of the Institute Cargo Clause(A) (All risk, subject to itemized exclusions). ◆ CIF now requires at least an insurance with the minimum cover of the Institute Cargo Clause (C) (Number of listed risks, subject to itemized exclusions) ◆ The rule Delivered at Terminal (DAT)has been changed to Delivered at Place Unloaded (DPU) to clarify that the place of destination could be any place and not only a "terminal" ◆ The Incoterms rules of Free Carrier (FCA), Delivered at Place (DAP), Delivered at Place Unloaded (DPU) and Delivered Duty Paid (DDP) now take into account that the goods may be carried without any third-party carrier being engaged, namely by using its own means of transportation. ◆ The *Incoterms 2020* now explicitly shifts the responsibility of security-related requirements and ancillary costs to the seller.

The 11 *Incoterms 2020* rules are presented still in two distinct classes: Incoterms rules for any **mode** or modes of transport; Incoterms rules for sea and inland waterway transport.

方式

The first group includes the seven Incoterms rules that can be used **irrespective of** the mode of transport selected, and of whether one or more than one mode of transport is employed. EXW, FCA, CPT, CIP, DAP, DPU and DDP fall under this class.

不考虑

In the second group, the **point of delivery** and the place to which the goods are carried to the importer are both ports, hence the label "sea and inland waterway" rules. FAS, FOB, CFR and CIF fall under this class.

交货点

Table 5-2 Two Classes of 11 *Incoterms 2020* Rules

For any mode or modes of transport		For sea and inland waterway transport	
EXW	EX WORKS 工厂交货	FAS	FREE ALONGSIDE SHIP 船边交货
FCA	FREE CARRIER 货交承运人	FOB	FREE ON BOARD 船上交货
CPT	CARRIAGE PAID TO 运费付至	CFR	COST AND FREIGHT 成本加运费
CIP	CARRIAGE AND INSURANCE PAID TO 运费及保险费付至	CIF	COST, INSURANCE AND FREIGHT 成本、保险费加运费
DAP	DELIVERED AT PLACE 所在地交货		
DPU	DELIVERED AT PLACE UNLOADED 卸货地交货		
DDP	DELIVERED DUTY PAID 完税后交货		

For either group, you, the exporter, bear **escalating** responsibilities and risks in the logistic process. See Table 5-2 and Figure 5-2 for detail.

不断升级的

For any mode or modes of transport　　For sea and inland waterway transport

Figure 5-2 Exporter's Obligations Under *Incoterms 2020* Rules

5.2 *Incoterms 2020* Rules in 4 Groups 分成四组的《2020 通则》术语

5.2.1 The "E" Group—EXW E 组——工厂交货

Table 5-3 The "E" Group—EXW E 组——工厂交货

Format of use (English)				使用格式（中文）			
EXW (insert named place of delivery) *Incoterms 2020*				EXW (插入指定交货地点) *Incoterms 2020*			
Term	**Export clearance**	**Import clearance**	**Contract of carriage**	**Contract of insurance**	**Place of delivery**	**Point of risk transfer**	**Mode of transport**
EXW	Ⓘ	Ⓘ	Ⓘ	Ⓘ	Ⓔ's premise or another named place	goods at disposal of Ⓘ	Any mode/ modes

(Note: Ⓔ stands for exporter and Ⓘ for importer, similarly hereinafter.)

"Ex Works" alone constitutes the first group of Incoterms rules for any mode or modes of transport. "Ex Works" means that you deliver when you place the goods at the disposal of the importer at your **premise** or at another named place (i.e., factory, warehouse, etc.). See Table 5-3 for its applicability and distribution of obligations and risks between the importer and the exporter. You do not need to load the goods on any **collecting vehicle**. Nor do you need to clear the goods for export, even if you are **in a position to do that**. Sounds simple? Yes. If you adopt this term, you have the least responsibilities and risks compared with what you have when you

场所

接货的车辆

有能力这样做

do with the other 10 rules. But it is rarely used for international business due to great obstacles for the importer in completing the transaction. A few exceptions include the following occasions:

准国内贸易
通关
出口许可证

- in domestic trade or **quasi-domestic trade**, such as between countries within a free trade area, where no **customs clearance** is needed.
- when you do not have **export license** but the importer is experienced in international logistics as well as in customs clearance for both export and import.
- when you do not have much experience in international logistics or customs clearance but the importer does, and is willing to bear the cost and risk.

实际上
要求

However, special care should be taken if you export on an EXW basis, because the importer just has limited obligations to provide you any information regarding the export. However, this information is often needed for such procedures as filing for tax refund. And you have no obligation to load the goods, even though you might be **practically** in a better position to do so. If you do load the goods, you do so at the importer's risk and expense. In case you are in a better position to load the goods, FCA, which **obliges** you to do so at your own risk and expense, is usually more appropriate.

5.2.2 The "F" Group—FCA, FAS, FOB F组——货交承运人、船边交货、船上交货

If you don't want to assume too many responsibilities or risks with logistics, you can adopt the "F" group—FCA, FAS and FOB, because you only need to deliver the goods at a specified place in your country in the specified way. FCA is suitable for any mode or modes of transport, while FAS and FOB are just for sea and inland waterway transport. See Table 5-4 for a comparison of their applicability and distribution of obligations and risks between the importer and the exporter.

交由他/她处置

Under FCA, you fulfill your responsibilities for delivery as long as you transfer the cargo to the carrier by **placing it at his/her disposal** at the specified place. This place has to be specified as clearly as possible because risks pass to the importer at this point. You are free of

Table 5-4 The "F" Group—FCA, FAS, FOB F组——货交承运人、船边交货、船上交货

Format of use (English)	使用格式（中文）
FCA (insert named place of delivery) *Incoterms 2020*	FCA (插入指定交货地点) *Incoterms 2020*
FAS (insert named port of shipment) *Incoterms 2020*	FAS (插入指定起运港) *Incoterms 2020*
FOB (insert named port of shipment) *Incoterms 2020*	FOB (插入指定起运港) *Incoterms 2020*

Term	Export clearance	Import clearance	Contract of carriage	Contract of insurance	Place of delivery	Point of risk transfer	Mode of transport
FCA	Ⓔ	Ⓘ	Ⓘ	Ⓘ	Specified place of exporting country	goods at disposal of carrier or forwarder	Any mode/ modes
FAS	Ⓔ	Ⓘ	Ⓘ	Ⓘ	On wharf/ barge that is alongside the ship	goods are alongside the ship	Sea/inland waterway transport
FOB	Ⓔ	Ⓘ	Ⓘ	Ⓘ	On the ship	goods are on board the ship	Sea/inland waterway transport

responsibilities for the goods in transit once you place the goods at disposal of the carrier, hence the name. Delivering to the carrier is equivalent to delivering to the importer. A modification of this rule in *Incoterms 2020* compared with *Incoterms 2010* is that it now provides the additional option to make an on-board notation on the bill of lading prior loading of the goods on a vessel.

Under FAS, as the name indicates, you must deliver the cargo alongside the ship. Please note, however, the word "alongside" is used **literally** here—you must move the cargo truly "alongside" the ship. **Landing** a container at the **container yard** is not "alongside" the ship, as a container yard normally covers a vast area at the port, which makes FAS **effectively** not appropriate for containerized cargoes. In another situation, where the ship is not **immediately** by the **dock**, to move your cargo "alongside" the ship, you need to use a **barge** to **forward** the cargo from dock to ship. To sum up, until the cargo is truly alongside the ship, your responsibilities and risks remain. Should the cargo break, catch fire, or fall into the sea before being alongside the ship, you are held responsible for it.

字面上的
放置 集装箱堆场
实际上
紧接地 码头
驳船 转运

Under FOB, your responsibilities and risks extend further until you move the cargo on board the ship. Once the cargo is so delivered, risks transfer to the importer and you are free. But like FAS, it has the same problem with containerized goods—containers are required to be placed at the container yard. However, as loading a ship is normally arranged by the port, you cannot **see to** the goods being truly moved "on board". So, if this term is used for containerized goods **anyway**, please **watch for** risks in the link from delivering to the carrier to moving the cargo truly "on board". Otherwise, use another term such as FCA for safety and convenience.

照料，照看
无论如何，即便这样
小心注意

5.2.3 The "C" Group—CPT, CIP, CFR, CIF C组——运费付至、运费保费付至、成本加运费、成本加运费加保费

Table 5-5 The "C" Group—CPT, CIP, CFR, CIF

C组——运费付至、运费保费付至、成本加运费、成本加运费加保费

Format of use (English)	使用格式（中文）
CPT (insert named place of destination) *Incoterms 2020*	CPT (插入指定目的地) *Incoterms 2020*
CIP (insert named place of destination) *Incoterms 2020*	CIP (插入指定目的地) *Incoterms 2020*
CFR (insert named port of destination) *Incoterms 2020*	CFR (插入指定目的港) *Incoterms 2020*
CIF (insert named port of destination) *Incoterms 2020*	CIF (插入指定目的港) *Incoterms 2020*

Term	Export clearance	Import clearance	Contract of carriage	Contract of insurance	Place of delivery	Point of risk transfer	Mode of transport
CPT	Ⓔ	Ⓘ	Ⓔ	Ⓘ	Specified place of exporting country	goods at disposal of carrier or forwarder	Any mode/ modes
CIP	Ⓔ	Ⓘ	Ⓔ	Ⓔ	Specified place of exporting country	goods at disposal of carrier or forwarder	Any mode/ modes
CFR	Ⓔ	Ⓘ	Ⓔ	Ⓘ	On the ship	goods on board the ship	Sea/inland waterway transport
CIF	Ⓔ	Ⓘ	Ⓔ	Ⓔ	On the ship	goods on board the ship	Sea/inland waterway transport

(Note: The underlined letters indicate that the insurance is compulsory for the designated party.)

Compared with the "F" group, if you wish to assume more responsibilities with logistics or if the importer requires you to do so, you can employ the "C" group—CPT, CIP, CFR, CIF. While CPT and CIP are applicable for any mode or modes of transport, CFR and CIF are only for sea and inland waterway transport. See Table 5-5 for a comparison of their applicability and distribution of obligations and risks between the importer and the exporter.

Common to FCA, CPT and CIP, you fulfill your responsibility for delivery once you transfer the goods by placing them under the disposal of the carrier. But CPT and CIP extend your responsibilities beyond those under FCA. Under CPT, you need to pay for the main carriage and under CIP, the main carriage plus insurance for this leg. However, please be noted that, paying for the main carriage, or the main carriage plus insurance for this leg doesn't mean you are held responsible for the safety of the goods until they reach destination. As mentioned above, risks transfer once you deliver to the carrier. Besides, according to *Incoterms 2020*, CIP is an Incoterms rule that now requires at least an insurance with the minimum cover of the Institute Cargo Clause (A) (All Risks, subject to itemized exclusions), instead of the Institute Cargo Clause (C) (Number of listed risks, subject to itemized exclusions) under *Incoterms 2010*. Table 5-6 shows you how to convert between FCA and CPT, or between FCA and CIP.

Table 5-6 Conversion Between FCA and CPT, or Between FCA and CIP

CPT= FCA + freight for the main carriage
CIP= FCA + freight for the main carriage + insurance premium for the main carriage

Common to FOB, CFR and CIF, you fulfill your responsibility for delivery once you move the goods on board the ship. But CFR and CIF extend your responsibilities beyond those under FOB. Under CFR, you pay for the sea freight and under CIF the sea freight plus the insurance for the sea leg. Similarly, paying for the sea freight, or the sea freight plus insurance for the sea leg doesn't mean you are held responsible for the safety of the goods until they reach destination.

As mentioned above, risks transfer once you deliver to the carrier. Table 5-7 shows you how to convert between FOB and CFR, or between FOB and CIF.

Table 5-7 Conversion Between FOB and CFR, or Between FOB and CIF

CFR = FOB+ sea freight CIF = FOB + sea freight + insurance premium for the sea leg

5.2.4 The "D" Group—DAP, DPU, DDP D组——所在地交货、卸货地交货、完税后交货

Table 5-8 The "D" Group—DAP, DPU, DDP
D组——所在地交货、卸货地交货、完税后交货

Format of use (English)	使用格式（中文）
DAP (insert named place of destination) *Incoterms 2020*	DAP (插入指定目的地) *Incoterms 2020*
DPU (insert named place of destination) *Incoterms 2020*	DPU (插入指定目的地) *Incoterms 2020*
DDP (insert named place of destination) *Incoterms 2020*	DDP (插入指定目的地) *Incoterms 2020*

Term	Export clearance	Import clearance	Contract of carriage	Contract of insurance	Place of delivery	Point of risk transfer	Mode of transport
DAP	Ⓔ	Ⓘ	Ⓔ	Ⓔ	Specified place of importing country	goods reach specified place, **NOT unloaded**	Any mode/ modes
DPU	Ⓔ	Ⓘ	Ⓔ	Ⓔ	Specified place of importing country	goods reach specified place, **unloaded**	Any mode/ modes
DDP	Ⓔ	Ⓔ	Ⓔ	Ⓔ	Specified place of importing country	goods reach specified place, **NOT unloaded**	Any mode/ modes

Under the "D" group of terms—DAP, DPU or DDP, you are required to deliver to the importer at his/her premise. Clearly, you bear the most responsibilities and risks under this group compared with other groups. DDP even asks you to clear the goods both for export and import and pay import duties. Insurance is optional for both sides, but, conceivably, it is highly suggested for your own sake. As a result, this group is not used too much, either, unless you are highly experienced in international logistics or you are doing business within a trade bloc, in which case, these terms give you a competitive edge over your rivals.

DAP asks you to deliver at any specified place of the importer's country, but not to unload the cargo. With DPU, other things being equal, unloading is your responsibility. With DDP, other things being equal with DAP, you must clear both export and import customs, pay import duty, but not unload. See Table 5-8 for a comparison of their applicability and distribution of obligations and risks between the importer and the exporter.

Notably, according to *Incoterms 2020*, FCA, DAP, DPU and DDP now take into account that the goods may be carried without any third-party carrier being engaged, but by the trader's own means of transportation. Under FCA, the importer may use his/her own means of transportation, while under DAP, DPU or DDP, the exporter may use his/her own.

Hopefully, by now, you may have gained a rough sense of similarities and differences among these Incoterms rules. From the "E" Group to the "D" Group, you bear escalating responsibilities and risks in the logistics process. For more details and differences from *Incoterms 2010*, please consult the original text of *Incoterms 2020*.

5.3 How to Use *Incoterms 2020*? 如何使用《2020通则》?

You cannot rest assured even if the incoterms rules are in place. Only by observing some important principles and using them wisely can you make the best of these rules.

5.3.1 Make Reference of Incoterms Rules in Your Sales Contract 在销售合同中引用贸易术语

If you want the *Incoterms 2020* rules to be applied to your contract, please make clear reference in your contract in order to avoid confusions with *Incoterms 2010*, as both are equally valid even though the new rules have been published and taken effect. This could be achieved through such words and **syntax**, "[the chosen Incoterms rule] 句法

+[named port, place of point] + *Incoterms 2020*." For example,

(1) CIF Shanghai Incoterms® 2020, or,

(2) DPU 611 Fifth Avenue New York, NY, 10022, US, Incoterms® 2020

5.3.2 Select the Appropriate Incoterms Rule 选择适宜的贸易术语

You need to select an Incoterms rule that is appropriate to the goods, to the means of their transport, and to the methods of payment and generally avoid extreme Incoterms rules. And the convention or practices at the specific port or place should also be considered.

♦ **Select an Incoterms rule that suits your goods** 选择适合你的货物的贸易术语

散装货物

码头

Bulk goods, such as coal, wheat, and iron ore, can be moved straight to the ship at specific **wharf**, while containerized goods cannot, which are normally landed on container yards before loading. Therefore, FAS, FOB, CFR, CIF can be used for bulk goods, but not quite satisfying for containerized goods.

♦ **Select an Incoterms rule that suits the mode of transport** 选择适合运输方式的贸易术语

门到门运输

Selecting an Incoterms rule that suits the mode of transport helps you clarify both your and the importer's respective obligations and reduce misunderstandings or disputes. For example, if the final destination is a named place on land, Incoterms rules that are applicable for sea transport, such as FAS, FOB, CFR, and CIF should be avoided. For container transport, Incoterms rules compatible with **door-to-door transport** is mostly preferred, such as DAP or DPU.

♦ **Select an Incoterms rule that suits the method of payment** 选择适合付款方式的贸易术语

As risk exposure is uneven between exporter and importer under certain methods of payment, selecting an Incoterms rule that suits the method of payment helps you reduce risk. For example, a potential risk of losing both money and goods exists under the payment method of cash on delivery by T/T (Chapters 9, 10 and 11). Taking control of the goods as long as possible by asking to arrange for transport helps to prevent this, in which case, CFR, CIF, CPT, DAP, DPU, etc. are more appropriate.

♦ **Avoid the extreme Incoterms rules 避免极端的贸易术语**

EXW and DDP are the most imbalanced Incoterms rules in terms of risk exposure, allocation of cost and obligations between importer and exporter. Therefore, they are not recommended except under special circumstances. For example, while EXW may mean the least risk, cost, and obligations for you, it imposes difficulties on you in filing for tax refund from the tax bureau. As the importer is to clear the goods even for export, it is not convenient for you to get the needed document for tax refund—**the copy of the customs clearance form for tax refund.** 出口报关单退税联 Similarly, DDP is not convenient for you to clear the goods for import.

5.3.3 Specify Your Place or Port as Precisely as Possible 尽可能精准地描述地址或港口名称

The chosen Incoterms rule can work only if the parties name a place or port, and will work best if the parties specify the place or port as precisely as possible. A good example of such precision would be: *"FCA 38 Cours Albert 1er, Paris, France Incoterms 2020"*.

5.3.4 Convert Between Incoterms Rules 在贸易术语之间转换

A proper chosen Incoterms rule not only safeguards your interests as exporters, but also makes a great marketing tool by taking care of the importer's needs.

5.3.4.1 Conversion 转换

Sometimes, you quote in one Incoterms rule, such as FOB, but the importer prefers another, such as CFR, CIF or any other of the 11 Incoterms rules. At other times, you want to initiate an adjustment with your price terms to obtain an order. In those cases, you need to convert from one rule to another. For that reason, you need to know the relationship between these rules and how to convert between them. Besides, **insurance premium** is often included in a price quotation, 保险费 and sometimes **commission**, too, which could make the conversion a 佣金

麻烦

little bit **messy**. Table 5-9 displays the formula used for converting between several Incoterms rules.

Table 5-9 Conversion Between Incoterms Rules

CFR=FOB+ sea freight	CPT=FCA+ main carriage freight
CIF=CFR+ insurance premium	CIP=CPT+ insurance premium

5.3.4.2 Insurance 保险

保险公司
被保险金额

Under terms of CIF or CIP, you must purchase insurance, which necessitates a calculation of the insurance premium—the money you pay to the **underwriter** to buy the insurance, which is often a percentage of **the insured amount**. The insured amount is your declared value of the goods and the most you can recover from the underwriter when risks materialize, which, according to *Incoterms 2020* and *UCP 600*, should be at least 110% of the CIF or CIP value of the merchandise. You may wonder why it is 110% instead of 100%. According to international conventions on marine cargo insurance, the 10% **markup** on the CIF or CIP value is **instituted** to allow for the expected profit that would have been realized without the risk incident. Sometimes the markup can be 20%-30%. The following formula will guide you through this process.

加成
制定

$$\text{insured amount} = \text{CIF or CIP value} \times (1 + \text{markup rate})$$

$$\text{insurance premium} = \text{insured amount} \times \text{premium rate}$$

Sometimes, you are quoting not in CIF or CIP price, but FOB, CFR or CPT price, but the importer authorizes you to purchase insurance on behalf of him/her, then you need to convert from an FOB or CFR price to a CIF price or from a CPT price to a CIP price before you can calculate the insurance premium and the insured amount. Take the CFR and FOB prices as examples, the insurance premium would be calculated as follows:

$$\begin{aligned}\text{insurance premium} &= \text{insured amount} \times \text{premium rate}\\ &= \text{CIF} \times (1+ \text{markup rate}) \times \text{premium rate}\end{aligned}$$

Which equals to,

$$\text{insurance premium} = (\text{CFR} + \text{insurance premium}) \times (1 + \text{markup rate}) \times \text{premium rate}$$

or,

$$\text{insurance premium} = (\text{FOB} + \text{sea freight} + \text{insurance premium}) \times (1 + \text{markup rate}) \times \text{premium rate}$$

Each of the above two formulas makes an equation that contains only a single unknown—the insurance premium, which can **be solved for** without much difficulty. From there you can further get the figure for the insured amount. 被解出

5.3.4.3 Commission 佣金

Suppose you are a manufacturer, and have concluded a deal with the importer through a trading company as the middleman. In line with trade conventions, you need to pay a commission to the trading company for its service in the deal, the amount of which may or may not be indicated in the price quotation, depending on the circumstances. Should the importer ask it be indicated, your price quotation could be something like this: "USD 1000/MT, CFRC2, Seattle, USA". Here, "C" stands for "commission", and "C2" tells the importer that the commission payable to the middleman is 2% of the FOB price for each metric ton. From your perspective, you need to do a calculation that starts with your **net price** (**the commission exclusive price**) and **the commission rate** required by the middle man to arrive at **the commission included price** for quoting to the importer. The following formula shows you the procedures. 净价 不含佣价 佣金率 含佣价

$$\text{commission included price} = \frac{\text{net price}}{(1 - \text{commission rate})}$$

This formula is deducted from the following formula:

$$\text{commission} = \text{commission included price} \times \text{commission rate}$$

$$\text{net price} = \text{commission included price} \times (1 - \text{commission rate})$$

5.4 Export Costs, Prices and Earnings 出口成本、价格和利润

But how do you arrive at your Incoterms price? And whether this price quotation makes a profit? Let's dig deeper.

5.4.1 Export Costs 出口成本

5.4.1.1 Effective cost for procurement 实际采购成本

Before you quote an Incoterms price to your customer, you need to know your cost, which differs depending on whether you are a manufacturer or a trading company. For a manufacturer, your total cost considers your production cost plus all domestic charges and fees for export. For a trading company, however, you have no production cost, but a procurement cost instead, plus all domestic charges and fees for export. And the tax refund system for export may complicate it a bit, often resulting in a different (often lower) effective cost for procurement than what you have paid for.

生产成本

- **production cost**: the cost to a manufacturer.

采购成本

- **procurement cost**: the cost to a trading company which procures goods from a manufacturer, pays the value-added tax, and gets the tax refund.

实际采购成本

- **effective cost for procurement**: the cost to the exporter once it gets the tax refund.

5.4.1.2 The tax refund system for export 出口退税制度

The tax refund for export is the money refunded by the tax authority to exporters for the value-added tax (VAT) they have paid in the production and distribution process. To ensure fair competition, importing countries generally require imports be subject to the same tax rate as domestically-produced goods, which means, whether or not the goods have been taxed by the exporting country, the importing country shall still tax them. Consequently, the main purpose of an exporting country's tax refund policy for export is to avoid double taxation on exports and to enhance a nation's competitiveness in foreign markets. The refund rate varies by product and may be adjusted by the government. According to WTO rules, this practice is not considered a **subsidy** as long as the amount of the refund does not exceed that of the tax paid. A tax refund effectively lowers an exporter's cost for export.

补贴

5.4.1.3 A trading company's effective cost for procurement一家贸易公司的实际采购成本

As we don't want to branch out to the production process in this course, let's focus on the cost of a trading company—your company will just do. Because of the tax refund expected, your total cost for export equals your procurement cost taking consideration of the tax refund, which results in an effective cost for procurement and is calculated as follows,

effective cost for procurement = procurement cost – tax refund

In the above formula, your procurement cost is the total amount of money you have paid to your supplier, which includes a value-added tax. So, the procurement cost is known, but you need to figure out the **net price of goods (VAT exclusive price)** from it in order to calculate the amount of tax refund you can get from the State Taxation Administration. Finally, subtracting the amount of tax refund from your procurement cost will arrive at your effective cost—how much money you have effectively spent in procuring the goods from your supplier.

净价（不含增值税的价格）

- Step 1: calculate the net price of goods as follows,

$$\text{net price of goods} = \frac{\text{procurement cost}}{(1+\ \text{VAT rate})}$$

This formula is deduced as follows:

$$\because\ \text{procurement cost} = \text{net price of goods} + \text{VAT}$$
$$= \text{net price of goods} + \text{net price of goods} \times \text{VAT rate}$$
$$= \text{net price of goods} \times (1+\text{VAT rate})$$

$$\therefore\ \text{net price of goods} = \frac{\text{procurement cost}}{(1+\ \text{VAT rate})}$$

- Step 2: calculate the amount of tax refund as follows,

tax refund = net price of goods × refund rate

- Step 3: calculate the effective cost for export as follows,

effective cost for procurement = procurement cost – tax refund

For a manufacturer, the effective cost for export is his/her production cost considering the tax refund.

在实际采购成本的基础上，出口总成本可以通过加总其他国内各种收费和费用来计算，这些收费和费用可能包括出口包装费、仓储费、内陆运杂费、检验费、海关费、码头操作费、单证费、银行费用、管理费用（用于旅行、接待和沟通等）等项目。

5.4.1.4 A trading company's total cost for export 一家贸易公司的出口总成本

On the basis of the effective cost for procurement, the total cost for export can be calculated by adding other domestic charges and fees, which may include such items as packaging, warehousing, inland freight and charges, inspection, customs clearance, terminal operation, documentation, banking charges, administrative cost (for travelling, reception, and communication, etc.), etc.

total cost for export = effective cost for procurement + domestic charges and fees

5.4.2 Export Prices 出口价格

要求的利润率

With the total cost for export, you are in a position to estimate your export price, an FOB or FCA price in most cases. From there, you may further calculate prices under other Incoterms rules. To sum up, your export price is a sum of three components: the effective cost for procurement, domestic charges and fees, and **required margins**.

the export price = total cost for export + required margins

Factors affecting your price include Incoterms rules selected, size of your customer's order, rate of tax refund, charges or fees and your expected margins, etc.

5.4.3 Export Earnings 出口利润

Two formulas are commonly used to see whether you make money through a transaction, and if you do, how much the profit margin is.

♦ **Exchange cost for export** 出口换汇成本

测量指标

If you quote the price and sign the contract in US dollar, a quick **test** tells whether you gain or lose from an export deal through the following formula:

$$\text{exchange cost for export} = \frac{\text{total cost for export in RMB}}{\text{total net revenue in USD}}$$

$$\text{出口换汇成本} = \frac{\text{出口人民币实际总成本}}{\text{出口美元总净收入}}$$

Exchange cost for export is the total cost for export in RMB spent in return for one US dollar, therefore, it can also be interpreted as "export cost per dollar". For a trading company like yours, the "total cost for export in RMB" in the **nominator** is the one we developed in 5.4.1.4, while the "total net revenue in USD" in the **denominator** takes the FOB net revenue in US dollar. Then you compare the result with the current exchange rate between USD and RMB. If the result is smaller than the exchange rate, the transaction makes a profit; otherwise, it is at a loss. Based on this result, you may adjust your price quoted to the importer and repeat this procedure until you come up with a price that can bring you a satisfying profit.

出口换汇成本是为换取 1 美元出口收入所花费的人民币总成本。对于一家像你们公司一样的贸易公司而言，公式**分子**中的"出口人民币总成本是我们在 5.4.1.4 中推导出的出口总成本。公式**分母**中的"出口美元净收入"等于美元表示的 FOB 净收入。将该计算结果与当前美元兑人民币汇率进行比较。如果结果小于当前汇率，则你的交易赚钱，否则亏损。根据这个结果，你可以调整你给进口商的报价，并重复这个过程，直到你提出一个可以给你带来满意利润的价格。

♦ **Profit margin for export 出口利润率**

You may use the following formula to calculate your profit margin of an export deal:

$$\text{profit margin for export} = \frac{\text{total net revenue in RMB} - \text{total cost for export in RMB}}{\text{total cost for export in RMB}}$$

Exercises 练习

I. True or False

1. The exporter is not obliged to cover insurance if the deal is under Incoterms DAP, but he/she is if under CIF. ( )
2. The exporter should cover the insurance under DPU for his/her own benefits. ( )
3. In *Incoterms 2020*, "delivery" means sending the cargo to the importer's premise. ( )
4. Under CIP, the exporter must pay the freight and insurance premium and bear all the risks until the goods reach the destination. ( )
5. The common feature of an FOB contract and an FAS contract is that the exporter must load the goods on a named ship. ( )

6. DPU requires the exporter to unload the cargo, while DAP and DDP do not. (　　)
7. EXW, DAP, DPU and DDP can be used for neighboring countries within a free trade area. (　　)
8. Since Incoterms rules are widely known in the **trade**, an international sales contract is based on *Incoterms 2020* **by default**, without the need to make refrence to it every time we sign a contract. (　　)

行业 默认

9. An international contract is legally binding on the importer and the exporter, while the Incoterms is not. (　　)
10. Now that *Incoterms 2020* takes effect, *Incoterms 2010* is no longer valid. (　　)

II. Multiple Choice Questions

1. Under CIP and CPT, the responsibility of booking shipping space or chartering a vessel should be taken by (　　) respectively.
   [A] exporter/exporter　　[B] exporter/importer
   [C] importer/importer　　[D] importer/exporter
2. Among *Incoterms 2020* rules, which rule represents the biggest obligation for the exporter? (　　)
   [A] EXW.　　[B] CIF.　　[C] DPU.　　[D] DDP.
3. What's the major difference between FOB and FAS? (　　)
   [A] The boundary of risk division.
   [B] The party responsible for space booking or ship chartering.
   [C] The party responsible for export clearance.
   [D] The party responsible for import clearance.
4. Which one of the following is a shared feature of CPT and CFR? (　　)
   [A] The exporter takes charge of arranging for carriage from the loading port to the unloading port and paying the sea freight.
   [B] The importer assumes all risks when the cargo is in transit.
   [C] The risk shifts with the completion of cargo delivery.
   [D] The exporter assumes all risks until the cargo reaches destination.

5. Which *Incoterms 2020* rule requires the exporter to be responsible for unloading the goods? (   )
   [A] DPU. [B] DAP. [C] DDP. [D] CIP.
6. Which *Incoterms 2020* rule is more appropriate for goods transported in containers? (   )
   [A] FAS. [B] FOB. [C] CIF. [D] CIP.
7. Which *Incoterms 2020* rule doesn't require the exporter to load the goods? (   )
   [A] EXW. [B] FCA. [C] CPT. [D] CIP.
8. Which *Incoterms 2020* rule requires the exporter to cover the cargo as per Institute Cargo Clause A? (   )
   [A] CIP. [B] CIF. [C] CPT. [D] CFR.
9. Which *Incoterms 2020* rule obliges the exporter to cover the goods with insurance? (   )
   [A] DDP. [B] CIP. [C] DDU. [D] DAP.
10. Which *Incoterms 2020* rule might pose difficulties for the exporter to clear customs? (   )
    [A] EWX and DDP. [B] FCA and DDP.
    [C] EXW and FAS. [D] FCA and DPU.

III. Case Study

1. An Indian importer has placed an order of a certain kind of **mother board** under FCA (Guangzhou Airport). The exporter delivered the goods to the carrier at the airport as scheduled. The airline received the goods and issued the air waybill. So, the exporter asked the importer to make payment. However, at this time, the market price of the goods fell. The importer then refused to pay, saying that he hadn't officially taken delivery and asked the exporter to have the goods shipped back home. This dispute resulted in a deadlock between the importer and exporter. Do you think the importer's statement is justified? 主板
2. A Russian customer ordered a batch of auto parts from an exporter in Northeast China who transported them to a place in Russia by rail under Incoterm DAP. When the goods arrived at the station and were unloaded, the importer found that the unloading charges were not paid and the quantity of goods was short, so the importer asked for a

deduction of the unloading charges and of an amount equal to the shortage from the total amount. The exporter claimed that he had loaded the goods in the right quantity and supported his claim with a series of documents. He suspected that the goods were stolen in transit and therefore refused the importer's request for a deduction and asked him to make a claim against the carrier. The questions are: (1) Is the importer's request for the exporter to pay for unloading justified? (2) Who should make a claim against the carrier?

IV. Problems Solving

马尼拉

1. Suppose you quote for a special type of steel plate at $1,800 per metric ton CIF **Manila** to a customer in the Philippines, with insurance coverage at 110% of the invoice value and the premium rate at 0.8%. But the customer requires a quotation at CFR Manila. How much should you quote to meet the customer's requirement?
2. Suppose you quote for a special type of steel plate at $1,800 per metric ton CIF Manila to a customer in the Philippines, with insurance coverage at 110% of the invoice value and the premium rate at 0.8%. But the customer requires an insurance coverage at 120% of the invoice value. How much should you quote to meet the customer's requirement?

无线路由器

3. Suppose you have quoted a commission exclusive price for a **wireless router** at CIF $25 Manila, while the customer asks for a quotation of commission inclusive price at CIFC4. What is the CIFC4 price if you want to keep your original net revenue?

巴基斯坦 卡拉奇

4. A Chinese business Nesco Steel Co., Ltd. is negotiating a deal of exporting a batch of steel pipe to a **Pakistani** customer. The export quotation is CFR **Karachi** $ 840/MT, and the customer counter-offers at CIFC5 Karachi $ 880/MT (assuming a premium rate of 1.5% and an insurance markup of 10%). If the Chinese business wants to keep its net export income unchanged, can it accept the counter-offer? How much should it quote?

Chapter 6 International Cargo Transport

第六章 国际货物运输

Learning Objectives:

- ◆ Pros and cons of major modes of international cargo transport
- ◆ How to dispatch goods via a certain mode of cargo transport
- ◆ How to calculate the freight for international cargo transport
- ◆ Contributions of containers and basics of container shipping

When deciding how to deliver the ordered goods to your customer, you have several options available. You can ship by sea, by air, by land or by a combined mode of transport from China to the importer's country. You must **weigh the pros and cons** of each mode considering the nature of goods, your destination and whether or not time is pressing. The major **concerns** in the decision include the capacity, speed, security and cost, etc. of a selected mode of transport.

权衡利弊

关切的事项

6.1 Ocean Transport 海上运输

Ocean transport refers to the shipping of goods by sea and broadly speaking, also include transport by inland waterways such as rivers or canals. It plays an important role in the development of international trade. More than two thirds of export and import goods worldwide and 90% of China's are shipped by sea. Ocean transport has obvious advantages compared with other modes of transport. Construction and maintaining costs are very low as most shipping routes are naturally formed. Therefore, it is comparatively economical for shipping **bulky** or low-valued goods such as coal, **ore**, grain, cotton, **timber**, salt, building materials, steel and petroleum, etc. However, it is less speedy and could be affected by bad weather or seasonal factors such as freezing of water in winter or reduction of water level in dry season. The varied depth of oceans, **canals** and ports also affects the navigation of some large vessels. Ocean transport is generally classified into two categories based on the business model: liner shipping and charter shipping. The former is like a bus, while the latter a taxi.

大件的，笨重的
矿石 木材
运河

6.1.1 Liner Shipping 班轮运输

A liner is a shipping service with a **regular** sailing route and follows a pre-established **schedule**. Liner transport is featured by fixed routes, **ports to call on**, schedules and **freight rates**. They are not absolutely fixed, but adjustments are not frequent.

规则的，固定的
时间表
停靠的港口
运费率，即运费单价

6.1.1.1 Liner vessel types 班轮运输船型

Cargoes can be containerized, **bulk** or **breakbulk**, which leads to the emergence of vessels for different purposes. Most liner shipping goes by containerships, accounting for about 80% of liner vessels worldwide. The other 20% are mainly: **general cargo vessels** and multipurpose vessels, which can accommodate both containers and breakbulk cargoes; car and truck carriers, designed specifically to handle passenger vehicles and trucks, but also tractors, bulldozers and the like; and **roll on/roll off ships**, which handle not only the drivable vehicles that are accommodated on car carriers, but also project and heavy lift cargoes that are typically too large or too heavy to be moved on container vessels, such as **wind turbines.**

散装货，大宗货 件杂货
杂货船，普通货船
滚装/滚卸船
风力涡轮机，风力发电机

6.1.1.2 Liner freight 班轮运费

A liner freight for a sailing route includes a **basic freight** and some **surcharges**. The basic freight covers transportation from the port of departure to the port of destination, inclusive of loading, unloading and **stowage and trimming expenses.** If your cargo does not fill up a full

基本运费
附加费
配舱和理货费

container, the liner normally starts with referencing a tariff before quoting you the basic freight rate. A **tariff** in the shipping industry is a pre-published schedule listing a set of criteria used for determining the appropriate **charge unit** for various categories of cargoes on a certain sailing route. Then the liner multiplies the basic rate for a type of cargo on that route by the quantity of the cargo in terms of the selected charge unit to arrive at the total basic freight. If your cargo does fill up a **full container load**, however, the liner applies a container rate, which will be discussed later in an independent section for containers. Let's first take a look at the criteria used in the tariff. 运价表 计费单位 整箱货

For a certain sailing route, freight for different categories of cargo in the tariff may be calculated by weight, measurement, value of the cargo or a combination of these criteria. The following letters are used to indicate the criterion applicable for a certain category.

♦ **"W" (weight)** 按重量计价

For categories of cargo marked with "W" in the tariff, the freight shall be calculated by gross weight of the cargo. The charge unit is ton, but often called a **weight ton**, which could be a metric ton (tonne), a long ton or a short ton, depending on whether you are calculating weight under the Metric System, the British Imperial System or the American Customary System. 重量吨

♦ **"M" (measurement)** 按体积/容积计价

For categories marked with "M" in the tariff, the freight shall be calculated by measurement of the cargo. The corresponding charge unit for these categories is often called a **measurement ton**, which is a cubic meter under the Metric System or 40 cubic feet under the British Imperial System and American Customary System. 尺码吨

♦ **"W/M" (weight/measurement)** 按重量与体积运费孰高计价

For categories marked with "W/M" in the tariff, the freight shall be calculated by a so-called **revenue ton (freight ton)**—either weight or measurement of the cargo, whichever produces greater freight revenue to the carrier. One revenue ton is 1 metric ton (tonne) (=1,000 kilogrammes) or 1 cubic meter. 运费吨

♦ **"A. V."** 从价计征

For categories marked with "A.V." (Ad Valorem) in the tariff, the freight shall be calculated by a percentage of the FOB price of the cargo. It often applies to goods of high economical values.

♦ **"W/M or A.V."** 按重量、体积或价值孰高计价

For categories marked with "W/M or A.V." in the tariff, the freight shall be calculated by either revenue ton or value of the cargo, whichever produces the greater revenue to the carrier.

♦ **"W/M plus A. V."** 按重量与体积运费孰高加从价运费

For categories marked with "W/M plus A. V." in the tariff, the freight rate is expressed in terms of revenue ton of the cargo, plus a certain percentage of the value of the goods.

♦ **Per unit** 计件运费

For categories marked with "per unit" in the tariff, the freight shall be calculated by number of the cargo, such as "per head" for cattle.

♦ **Open rate** 议价运费

Open rate applies when the freight rate can be negotiated between the liner and the shipper.

Calculating liner freight can be challenging, as it may include a number of surcharges. Why are there so many surcharges? The answer, from a liner's view, is because the basic freight rates, being relatively fixed, cannot respond in time to specific circumstances regarding the cargo, the shipping process, or fluctuations in the shipping market. Currency adjustment factor and bunker surcharge are two examples. The former compensates the liner for a **corrosion** (腐蚀) of its profits caused by a depreciation of the currency the freight is quoted in and the latter for the same caused by a rising price of the fuel in the international market. The major surcharges are listed below.

- **Currency adjustment factor (CAF)** 货币调整系数
- **Bunker surcharge or bunker adjustment factor (BAF)** 燃油附加费或燃油调整系数
- **Extra charge for heavy lifts** 超重费
- **Extra charge for over lengths** 超长费
- **Direct additional** 直航附加费
- **Port congestion surcharge** 港口拥堵费
- **Transshipment surcharge** 转运附加费
- **Optional fees** 选港费
- **Terminal handling charges** 港口操作费

- **Alternation of destination surcharges** 变更港口附加费
- **Destination delivery charge** 到港提货费

6.1.2 Charter Shipping 租船运输

An overwhelming majority of ocean transport goes by liner. However, liner shipping cannot satisfy all the needs for international transport. A number of factors may prevent you from shipping by a liner. For example, there is no direct ship to your port of destination, or no liner service at all for cargoes of certain physical nature, sizc or quantity, such as some low-value or price–sensitive commodities. In these cases, you may hire a vessel just for your service. This is called charter shipping or **tramp shipping**. The word "charter" can be used both as a noun and a verb. As a verb, it means "to hire a vehicle for one's own use". If you go by charter shipping, neither the route nor the loading port, unloading port or sailing date is fixed. Different from a standard shipping contract under liner shipping, you sign a unique contract with the ship owner, which is called a **"charter party"**, and you, the shipper, will be the **"charterer"**. Both you and the ship owner's rights and obligations are negotiated and stipulated in the charter party.

不定期运输
租船合同
承租人

6.1.2.1 Types of charter shipping 租船运输的类型

You may charter a vessel under different charter parties, such as:

♦ **Voyage charter 航次租船**

This is a charter party under which the ship owner places the vessel at the disposal of the charterer for one or more voyages, and is responsible for the operation of the vessel. It could be a **single voyage charter**, a **return voyage charter** or a **successive voyage charter**.

单程租船
往返租船 连续租船

♦ **Time charter 定期租船**

This is a charter party under which the ship owner **leases** his/her vessel and **crew** to the charterer for a stipulated period of time. The charterer pays for the fuel and port charges in addition to the charter freight.

租出
所有船员

♦ **Bare boat charter 光船租船**

This is a charter party under which an individual or **legal entity** is generally **vested with temporary ownership** of the boat. "Bare boat" describes a ship without a crew or a **master**. The charterer is in charge

法律实体，法人
被授予临时的所有权
船长

of crewing and operating the ship within a relatively longer period of time, usually a number of years.

6.1.2.2 Charter freight 租船运费

根据

Charter freight is adjusted **as per** demand and supply on the freight market. Depending on terms of your charter party, you may pay it before departure, at destination, or partly before departure and partly at destination. And who pays for loading and unloading should also be clarified in the contract. The following terms are often used for simplifying the negotiation:

- Liner terms: The ship owner pays for both loading and unloading, as in a liner service.
- Free In (FI): The ship owner pays for unloading, but not loading. Note that "free" means that the ship owner is free of loading. The same applies to the following terms.
- Free Out (FO): The ship owner pays for loading, but not unloading.
- Free In and Out (FIO): The ship owner pays for neither loading nor unloading. Under this term, who pays for the **stowage and trimming** expenses should be further clarified. The abbreviation of "FIOST" indicates that the ship owner pays for none of the loading, unloading, stowing and trimming expenses, which shall all be borne by you—the charterer.

理舱和平舱

装卸货日数

滞期费

速遣费

留置权

Time spent for loading and unloading means a lot to ship owners. To increase efficiency, a charter party often stipulates an allowed number of days for the task, called **lay day**, beyond which, you normally have to pay a **demurrage** to the ship owner, but if it is advanced, the ship owner may reward you with a **dispatch**. Notably, however, in case the freight is not paid off, the ship owner can exert a **lien**—keeping the cargo on board until the freight is paid off, which often makes a charter party bill of lading unpopular with banks under a letter of credit transaction.

6.2 Air Transport 航空运输

Shipping by air is fast but expensive. It is often used for cargoes of high value but low volumes.

6.2.1 Advantages and Disadvantages 优点和缺点

Air transport is faster for shipping high-value or perishable goods such as fruits, seafood, flowers, etc. Among others, efficient customs clearance also contributes to its fast transit. As it is faster, packaging cost can be reduced and insurance premiums are lower compared with other modes of transport. It is accessible to most areas despite obstructions of land or sea.

However, air transport is expensive. The carrying capacity of air crafts is also limited and thus not suitable for shipping bulky, heavy and cheaper goods. It may be influenced by bad weather and cause delay in shipment and delivery.

6.2.2 Types of Air Transport 航空运输的种类

Like ocean transport, air transport is also classified into several categories based on business models such as:

♦ **Scheduled carriage** 班机运输

Scheduled carriage is operated by airlines on a daily or less frequent schedule between fixed airports.

♦ **Chartered carriage** 包机运输

Chartered carriage is the hire of an aircraft by a shipper to deliver cargoes. It suits cargoes of large quantities or of different shippers **bound for a common destination**. 去往同一目的地

♦ **Consolidated carriage** 集合运输

Consolidated transport arises when your freight forwarder has regular consignments to be air-shipped from one particular airport to another. As a result, he/she may obtain preferential bulk rate from the airline based on the overall weight and measurement of the expected cargoes. The problem with consolidations, however, is that flights for the consolidated carriage are only available on certain days of a week, which might delay your shipping plans.

♦ **Air courier service** 航空快递服务

An air courier service is an expedited air freight service covering customs clearance and land transport at both ends. It suits the need for shipping documents or goods of light but higher economic value. That is why it is also called a desk-to-desk service.

6.2.3 Air Freight 航空运费

Similarly with ocean shipping, when calculating air freight, both the total weight and total volume are taken into consideration. You need to apply a formula to convert the total volume of a shipment into an equivalent weight and compare it with the real weight of the cargo or vice versa. Whichever figure is larger would be selected by the airline as the one for calculating air freight. The formula for converting from volume to equivalent weight is $1\ m^3 = 167\ kg$ (for converting from weight to equivalent volume, the formula is $1\ kg = 6{,}000\ cm^3$).

The procedures for calculating air freight are as follows (see Table 6-1):

Table 6-1 Procedures for Calculating Air Freight

① First, calculate the total weight and total volume of your shipment. ② Then convert the total volume into equivalent weight based on the formula: $1\ m^3 = 167\ kg$ ③ Compare the real weight and the equivalent weight converted from total volume and then choose the one that is larger. ④ Apply the corresponding freight rate to the larger figure. For example, suppose you have three cartons for shipment which weigh a total of 110 kg and the measurement of each is 1.0 m (L) *0.5 m (W) *0.5 m (H) (L = length, W = width, H = height), so the total volume of the three cartons would be $1.0*0.5*0.5*3=0.75\ m^3$. Then multiply $0.75\ m^3$ by 167 to convert the total volume of the cargo into its equivalent weight. The result is 125.25 kg. Since the equivalent weight is greater than the real weight of 110 kg, it would be the one used by the airline to calculate the air freight. If the corresponding air freight rate for this weight in the air freight tariff is $ 41, the total air freight would be $ 41/kg*125.25 kg = $ 5,135.25.

6.3 Land Transport 陆路运输

Lang transport, comprising mainly rail and road transport, can ship cargoes between regions that are connected by land, such as between inland cities and seaports or airports, between neighboring countries or used as land bridge that crosses continents. It can be employed either independently for international shipping, or as a feeding vehicle for ocean or air transport, particularly under multimodal transport. Though at a lesser scale than the other modes, with the proliferation of free-trade agreements worldwide, it is likely to see a marked growth among countries in the same geographical area and may even become the dominant mode within certain regions, opening up opportunities for trade to new corners of the world.

6.3.1 Rail Transport 铁路运输

Rail transport can be used both for domestic and international shipping. In international shipping, it can be used for shipping cargoes between inland areas and seaports or airports or between neighboring countries like China and Russia, or Germany and Poland. However, when you need to ship cargoes between China and Germany, as the railway crosses several countries, you need to complete many formalities, unless China has signed **conventions** or agreements with other countries along the railway. Such conventions or agreements include ***Convention Concerning International Carriage of Goods by Rail*** **(CIM)** and ***Agreement on International Railway Freight Transportation*** **(SMGS)**. China joined the latter in 1954.

公约

《国际铁路货物运输公约》，简称《国际货约》

《国际铁路货物联运协定》，简称《国际货协》

Rail transport is faster than ocean transport and the capacity is satisfying. It is less affected by bad weather or seasonal factors and the cost is just marginally higher than that for ocean transport and far lower than that for air transport. In recent years, the China-proposed **Belt and Road Initiative has spurred** transaction values by rail, thanks to the **slash** in transit time achieved by **China Railway Express (CRE)**. A journey from Zhengzhou to Hamburg by China Railway Express now takes only 16~18 days, compared with 30~45 days of a similar journey by sea. As of 2021, China Railway Express has completed 41,000 journeys to and from Europe, with destinations expanded to 168 cities in 23 countries in Europe. In 2021 alone, 7,377 journeys were completed, delivering cargoes of 707,000 TEUs to Europe, representing a **year-on-year** increase of 43% and 52% respectively.① CRE's major railway stations of departure include Zhengzhou, Xi'an, Chongqing, Chengdu and **Urumqi**. These stations have opened up great opportunities of trade for inland cities. However, further development of international rail transport is highly dependent on the improvement

"一带一路"倡议

刺激

大幅削减 中欧班列

同比

乌鲁木齐

① Source: CCTV news.

of railway infrastructure of countries along the way and their cooperation in the **harmonization** of international railway conventions.

协调

6.3.2 Road Transport 公路运输

Road transport, with the biggest advantage of being flexible, can also be used both for domestic and international shipping. For example, it can be used for delivering goods between warehouses and sea port/airport or railway stations, or between neighboring countries, including those within a trade bloc, such as neighboring countries in the European Union. According to Eurostat, road transport is often the most flexible and common mode of transporting goods within the EU, as there is an extensive motorway network for a seamless transition when crossing national borders. However, shipping by road is also dependent on the infrastructure of the countries in question, but a big plus is its door-to-door service, making it accessible to rural or remote areas.

6.4 Multi-Modal Transport 多式联运

Facilitated by a wide adoption of containers in international shipping, multi-modal transport can move goods from origin to destination by a combination of several modes of transport (by sea, rail and road, for example) under a single contract without handling of the freight when modes shift. It is often carried out by a **Multi-Modal Transport Operator (MTO)** who, as the carrier, normally concludes a multi-modal transportation contract with the shipper and is liable for the entire transportation process. It is often associated with **full-container-load (FCL)** transport as containers travel from origin to destination without being opened in transit, although it can also apply to **less-than-container-load (LCL)** cargoes.

多式联运经营人

集装箱整箱运输

集装箱拼箱货

If you transport this way, you can expect to save cost and speed up payment collection as your goods, benefiting from limited handling in transit, move faster and are less likely to be stolen or damaged, which helps to enhance your competitiveness in the international market and enables you to sell to farther markets. The transportation process is also simplified as you need only to deal with the MTO in all matters relating to transport, including settlement of claims for loss, damage or delay in the delivery. However, its limitations are obvious, too. First, as the MTO is fully liable for you in the whole journey, selecting an experienced MTO is vital to a smooth journey. Second, a limited number of both multimodal routes and experienced MTOs tends to **hike up** the freight rate, **offsetting** some reduction in cost brought about by faster transit and less damages to or loss of your goods.

推高
抵消

6.5 Container Transport 集装箱运输

If you have ever seen a container, you may find that it is nothing but a big "box", yet it has a legendary story with a short history. Before the **advent** of containers, cargoes come in various shapes, packages and weights. Loading and unloading a ship was labor-intensive, **backbreaking** and time-consuming. The idea of using a big "box" to hold cargoes of varied natures and shapes was pioneered in 1956 by **Malcom McLean**, owner of a trucking company in North Carolina, the United States. His idea has revolutionized international shipping ever since. As the big "boxes" were finally decided to be in standardized measurements, they can be **stacked** on top of one another **neatly** and for many **layers** so that port **cranes** can process them efficiently. Containers' **prevalence** in ocean shipping drives revolution of the shipbuilding industry as well, making container ships universal and larger day by day. It also helps to achieve "**one-stop**" delivery for international buyers by linking different modes of transport while reducing handling of cargoes to the minimum.

出现，问世
艰苦繁重的
马尔科姆·麦克莱恩
堆放 整齐的 层
起重机 普及
一站式

Properly speaking, container transport is not a mode of transport but an instrument to link various modes of transport. Therefore, it can be employed by any mode of transport (by sea, air, rail or road, etc.) Though it is mostly used for FCL/FCL transport as containers travel from end to end without being opened in transit, it also applies to LCL/LCL cargoes. Door-to-door service is also available. Transport by means of containers reduces costs and time for loading and unloading, and protects the shipments from **pilferage** and damage in handling. The

盗窃

capacity is large. Therefore, it has become the most popular means of transport today for shipping goods internationally.

6.5.1 Container Sizes and Shipping Terminologies 集装箱尺寸和运输术语

Before you ship goods via containers, you must know the common sizes of containers and important terminologies in container shipping (see Figure 6-1 and Table 6-2).

集装箱大小和尺寸

- **Container sizes and dimensions:**

Figure 6-1 Common Sizes of Containers

Table 6-2 Common Container Sizes and Dimensions

有效载荷

	20-foot containers	
	General purpose containers	Reefer containers
Interior dimension	5.905 M×2.350 M×2.392 M	5.485 M×2.275 M×2.260 M
Max. **payload**	25 TNE	21 TNE
Cubic capacity	33 CBM	27 CBM
	40-foot containers	
Interior dimension	1.204 M×2.350 M×2.392 M	1.158 M×2.275 M×2.415 M
Max. payload	29 TNE	26 TNE
Cubic capacity	67 CBM	58 CBM
	40-foot high cube containers	
Interior dimension	1.204 M×2.350 M×2.697 M	1.162 M×2.290 M×2.500 M
Max. payload	29 TNE	26 TNE
Cubic capacity	76 CBM	66 CBM

- **Container Yard (CY):** The area **adjacent to** the vessel **berth** where containers are delivered to or received from the vessel, or delivered to and received from inland carriers. 集装箱堆场，货柜场 附近 泊位
- **Container Freight Station (CFS):** A facility at which LCL cargoes are received from merchants for loading into containers or at which LCL cargoes are unloaded from containers and delivered to merchants. 集装箱货运站
- **DOOR:** The **consignor** or **consignee**'s warehouse where the cargo is loaded or unloaded. 门 发货人 收货人
- **Full Container Load (FCL):** A **shipment** that fills up a container's allowable maximum weight or measurement. In practice, however, FCL in ocean shipping does not always mean packing a container to its full payload or full capacity. It means that the entire container load **is bound for** one consignee. 整箱货，整柜货 一批货 驶往
- **Less than Container Load (LCL):** A shipment that is not large enough to fill up a standard cargo container so that it has to share a container with other consignors' cargoes which are bound for the same destination. 拼箱货，拼柜货
- **Twenty-Foot Equivalent Unit (TEU):** A measure of the cargo capacity of container ships or container terminals based on the size of a standardized container of 20 feet in length. 二十英尺标准箱（柜）

6.5.2 Classifications of Container Shipping 集装箱运输方式分类

The following groups of abbreviations describe the major types of a container's journey:

- **CFS/CFS**—from container freight station at exporting country to container freight station at importing country 集装箱货运站到集装箱货运站
- **CY/CY**—from container yard at exporting country to container yard at importing country 集装箱堆场到集装箱堆场
- **CFS/CY**—from container freight station at exporting country to container yard at importing country 集装箱货运站到集装箱堆场
- **CY/CFS**—from container yard at exporting country to container freight station at importing country 集装箱堆场到集装箱货运站
- **DOOR-DOOR**—from exporter's warehouse to importer's warehouse 门到门

6.5.3 Container Freight Rates 集装箱费率

To calculate the basic freight for container shipping on a liner service, the first step often involves a decision between two options—full container load or less than container load, as freight rates charged vary between the two options. A full container load applies to a shipment that can fill up one or more containers, while a less than container load cannot fill up an entire container but has to share one with other consignors' cargoes. For a full container load, a liner normally applies a flat rate regardless of the commodity being carried, as long as the cargo is permitted and not dangerous. For a less than container load, the liner also refers to the tariff for determining the freight rate, as what is discussed before.

Let' take a 20-foot container as an example and see how this is done (see Table 6-3).

Table 6-3 Procedures for Calculating Basic Freight for Container Shipping

① Calculate the total weight and total measurement of your shipment. ② Divide the total weight of your shipment by the maximum payload of a 20-foot container to see how many containers you need. Record that figure as X. ③ Divide the total measurement of your shipment by the cubic capacity of the same container size to see again how many containers you need. Record that figure as Y. ④ Compare X and Y. The bigger one of the two will be the number of containers you need. ⑤ If the bigger one of X and Y is greater than one, the shipment makes a full container load, then multiply this figure by the corresponding freight rate for a full container load. ⑥ If the bigger one of X and Y is smaller than one, the shipment makes a less than container load and the corresponding freight rate for that commodity dictated by the tariff will apply. However, in this case, you may still calculate the freight under a full container load and compare to see which option saves more money. **Notes:** For full container load, sometimes you may still need to calculate the freights under containers in other sizes to see which container size helps you save the most on freight. See exercise for this chapter (Calculation 1 and 2).

Nowadays, logistic companies often publish their container freight rates online. You may calculate on your own or turn to a freight forwarder for help. The number of packages a container can hold is limited by both its payload and cubic capacity. As long as the shipment is not beyond both limits, a flat freight rate is charged for a route. Try this site for a quotation of sea freight rate for FCL or LCL: https://www.ufsoo.com/

Exercises 练习

I. True or False

1. Compared with other modes of international transport, the freight rate of ocean transport is lower while the transit time is longer. (　)
2. Liner freight doesn't cover stevedore charges. (　)
3. "Freight" and "Freight rate" means the same for cargo transport. (　)
4. For goods marked "A.V" in the freight tariff, the freight is calculated based on the EXW price of the goods concerned. (　)
5. "Bare boat" refers to a ship without any crew or captain. (　)
6. Liner freight includes a basic freight and some surcharges. (　)
7. Weights are always measured in tons, both for air shipping and ocean shipping. (　)
8. It now takes about 18 days from Zhengzhou to Hamburg, which greatly reduces the time of goods in transit. (　)
9. Multi-modal transport is mostly used for FCL container transport. (　)
10. Containers can be used for any mode of transport. (　)

II. Multiple Choice Questions

1. The mode of transport mostly used for China's import and export is (　　).
   [A] international multi-modal transport
   [B] ocean and inland waterway transport
   [C] air transport
   [D] land transport
2. Which of the following commodity does not need air-shipping? (　　)
   牛油果 [A] **Avocado**.
   车厘子 [B] **Cherry**.
   蓝莓 [C] **Blueberry**.
   开心果 [D] **Pistachio**.
3. Which one of the following might use a different charge unit for calculating freight from other commodities? (　　)
   [A] Cotton.
   羽绒服 [B] **Eiderdown coat**.
   海绵 [C] **Sponge**.
   水泥 [D] **Cement**.
4. (　　) is the document usually used by Chinese exporters for the transport of goods to Western Europe via the **Eurasian Land Bridge**. 亚欧大陆桥
   [A] A railway consignment note
   [B] An air waybill
   [C] An ocean bill of lading
   [D] A cargo receipt
5. The term for a "door-to-door" service by container transport is (　　).
   [A] FCL/FCL
   [B] FCL/LCL
   [C] LCL/FCL
   [D] LCL/LCL
6. Which is (are) the CORRECT description(s) of a liner transport? (　　)*
   [A] Fixed route and ports.
   [B] On a regular basis.
   [C] Cargo handling charges covered in the liner freight.
   [D] Flexible with types and quantity of cargo carried.

7. Which one of the following is NOT a type of charter transport? ( )
   [A] Time charter.
   [B] Voyage charter.
   [C] Bare boat charter.
   [D] Container charter.
8. Which is (are) the feature(s) of an international multi-modal transport? ( )*
   [A] A single multi-modal transport document is used.
   [B] There must be two or more distinct and coherent modes of transport.
   [C] The MTO is responsible for the entire journey.
   [D] A single freight rate is applied to the entire journey.
9. Liner freight is charged against a variety of standards, depending on the category of the cargo. ( ) is the standard that determines the freight rate against the weight, measurement or value of a cargo, whichever is the highest.
   [A] W/M
   [B] W/M OR AD VAL
   [C] AD VAL
   [D] OPEN RATE
10. Following the Belt and Road Initiative, ( ) has been given a spur.
    [A] ocean transport
    [B] air transport
    [C] international railway transport
    [D] international multi-modal transport

III. Calculations

1. Suppose your company has entered a deal of exporting 8,150 pieces of down jackets from Tianjin to New York. The packaging unit is carton. Each carton contains 20 pieces, with a gross weight of 34 kg, a net weight of 30 kg, and a volume of 0.28616 CBM per carton. Please calculate the total gross weight and total volume, and then the

sea freight for 20’ sized container, 40’ sized container and for LCL respectively and compare which option is the most cost-effective. Suppose the sea freight rate from Tianjin to New York found from the website of a logistics company is: $3,702 for 20’ container, $4,674 for 40’ container; and $47 for ordinary LCL by volume (MTQ) and $59 by weight (TNE).

2. Suppose your company has entered a deal of exporting 2,150 pieces of down jackets from Tianjin to Vancouver. The packaging unit is carton. Each carton contains 20 pieces, with a gross weight of 34 kg, a net weight of 30 kg, and a volume of 0.28616 CBM per carton. Please calculate the total gross weight and total volume, and then the sea freight for 20’ sized container and LCL respectively and compare which option is more cost-effective. Suppose the sea freight rate from Tianjin to Vancouver found from the website of a logistics company is: $1199 for 20’ container, and $92 for ordinary LCL by volume (MTQ) and $86 by weight (TNE).

Chapter 7 Transport Documents

第七章 运输单据

Learning Objectives:

- Bill of lading—the transport document for ocean transport
- Other transport documents for ocean, air, and land transport
- Multimodal bill of lading and through bill of lading

Once you have dispatched the goods for international shipping, a certain type of transport document will be issued, which is generally more critical than a domestic counterpart, such as those when you send things by domestic couriers. In this chapter, let's learn about the transport documents under different modes of transport.

7.1 Bill of Lading[①] 海运提单

When you deliver the goods via ocean transport, upon your request, the **carrier** or its agent normally issues a bill of lading (B/L, BL or BoL) to you or the importer, depending on the Incoterms rule employed. It is one of the most crucial documents in international trade to ensure that exporters receive payment and importers receive the merchandise.

承运人

---

① The word "lading" means "loading", both words being derived from the Old English word *hladan*. "Lading" specifically refers to the loading of cargo aboard a ship (despite the etymology, "bills of loading" is not a synonym for "bills of lading").

7.1.1 What is a Bill of Lading? 海运提单是什么?

A bill of lading is a document issued by a carrier or its agent to acknowledge receipt of cargo for shipment. However, more than that, it must be transferrable and serve three functions:

货物收据

(1) It is a **receipt for the goods**. The carrier acknowledges that it has received the goods and will accept responsibility for the goods until they reach their port of destination.

运输合同

(2) It is a **contract of carriage**. The carrier agrees with the shipper—either you or the importer, depending on the Incoterms rule employed, to transport the goods from one port to another for a given amount of money. It contains or evidences the terms of contract of carriage.

物权凭证

释放

(3) It is a **document of title**. Representing legal ownership of the goods, it can be transferred to represent the transference of ownership of the goods. It is also the document that the carrier needs to authorize the **release** of the goods at the port of destination.

《跟单信用证统一惯例》国际商会第600号出版物

多式联运提单

联合提单

According to various treaties, conventions or practices on marine cargo transport, these are three commonly acknowledged criteria for identifying a B/L. A document that has fulfilled all the three roles is almost certainly a B/L, but one with any of the three roles absent rarely is. ***UCP 600*** defines a B/L as the transport document used only for port-to-port sea shipments, rather than one for air or land shipments. Additionally, for shipment delivered by more than one mode of transport, the shipping document is called a **multimodal bill of lading** or a **combined bill of lading**. It could be issued as a title document or one that is not.

7.1.2 How to Fill out a Bill of Lading? 如何填写海运提单?

拖，拉

信息栏

A B/L is a legal document that has to be filled out before a shipment is **hauled**. Having this document signed protects both the carrier and the shipper as it contains detailed information about whatever is being shipped. It is also relevant to purchasing cargo insurance. However, it can be quite a complicated task to fill it out correctly. With so many **fields** on the bill, one tends to be overwhelmed at first sight. But take it easy. Figure 7-1 and Table 7-1 provide a detailed instruction on how to fill out the document. And in most cases, you don't need to fill out all the fields, but just the indispensable ones as shown in Figure 7-1.

<table>
<tr><td colspan="2">1. Shipper
TIANJIN BINHAI IMPORT & EXPORT CO., LTD.
NO.188 HAIHE ROAD, BINHAI DISTRICT, TIANJIN,
P. R. CHINA</td><td>2. BL No. SINOTRANS-CAS-20056</td></tr>
<tr><td colspan="2">3. Consignee or order
TO ORDER</td><td rowspan="4">中国对外贸易运输总公司
CHINA NATIONAL FOREIGN TRADE TRANSPORTATION GROUP
OCEAN BILL OF LADING
SHIPPED on board in apparent good order and condition (unless otherwise indicated) the goods or packages specified herein and to be discharged at the mentioned port of discharge or as near thereto as the vessel may safely get and be always afloat.
The weight, measure, marks and numbers, quality, contents and value, being particulars furnished by the Shipper, are not checked by the Carrier on loading.
The Shipper, Consignee and the Holder of the bill of lading hereby expressly accept and agree to all printed, written or stamped provisions, exceptions and conditions of this bill of lading, including those on the back hereof.
IN WITENESS WHERE of the number of original BLs stated below have been signed, one of which being accomplished the other(s) to be void.</td></tr>
<tr><td colspan="2">4. Notify Party
SINGAPORE WONKA TRADING COMPANY LTD
67 ANG MO KIO AVENUE 8 SINGAPORE 560250</td></tr>
<tr><td>5. Pre-carriage by</td><td>6. Port of Loading
TIANJIN CHINA</td></tr>
<tr><td>7. Vessel and Voy. No.
DONG FENG V.133</td><td>8. Port of Transshipment</td></tr>
<tr><td>9. Port of Discharge
SINGAPORE</td><td>10. Final Destination
SINGAPORE</td><td>11. For arrival info & release of cargo contact</td></tr>
</table>

12. Marks & Nos.	**13. No. of cont. or pkgs.**	**14. Description of packages and goods**	**15. Gross weight (kgs.)**	**16. Measurement (cbm)**
SWTC SINGAPORE NO.1-30 TBIM-SWTC-09	30 CARTONS	SWIMMING SUITS 30 CARTONS CREDIT NUMBER: KOS879 DATE OF CREDIT: 20220510 THE NAME OF ISSUING BANK: BANK OF CHINA SINGAPORE	1,260 KGS.	25.20 M^3

<table>
<tr><td colspan="3">17. Total number of Containers or other Packages or units received by the Carrier (in words)</td><td colspan="3">SAY TOTAL THIRTY CARTONS ONLY</td></tr>
<tr><td>18. Freight and charges</td><td>19. Revenue tons</td><td>20. Rate</td><td>21. Per</td><td>22. Prepaid</td><td>23. Collect</td></tr>
<tr><td rowspan="2">24. Exchange rate</td><td>25. Prepaid at
TIANJIN CHINA</td><td colspan="2">27. Payable at</td><td colspan="2">28. Place and date of issue
JUNE 15, 2022 TIANJIN CHINA</td></tr>
<tr><td>26. Total prepaid in national currency</td><td colspan="2">29. No. of original B(s) /L
Three (3)</td><td colspan="2" rowspan="3">32. Signature
Signed for or on behalf of the Master
张楠
as Agent</td></tr>
<tr><td colspan="4">30. LADEN ON BOARD THE VESSEL
Date June 15, 2022 By</td></tr>
<tr><td colspan="4">31. CONTAINER/SEAL NO. MBLU4459040/771126/CY-CY</td></tr>
</table>

Figure 7-1 A Sample Bill of Lading

Table 7-1 How to Fill out a Bill of Lading

1. **Shipper (From)**: Fill in the company name and address of the shipper (consignor).
2. **Bill of lading number**: A unique control number to reference the bill of lading.
3. **Consignee or order**: There are generally three ways to fill out this field with significantly different effect, which will be explained in the next section:
   (a) Fill in the company name and address of the consignee, or
   (b) Fill in "bear", "holder" or left blank, or
   (c) Fill in "to order" or "to order of ×××"
4. **Notify party**: Fill in the complete information for the recipient of the shipment, if different from the consignee.
5. **Pre-carriage by**: In the case of transshipment or multimodal combined transport, fill in the transport mode and vehicle name prior to the main carriage. Leave blank if no transshipment or multimodal transport is employed.
6. **Port of loading**: Fill in the port where the cargo will be loaded. E.g., Port of Loading: Tianjin. You may also be required to fill in the country.
7. **Vessel and voyage number**: Fill in the vessel name and voyage number which will be delivering the shipment to the consignee at destination.
8. **Port of transshipment**: In the case of transshipment, fill in the port where transshipment occurs.
9. **Port of discharge**: Fill in the port where the cargo will be arriving. E.g., Port of discharge: Singapore. You may also be required to fill in the country.
10. **Final destination**: Fill in the city where the carrier will be delivering the cargo to the consignee.
11. **For arrival info & release of cargo contact**: Fill in the name of the agent the consignee should contact to obtain cargo release, arrival notices, etc., at destination. Note that these agents may offer customs clearance and delivery services but are not obliged to fulfill them.
12. **Marks & numbers**: Fill in the shipping marks and the total number of packages per line item, whether the packages are consolidated on a pallet or in an outer container.
13. **No. of containers and/or packages**: Fill in the total number of containers, and/or packages.
14. **Description of packages and goods**: Fill in the description of each line item, noting the type of package (boxes, barrel, etc.) and the quantity per package. There must be a separate line item for each different freight classification description. If more than one type of packaging is used per freight classification, a separate entry must be used for each type of package. Also include handling instructions (i.e., fragile, should be kept cool, etc.)
15. **Gross weight**: Fill in the total gross weight for each line item.
16. **Measurement**: Fill in the total measurement for each line item.
17. **Total number of Containers or other Packages or units received by the Carrier (in words)**: Fill in this information in words.
18. **Freight and charges**: Fill in the total amount of freight and charges to ship the cargo.
19. **Revenue tons**: Fill in the revenue tons of the cargo.
20. **Rate**: Fill in the freight rate for each line item on the bill of lading.
21. **Per**: Fill in the unit for the freight rate, such as container or revenue ton.

continued

22. **Prepaid**: Fill in the amount prepaid by the shipper.
23. **Collect**: Fill in the amount to be collected for the merchandise itself. Be sure to include the freight charges.
24. **Exchange rate**: Fill in exchange rate between currencies (i.e., USD, EUR, etc.).
25. **Prepaid at**: Fill in the city name where the freight is prepaid.
26. **Total prepaid in national currency**: Fill in the total freight prepaid in the national currency.
27. **Payable at**: Fill in the city name where the freight is to be collected by the carrier.
28. **Place and date of issue**: Fill in the city and date of where and when the BL is issued.
29. **Number of Original BLs**: Fill in the number of original BLs for the entire shipment.
30. **Laden on board the vessel date & by**: Fill in the on-board date and the carrier's name.
31. **Container/seal number**: Fill in the container or seal number.
32. **Signature**: The authorized representative of either the carrier or its agent may sign the bill of lading. His/her signature is sealed here and should indicate whether he/she has signed for or as agent of the carrier. A bill of lading with signature of the carrier's authorized representative is usually known as a Master BL and the one with signature of its agent as a House BL.

7.1.3 How Does a Bill of Lading Work? 海运提单如何运作?

The workflow of a typical B/L under a letter of credit normally consists of the following steps as described in Figure 7-2:

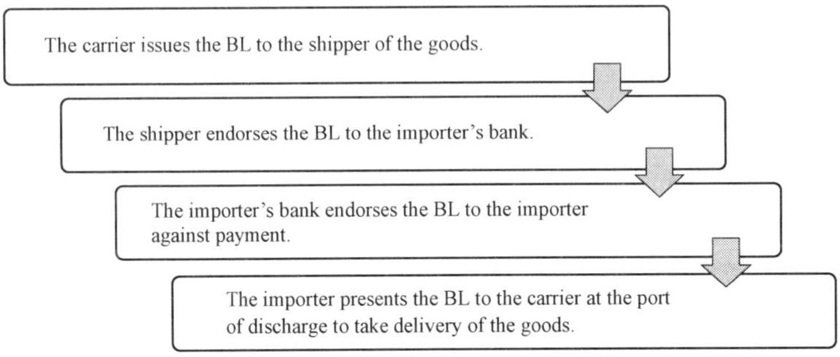

Figure 7-2 Workflow of a Bill of Lading

7.1.3.1 Issue a bill of lading 签发提单

A B/L should be issued by the carrier or its agent once the goods have been loaded on board the ship. The on-board date is normally regarded as the date of issue. In practice, generally 2 or 3 originals are issued. Only the originals can be used for taking delivery, and when any one original is used for taking delivery, all the other originals cease to be effective.

7.1.3.2 Avoid advanced & ante-dated bill of lading 避免预签提单和倒签提单

The date of issue is crucial for a B/L and should be correctly filled out. In practice, however, two behaviors regarding this date are common but not quite ethical, which you should try to avoid: asking the carrier to issue an advanced B/L or an ante-dated B/L.

♦ **Advanced bill of lading 预签提单**

An advanced bill of lading is a B/L issued by the carrier whilst the goods have not been shipped. It is often used when the date stipulated in the letter of credit for **presenting** the B/L and other documents is almost **due**, but the shipper has not yet got goods ready for shipment. In order to present documents including the B/L to the bank within the stipulated **period for presentation**, the carrier sometimes issues an advanced B/L at the request of the shipper. This **poses a risk** to the carrier—if for a certain reason the cargo is not loaded or not completely loaded, it has a responsibility to the consignee.

提交

到期

交单期

构成风险

♦ **Ante-dated bill of lading 倒签提单**

An ante-dated bill of lading is a B/L that **bears** a date of issue that is prior to the actual date of shipment, such as a B/L date of Sept. 15th for an actual shipping date of Sept. 20th. This occurs mostly when the shipment is delayed. In order to comply with either the contract or the letter of credit, the carrier sometimes issues an ante-dated B/L at the request of the shipper. As this may mislead the consignee to believe that the cargo shall arrive **sooner** than actually is, the carrier must be fully aware of the risks involved—the consignee may **file litigation** against it for **losses incurred**.

记载

更早

提起诉讼

所造成的损失

7.1.3.3 Transfer a bill of lading 转让提单

A straight B/L requires that the shipment be made to the named consignee in the **consignee box**. This type of B/L cannot be transferred. A bearer or holder B/L can be transferred to anyone merely by delivering to the person or company. A "to-order" B/L can be transferred to a named or any person or company by **endorsement**—making notations at the back of the B/L about how to transfer it. Generally, there are three types of endorsement representing three ways of transferring the B/L:

收货人框

背书

♦ **Restrictive endorsement**: The endorser can transfer the B/L to a named **endorsee** who cannot further transfer the B/L. 限定背书 被背书人

Deliver to Singapore Wonka Trading Co., Ltd.	→	the endorsee (who cannot further transfer)
李明	→	authorized representative of **endorser** 背书人
For Tianjin Binhai Import & Export Co., Ltd.	→	endorser
July 20, 2022	→	date of endorsing

♦ **Order endorsement**: The endorser can transfer the B/L to a named endorsee who can further transfer the B/L. 指示背书

Deliver to Order of Bank of China, Tianjin Branch	→	the endorsee (who can further transfer)
李明	→	authorized representative of endorser
For Tianjin Binhai Import & Export Co., Ltd.	→	endorser
July 20, 2022	→	date of endorsing

♦ **Blank endorsement**: The endorser can transfer the B/L to anyone who can further transfer it by delivering it to anyone else. 空白背书

	→	the endorsee (who can further transfer by delivery)
李明	→	authorized representative of endorser
For Tianjin Binhai Import & Export Co., Ltd.	→	endorser
July 20, 2022	→	date of endorsing

7.1.4 Types of B/Ls 海运提单的种类

B/Ls can be classified into many types and take many forms, depending on the criterion used.

7.1.4.1 On-board & received-for-shipment bill of lading 已装船提单和备运提单

♦ **On-board bill of lading 已装船提单**

An on-board B/L indicates that the merchandise has been received in good order and condition from the named shipper (consignor) and physically loaded onto a vessel on the stated date. An on-board B/L is normally more popular with banks than a received-for-shipment B/L in the case of a **negotiation for payment**. 议付货款

♦ **Received-for-shipment bill of lading 备运提单**

A received-for-shipment B/L indicates that the merchandise has been received, but not necessarily loaded onto a vessel. Typically, it is issued by a freight forwarder at a port or **depot**. It can be exchanged for an on-board BL upon being loaded.

运输终端

7.1.4.2 Clean & unclean bill of lading 清洁提单和不清洁提单

♦ **Clean bill of lading 清洁提单**

A clean B/L is one on which the carrier doesn't make any **adverse** remarks or notations (called "clauses") about the condition, packaging, or quantity of the goods. Importers and their banks typically make payment on condition of a clean B/L under a letter of credit transaction.

不利的，不良的

♦ **Unclean bill of lading 不清洁提单**

An unclean B/L is one with adverse remarks or notations (called "clauses") having been made by the carrier indicating that the goods received for shipping (or their packaging) look wet, damaged, in doubtful condition, or not of correct quantity. Importers and their banks normally do not accept an unclean B/L for payment under a letter of credit transaction. An unclean B/L is also called a **claused B/L**, dirty B/L, or foul B/L. Expressions that denote an unclean B/L could be "packaging is not sufficient for the sea journey", "goods which are properly stored at the port of loading have been shipped on board and partially wet and not in good condition", etc.

条款提单

7.1.4.3 Order, straight and bearer bill of lading 指示提单，记名提单和持有人提单

一份指示提单规定，货物的交付凭某人指示，这个人可以是托运人、收货人、相关的银行、承运人，等等。有时仅仅注明“凭指示”，这通常是指“凭托运人指示”。用于命名收货人的常用表达式是“交付给×或凭其指示”“凭×的指示”。

♦ **Order bill of lading 指示提单**

An order B/L states that delivery is to be made to the order of someone, who could be the shipper, the consignee, a related bank, the carrier, etc., or sometimes just "to order", which usually indicates "to order of the shipper". A common expression used for naming the consignee is "to × or his/her order" "to the order of ×".

♦ **Straight bill of lading 记名提单**

A straight B/L states explicitly the consignee of the merchandise without using words like "to order" and therefore is non-negotiable.

记名提单明确规定了商品的收货人，而不使用“凭指示”之类的字眼，

Under a straight B/L, the carrier delivers the shipment to the consignee against presentation of identification. It is used mostly when the goods have been paid for or when payment is not required (such as in the case of donations or gifts).

因此是不可议付的。在记名提单下，船公司在收货人出示身份证明的情况下将货物交付给收货人。它主要用于当货物已经支付或不需要付款时（例如，在捐赠或礼物的情况下）。

♦ **Bearer bill of lading 持有人提单**

A bearer B/L is one on which no consignee is named so that delivery is to be made to the bearer of the B/L, namely, whomever holds the bill. Understandably, it is seldom used due to huge risk involved.

持有人提单是提单上没有指明收货人的提单，因此，货物将交付给提单的持有人，即谁持有就交付给谁。正如你可以想象的，它很少使用，因为这种提单包含巨大风险。

7.1.4.4 Liner bill of lading & charter party bill of lading 班轮运输和租船合同提单

♦ **Liner bill of lading 班轮运输提单**

If you are shipping a small amount of cargo, you normally arrange for a liner to transport the goods and get an ordinary B/L—a liner B/L.

♦ **Charter party bill of lading 租船合同提单**

If you need the entire (or a very substantial part) capacity of a vessel, you may need to charter the vessel, and enter into a charter party with the ship owner. Under this agreement, the transport document is issued by the master (the captain) to you, the charterer, and is called a "charter party bill of lading".

A charter party B/L under a transaction by letter of credit is usually unpopular with a bank, as the credit is **subject to** the charter party between the charterer and the ship owner. The ship owner often has a right to lay claim to the cargo aboard the ship in case of a dispute with the charterer. For this reason, bankers generally refuse to accept a charter party B/L as **collateral** for loans, or for payment under a letter of credit. Conceivably, a charter party B/L could not be presented as a **substitute** for a **marine** or port-to-port B/L if the latter is **expressly** required in the credit.

受到……制约

抵押品

替代品　海运　明确地

7.1.4.5 Freight prepaid & freight collect bill of lading 运费预付提单和运费到付提单

♦ **Freight prepaid bill of lading 运费预付提单**

A sales contract sometimes requires that the B/L be marked "freight prepaid", the reason being that, in case the sale is under CIF, the importer wants to make sure that the freight has already been paid by the exporter (usually the shipper) and that the carrier will not attempt to **claim freight** from the importer or exercise a **lien** on the merchandise at the port of destination.

收取运费　留置权

If the importer pays by letter of credit, bankers normally only accept a transport document with words expressly indicating whether or not the freight has been paid, such as with a **stamp** of "Freight Prepaid" or "Freight Collect", or with the information indicated by other means.

印章

♦ **Freight collect bill of lading 运费到付提单**

A freight-collect B/L is one under which the freight is to be paid at the port of destination such as in the case of an FOB-based transaction.

7.1.4.6 Long form & short form bill of lading 长式提单和短式提单

♦ **Long form bill of lading 长式提单**

A long form B/L is one with the terms and conditions of carriage (the rights, responsibilities of the carrier and the shipper) printed on the back of the B/L. These terms are **governed** generally either by the **former *Hague Rules***, the more recent ***Hague-Visby Rules***, or the ***Hamburg Rules***, etc. for international shipping.

管辖
前《海牙规则》
《海牙-维斯比规则》
《汉堡规则》

♦ **Short form bill of lading 短式提单**

A short form B/L is one without the terms and conditions of carriage (the rights, responsibilities and liabilities of the carrier and the shipper) printed on the back of the document. Otherwise, it is no different from the long form B/L. Whether or not these terms and conditions are printed on the back, the shipper and the carrier **are bound** by the conditions of carriage, governed generally by the same rules for international shipping mentioned above.

被约束

7.1.4.7 Stale bill of lading & telex/email-released bill of lading 过期提单和电放提单

♦ **Stale bill of lading 过期提单**

When you and the importer are in neighboring or nearby countries, due to the short distance between the countries and inefficiency in transmitting the B/L, a possibility exists that the cargo reaches the destination before the B/L does, or the B/L is presented for negotiation beyond a reasonable period of time. In such cases, the B/L becomes **stale**, hence the name—stale bill of lading. In the first case scenario, there is possibility that you might not get paid on time or not get paid at all. In the second, the importer cannot take delivery of the goods on time, has to pay additional fees or charges such as demurrage and warehousing fees, and may suffer losses caused by the fluctuation of the merchandise's price. To prevent these adverse situations, you'd better take precautions to prevent a B/L from becoming stale. 过期的

♦ **Telex/email-released bill of lading 电放提单**

When a B/L is expected to be "stale", one of the solutions is filing an application to the carrier for a telex or email release of the B/L, which allows the consignee to take delivery of the merchandise without presenting an original B/L but a copy of the original instead. However, as this poses great risk for the carrier, it often requires a **letter of indemnity** from you in order to exempt itself from liabilities should the cargo be released not to the proper party. Then it shall keep the full set of original B/Ls with itself or its agent, and send a message to its agent at the port of destination via telex or email, permitting the consignee to take delivery of the goods with a copy of the original B/L. 保函

7.2 Other Transport Documents 其他运输单据

Other transport documents include waybills such as sea waybills and air waybills and consignment notes such as those for rail and road transport. Different from a bill of lading, they are non-negotiable documents.

7.2.1 Waybills and Consignment Notes 运单和托运单

As B/Ls represent ownership of the cargo, they are negotiable transport document, meaning that they can be transferred when the cargo is in transit at sea. Transferring the B/L signifies selling the goods. This feature of a B/L meets the needs of international trade by sea. But sometimes neither you nor the importer has the need to transfer the transport document, for example, when the importer has no intention to sell the goods in transit; when you buy or ship goods for yourself, or sell to a branch, a **subsidiary** or a regular or trusted customer. In these cases, a non-negotiable transport document, such as a sea waybill, an air waybill, a rail consignment note or a road consignment note, etc. can be employed, depending on your mode of transport.

子公司

These waybills or consignment notes share three important traits: They are the carrier's receipt of goods and contract of carriage, but not document of title. They simplify transport and can be employed under certain circumstances, but they also pose risks and inconveniences for traders. For example, as they are not documents of title, they are not negotiable. Carriers thus can release the cargo to the consignee without requiring the original transport document from the latter, making it impossible for you to claim payment from the importer by controlling the cargo. And you must watch for the possibility that the importer takes delivery by simply proving his/her identity without making payment. This may even occur under a letter of credit. When that does occur, the credit effectively loses validity. Consequently, bankers are often reluctant in granting letters of credit to importers when this type of non-negotiable transport documents is employed for presentation, which in turn impedes the expansion of international trade. This is just the problem with further expansion of the China Railway Express.

7.2.2 Sea Waybills 海运单

A sea waybill is a shipping document that is essentially not a B/L but only the receipt of goods and contract of carriage. It looks remarkably like a B/L, especially in two important ways: First, the front of the document generally bears a description of the quantity and condition of the goods; Second, the back of the document lists the terms of the contract of carriage.

They differ from B/Ls in that, rather than indicating that the goods in question are to be delivered to the order of the shipper or someone else, they often expressly state that the cargo is to be delivered only to the consignee. This is achieved in a number of ways. For example, the document may bear the words "non-negotiable", or omit the word "order" from the consignee box, and state **explicitly** that the cargo will be delivered to the consignee or its authorized representative against proper proof of identity and authorization. Alternatively, the consignee box might indicate explicitly that the document is "not to order". The document may also simply omit the consignee box altogether, stating expressly that the goods is to be delivered "to the party nominated by the charterer or his/her authorized agent". 明确地

When you use a sea waybill, the major advantage is that the importer does not need to present the original document to the carrier for taking delivery; he/she only needs to prove his/her identity as the named consignee on the front of the document. Certainly, the importer may stipulate a **tender** for the document in the sales contract or letter of credit. However, he/she does not need physical possession of the document to gain access to the cargo. Consequently, if the document is delayed, it causes none of the problems associated with non-presentation of a B/L. This feature is often stated explicitly in clauses of varying complexities. In the most basic terms, the document may state that "delivery of the goods will be made to the consignee or his/her authorized representative upon proper proof of identity and authorization without the need of presenting or surrendering a copy of this waybill". The document may further state that "the carrier is to exercise due care to ensure that delivery is made to the proper party. However, in case of incorrect delivery, no responsibility will be accepted unless due to fault or negligence on the part of the carrier". 保管人

7.2.3 Straight B/Ls and Waybills Compared 记名提单和运单比较

Waybills and some straight B/Ls are not documents of title. These documents merely show the names of the shipper and consignee. Since a straight B/L and a waybill only **envisage** delivery be made to the named consignee, the importer doesn't need to present the document 预想，设想

Non-Negotiable Sea Waybill

Consignor (name, address, tax reference)	Shipper's reference	Bill of lading number
	Forwarder's reference	
	Unique consignment reference	
Consignee (name, address, tax reference)	Carrier (name, address, tax reference)	
Notify party (name, address, tax reference)	Additional notify party (name, address, tax reference)	

Pre-carriage by	Place of receipt	
Vessel/voyage no,	Port of loading	
Port of discharge	Final place of delivery by on-carrier	

Marks and numbers, transport unit id	Number and kind of packages; shipping description of goods	Gross weight	measurement

Container no(s);seal no(s)	Freight details; charge	Rate	Per	Prepaid	Collect

	Freight payable at	Carrier's name
	Number of original Bill of Lading	Place + (ISO code) and date of issue (yyyy-mm-dd)
Received for carriage as above in apparent good order and condition, unless otherwise stated hereon The goods described in the above particulars		Authenticating signature

Figure 7-3　A Sample Sea Waybill

Shipper's Name and Address | Shipper's Account Number

Not Negotiable

Air Waybill 中国东方航空公司

ISSUED BY CHINA EASTERN AIRLINES

Copies 1, 2 and 3 of this Air Waybill are originals and have the same validity

Consignee's Name and Address | Consignee's Account Number

It is agreed that the goods described herein are accepted in apparent good order and condition (except as noted) for carriage SUBJECT TO THE CONDITIONS OF CONTRACT ON THE REVERSE HEREOF, ALL GOODS MAY BE CARRIED BY ANY OTHER MEANS INCLUDING ROAD OR ANY OTHER CARRIER UNLESS SPECIFIC CONTRARY INSTRUCTIONS ARE GIVEN HEREON BY THE SHIPPER. THE SHIPPER'S ATTENTION IS DRAWN TO THE NOTICE CONCERNING CARRIER'S LIMITATION OF LIABILITY. Shipper may increase such limitation of liability by declaring a higher value for carriage and paying a supplemental charge if required.

Issuing Carrier's Agent Name and City

Accounting Information

Agent's IATA Code | Account No.

Airport of Departure (Addr. of First Carrier) and Requested Routing

Reference number | Optional Shipping Information

To | By First Carrier | Routing and Destination | To | by | To | by | Currency | CHGS Code | WT/VAL (PPD, COLL) | Other (PPD, COLL) | Declared Value for Carriage | Declared Value for Customs

Airport of Destination | Flight/Date | For Carrier Use only | Flight/Date | Amount of Insurance | INSURANCE-If carrier offers insurance and such insurance is requested in accordance with the conditions thereof indicate amount to be insured in figures in box marked "Amount of Insurance".

Handling Information

SCI

No. of Pieces RCP	Gross Weight	Kg Lb	Rate Class / Commodity Item No.	Chargeable Weight	Rate/ Charge	Total	Nature and Quantity of Goods (incl. Dimensions or Volume)

Prepaid | Weight Charge | Collect

Other Charges

Valuation Charge

Tax

Total Other Charges Due Agent

Shipper certifies that the particulars on the face hereof are correct and that insofar as any part of the consignment contains dangerous goods, such part is properly described by name and is in proper condition for carriage by air according to the applicable Dangerous Goods Regulations Charges at Destination

Total Other Charges Due Carrier

Signature of Shipper or His Agent

Total Prepaid | Total Collect

Currency Conversion Rates | CC Charges in Dest. Currency

Executed on (date) At (place) Signature of Issuing Carrier or as Agent

For Carrier's Use Only at Destination | Charges at Destination | Total Collect Charges

AWB No.

Figure 7-4 A Sample Air Waybill

for taking delivery. However, if a straight B/L expressly states that "delivery shall only be made against presentation of an original B/L", this requirement turns the straight B/L into a title document and should be complied with. Most waybills, however, expressly state that presentation is not required for taking delivery (see Figure 7-3 and Figure 7-4).

7.3 Multi-Modal Bill of Lading & Through Bill of Lading 多式联运提单和直达提单

These B/Ls apply when the carriage covers at least two modes of transport.

A multi-modal transport B/L or combined B/L, is one under which the carrier, namely, the Multi-Modal Transport Operator (MTO), generally the sea carrier, as the "one-stop shop" to the shipper, arranges and is liable for the transport of the cargo in the entire journey. In practice, he/she typically **sub-contracts** some legs of or the whole carriage to others. It can be issued either in a negotiable form or a non-negotiable form.

分包

A through B/L is one under which the main carrier undertakes to perform one portion of the carriage, such as the sea leg, and also to arrange, as agent, an additional leg, such as the road carriage onward from the port of destination.

Exercises 练习

I. True or False

1. An ante-dated B/L is usually used when the shipping date stipulated in the letter of credit is due but the shipper has not got the goods ready for shipment. (   )
2. Advanced B/Ls and ante-dated B/Ls may lead to litigation, so they are not common practice in ocean transport. (   )
3. Not all transport documents are transferable. (   )
4. Bankers generally refuse to accept charter party B/Ls under a letter of credit. (   )

5. If a B/L is required according to a letter of credit, the master B/L should be presented. ( )
6. Bearer B/Ls are rarely used because it involves great risk. ( )
7. Usually, bankers only pay for clean B/Ls under a letter of credit. ( )
8. An order B/L delivers the cargo straight to the importer. ( )
9. Short form B/Ls are seldom accepted by bankers under a letter of credit. ( )
10. If the importer is to take delivery of the goods with a sea waybill, the original of the document must be presented to the carrier. ( )

II. Multiple Choice Questions

1. The title of a B/L refers to the ( ).
   [A] shipper
   [B] consignee
   [C] notify party
   [D] port of loading
2. In practice, a B/L is mostly ( ).
   [A] issued as a straight B/L
   [B] issued as a bearer B/L
   [C] made out to order
   [D] issued with the title left blank
3. Which one of the following statements is INCORRECT about an ocean B/L ? ( )
   [A] It is a receipt of goods.
   [B] It evidences the contract of carriage.
   [C] It is a document of title.
   [D] It is an unconditional payment order.
4. In accordance with *UCP 600*, the issuing date of an ocean B/L shall be ( ).
   [A] the date on which loading begins
   [B] the date on which loading is complete
   [C] any date on which the cargo is loaded onto the vessel
   [D] the date of loading in the contract of carriage

5. Of the following transport documents, (　　) can simultaneously serve as a receipt of goods, a contract of carriage and a document of title.
   [A] a railway consignment note
   [B] an air waybill
   [C] an ocean B/L
   [D] a sea waybill
6. Which one of the following statements about a multi-modal B/L is TRUE? (　　)
   [A] A multi-modal B/L is always non-negotiable.
   [B] A multi-modal B/L can be issued as a negotiable document.
   [C] A multi-modal B/L can always be transferred.
   [D] A multi-modal B/L can never be transferred.
7. If an ocean B/L under a letter of credit bears "TO ORDER" in the consignee box, (　　) is entitled to endorse the B/L the first time.
   [A] the shipper
   [B] the issuing bank
   [C] the importer
   [D] the negotiating bank
8. According to *Incoterms 2020*, under FCA and by ocean transport, (　　). *
   [A] the exporter cannot get an "on-board" B/L, because when the cargo is placed at the disposal of the carrier, it mostly hasn't been loaded "on board"
   [B] the exporter's violation of the contract and the letter of credit is inevitable if both require an " on-board" B/L
   [C] the importer can authorize his/her freight forwarder to issue an "on-board" B/L when the cargo is placed at the disposal of the forwarder
   [D] the exporter, if allowed by the importer, can expect to be issued an "on-board" B/L when the cargo is placed at the disposal of the forwarder

9. Which one of the following transport documents requires the importer to present the original document for taking delivery? ( )
   [A] A straight B/L.
   [B] A sea waybill.
   [C] An air waybill
   [D] An order B/L.
10. The shipper's endorsement is required when the consignee box of the ocean B/L is shown as ( ).
   [A] TO ORDER
   [B] ABC COMPANY
   [C] TO ORDER OF ISSUING BANK
   [D] TO ORDER OF APPLICANT

III. Case Study

1. An exporter Qingdao Herui Organic Agriculture Development Co., Ltd. entered into a deal of selling **scallion** to a Hong Kong trading company F.O.H Food Trading (H.K.) Co., Ltd. under Incoterm FOB **Ningbo**, but the Hong Kong trader resold the goods in no time to a Korean company Kinsta Food Trading, Co., Ltd. under Incoterm CFR **Pusan**. The letter of credit opened by F.O.H required the goods be loaded at Port of Ningbo under FOB and discharged at Port of Pusan and the B/L indicate "Freight Prepaid". Why did the Hong Kong trader order such a requirement? What should the exporter do?

   大葱

   宁波

   釜山

2. Squirrelsmile Nuts Co., Ltd., a Chinese exporter from the inland city of **Zunhua**, Hebei Province, entered a deal of exporting a batch of **chestnuts** to Italy via ocean transport from Port of Tianjin to Port of Naples under *Incoterms 2010* rule FCA Zunhua, and payment by L/C.[①] The documents required for presentation included an "on board" B/L. However, when the exporter delivered the goods to his carrier at the local place, he could not get the "on board" B/L, as the merchandise hadn't been loaded truly on board. What do you think the company can do to cope with this issue?

   遵化

   栗子

① https://baijiahao.baidu.com/s?id=1677896676032968280&wfr=spider&for=pc

Chapter 8 International Cargo Transport Insurance

第八章 国际货物运输保险

Learning Objectives:

◆ Marine cargo transport insurance
◆ Cargo insurance under other modes of transport
◆ *China Insurance Clauses* and *Institute Cargo Clauses*
◆ Procedures in purchasing a cover and filing a claim
◆ Principles of indemnification

In international trade, your cargo travels long distances between countries or regions. Beyond the physical control of you and the importer, it may be subject to various kinds of risks ***en route***, such as a hurricane, a lightning strike, unexpected accidents or water damage. Purchasing cargo insurance can reduce your loss if any of the risks **materializes**. Cargo insurance is a contract **whereby the insurer**, on the basis of a **premium** paid, undertakes to **indemnify the insured** against loss from certain risks or **perils** to which the cargo insured may be exposed. It is a type of **property coverage** that is comparable to other types of property coverage such as car and homeowner's insurance which are purchased to protect the financial interests of the owner of the vehicle or house.

在途中

发生　凭此　保险人，保险公司　保险费

赔偿被保险人　重大危险

财产保险

In international trade, one of two sets of **insurance clauses** is commonly adopted: ***China Insurance Clauses (CIC)*** **by People's Insurance Company of China**, and ***Institute Cargo Clauses (ICC)*** **by**

保险条款

中国人民保险公司的《中国保险条款》

伦敦保险学会的《协会货物条款》

London Insurance Institute. Traders can stipulate their insurance terms in the sales contract as per either one of them. In this chapter, we shall mainly focus on the former and briefly touch on the latter. In China, the People's Insurance Company of China (PICC), established in 1949, is the sole state-owned insurance company which **underwrites** almost all kinds of insurance and has agents in almost all main ports and regions over the world. Since its establishment, it has become **customary** for Chinese traders to have their imports insured with PICC as per *CIC*. Exports can be insured with foreign insurance companies as per *ICC*, or with PICC as per *CIC* when accepted by the importer.

承保

惯例的

下文将依次介绍中国人民保险公司《中国保险条款》下的《海运货物保险条款》《航空货运保险条款》《陆运货物保险条款》和《邮包货运保险条款》，并简要比较《协会货物条款》和《中国保险条款》。

In what follows, I will successively introduce the *Ocean Marine Cargo Clauses*, *Air Cargo Clauses, Overland Cargo Clauses* and *Parcel Post Clauses* under *CIC* by PICC and briefly compare *ICC* with *CIC*.

8. 1 Marine Cargo Transport Insurance 海上货物运输保险

When you ship by sea, be aware of risks from different sources. When any one of them materializes, it causes you a loss, resulting in some expenses. Marine cargo transport insurance exists and develops to help you recover part or all of your losses.

8.1.1 Risks, Losses and Expenses Covered 所保风险、损失及费用的种类

内在的，固有的

Considering the **inherent** logic from risks to losses, and from losses to expenses, we will be following the same logic in this section (see Figure 8-1).

8.1.1.1 Risks: marine perils and extraneous risks 风险：海上风险和外来风险

♦ **Marine perils 海上风险**

海上风险

Two types of risks are covered under *CIC* marine cargo insurance. One is related with the cargo's status at sea, namely **marine perils**, which

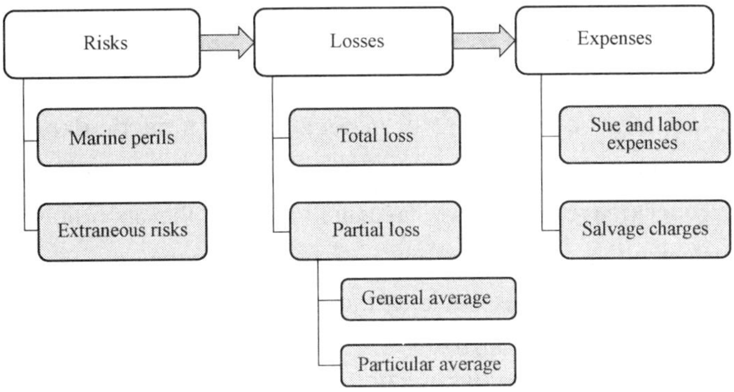

Figure 8-1 Risk, Losses, and Expenses

include both **natural calamities** and **fortuitous (unexpected) accidents** at sea. Heavy weather, lightening, tsunami, earthquake, volcanic eruption, etc. are examples of natural calamities, while fortuitous accidents may be a fire, an explosion, the vessel's being stranded, grounded, sunk or capsized, or its collision with icebergs or other objects, etc. 自然灾害 意外事故

♦ **Extraneous risks 外来风险**

The other type, called extraneous risks, has nothing to do with the cargo's status at sea—the cargo **is susceptible to** these risks even if it is placed at any other places. "Extraneous" means "not directly connected with the particular situation you are in or the subject you are dealing with". Causes of extraneous risks can be of a **general nature** or a **special nature**. **General extraneous risks** include theft and pilferage, contamination, leakage, sweating and/or heating, taint of odor, rusting, hook damage, short-delivery and non-delivery, shortage in weight, clashing, etc. **Special extraneous risks** include war, strike or failure to deliver due to some special laws or regulations. 容易受……影响 一般性的 特殊性的 一般外来风险 特殊外来风险

8.1.1.2 Losses: total loss and partial loss 全部损失和部分损失

♦ **Total loss 全部损失**

Two types of losses are covered by marine cargo insurance under *CIC*—a total loss and a partial loss. A total loss can be an **actual total loss** or a **constructive total loss**. An actual total loss is the complete loss of the insured cargo in value. A constructive total loss is a situation where the **salvage** cost of the damaged cargo exceeds the salvaged value of the cargo and simply abandoning the cargo is more cost-effective. Most insurance policies **provide** that indemnity for the total loss is up to the insured amount. 实际全损 推定全损 拯救 规定

♦ **Partial loss 部分损失**

单独的　共同的
单独海损分摊
共同海损分摊　单独海损
共同海损

If the loss is less than the total cost, it is called a partial loss. A partial loss may be **particular** or **general**, called a **particular average loss** and a **general average loss**, respectively, or just a **particular average** and a **general average**. Here "average" means "the apportionment of financial liability resulting from loss of or damage to a ship or its cargo". This sense dates back to the ancient French language in the marine transportation industry.

♦ **General average 共同海损**

联系

分摊

A general average loss is based upon a relationship between the ship owner and all the shippers who have cargoes aboard the same vessel on a particular voyage. All these parties are **bound** together on the voyage. When an entire ship is threatened by a marine peril or some other hazard, to save the ship and the cargoes, part of the cargoes or the vessel have to be abandoned or sacrificed. In such an emergency, the master may declare an action of general average. If it was your cargo that had been voluntarily sacrificed, whoever's property was saved must proportionally **apportion** your loss before he/she could claim for recovery from his/her insurance company.

But some conditions must be satisfied before the master can declare a general average loss:

(1) There must be an extraordinary situation.

(2) The peril must be real and not imaginary.

(3) The loss must be voluntary and deliberate.

谨慎的

(4) The sacrifice must be made **prudently**.

(5) The purpose is to save the whole voyage.

(6) The act should be successful at least partially.

♦ **Particular average 单独海损**

A particular average loss refers to a damage or loss suffered by part of the cargoes. For example, if a storm or fire damaged your cargo, but no one else's cargo had to be sacrificed to save the vessel, you would be suffering from a particular average loss. In this case, you should turn to your insurance company for indemnity, provided your insurance policy covers the specific type of loss suffered.

8.1.1.3 Expenses: sue and labor expenses & salvage charges 施救费用和救助费用

Marine cargo insurance also covers expenses incurred to avoid or reduce the damage to or loss of the insured cargo. These expenses mainly come in two types. One is the sue and labor expenses incurred when the insured, the employee or the **assignee** take necessary and proper measures to minimize or avoid losses caused by the risks covered in the insurance policy. The other is the salvage charges incurred when a third party (a party other than the insurer and the insured) takes such measures to reduce or avoid the damages or losses. 受让人

8.1.2 Insurance Coverage 海险的主要种类

There are mainly two types of coverage under *CIC*, **basic coverage** and **additional coverage**. Basic coverage includes **Free from Particular Average (FPA), With Particular Average (WPA)** and **All Risks**. The relationship between them resembles that of a Russian Doll—FPA comprises 8 types of basic coverage while WPA is built upon FPA plus one more type, and All Risks upon WPA plus general additional coverage (see Figure 8-2). 基本险 附加险 平安险 水渍险 一切险

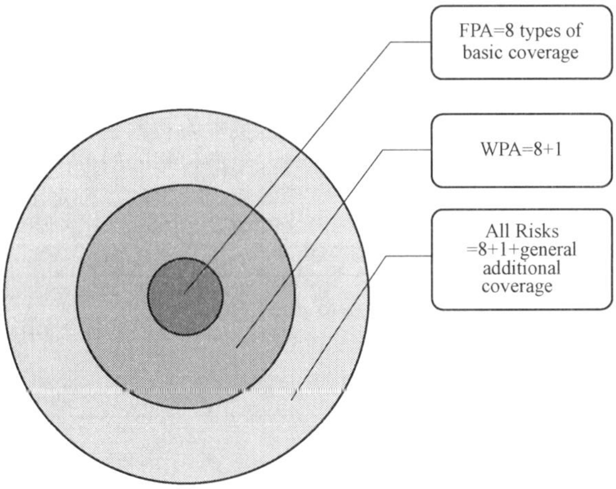

Figure 8-2 Relationship Between Basic Coverage Under *CIC*

Additional coverage is classified into **general additional coverage** and **special additional coverage**, corresponding respectively to general additional risks and special additional risks. Neither can be covered alone; they must go with basic coverage, though general additional risks have already been covered under All Risks. 一般附加险 特殊附加险

8.1.2.1 Basic coverage 基本险

♦ **FPA (Free from Particular Average) 平安险**

FPA（平安险）是一种保障范围有限的保险，它为包括自然灾害和意外事故在内的海上风险造成的全损和共同海损提供保险。它字面意思表示单独海损不予赔付，但随着海洋货物保险的发展，某些单独海损（部分损失）现在可以赔付，包括那些由意外事故单独或意外事故和自然灾害共同造成的单独海损（部分损失）等。其具体的八个保险范围如下：

FPA is a type of limited coverage which covers total losses and general averages arising from marine perils including natural calamities and fortuitous accidents. It literally means that particular averages are not covered, but with the real-world development of marine cargo insurance, some particular averages (of a partial loss nature) are now recoverable, including those caused by fortuitous accidents alone or by fortuitous accidents and natural calamities combined, etc. The specific eight types of coverage are listed as follows (see Table 8-1):

Table 8-1 Basic Coverage Under FPA

FPA covers	平安险的保障范围
① Total or constructive total loss of the whole consignment hereby insured caused in the course of transit by natural calamities: heavy weather, lightning, tsunami, earthquake and flood. In case a constructive total loss is claimed for, the Insured shall abandon to the Company the damaged goods and all his/her rights and title pertaining thereto. The goods on each lighter to or from the seagoing vessel shall be deemed a separate risk. Constructive total loss refers to the loss where an actual total loss appears to be unavoidable or the cost to be incurred in recovering or reconditioning the goods together with the forwarding cost to the destination named in the Policy would exceed their value on arrival.	① 被保险货物在运输途中由于恶劣气候、雷电、海啸、地震、洪水自然灾害造成整批货物的全部损失或推定全损。当被保险人要求赔付推定全损时，须将受损货物及其权利委付给保险公司。被保险货物用驳船运往或运离海轮的，每一驳船所装的货物可视作一个整批。推定全损是指被保险货物的实际全损已经不可避免，或者恢复、修复受损货物以及运送货物到原定目的地的费用超过该目的地的货物价值。
② Total or partial loss caused by accidents the carrying conveyance being grounded, stranded, sunk or in collision with floating ice or other objects as well as fire or explosion.	② 由于运输工具遭受搁浅、触礁、沉没、互撞、与流冰或其他物体碰撞以及失火、爆炸意外事故造成货物的全部或部分损失。
③ Partial loss of the insured goods attributable to heavy weather, lightning and/or tsunami, where the conveyance has been grounded, stranded, sunk or burnt. irrespective of whether the event or events took place or after such accidents.	③ 在运输工具已经发生搁浅、触礁、沉没、焚毁意外事故的情况下，货物在此前后又在海上遭受恶劣气候、雷电、海啸等自然灾害所造成的部分损失。

continued

FPA covers	平安险的保障范围
④ Partial of total loss consequent on falling of entire package or packages into sea during loading, transshipment or discharge.	④ 在装卸或转运时由于一件或数件整件货物落海造成的全部或部分损失。
⑤ Reasonable cost incurred by the insured on salvaging the goods or averting or minimizing a loss recoverable under the Policy, provided that such cost shall not exceed the sum insured of the consignment so saved.	⑤ 被保险人对遭受承保责任内危险的货物采取抢救、防止或减少货损的措施而支付的合理费用，但以不超过该批被救货物的保险金额为限。
⑥ Losses attributable to discharge of the insured goods at a port of distress following a sea peril as well as special charges arising from loading, warehousing and forwarding of the goods at an intermediate port of call or refuge.	⑥ 运输工具遭遇海难后，在避难港由于卸货所引起的损失以及在中途港，避难港由于卸货，存仓以及运送货物所产生的特别费用。
⑦ Sacrifice in and contribution to general average and salvage charges.	⑦ 共同海损的牺牲、分摊和救助费用。
⑧ Such proportion of losses sustained by the shipowners as is to be reimbursed by the cargo owner under the contract of affreightment "Both to Blame Collision" clause.	⑧ 运输契约订有"船舶互撞责任"条款，根据该条款规定应由货方偿还船方的损失。

♦ **WPA (With Particular Average)水渍险**

WPA is a type of wider coverage than FPA which literally means particular averages are covered. In addition to the eight types of coverage under FPA, it also covers **partial loss or damage attributable to natural calamities.**

水渍险比平安险承保范围要广一些，它字面意思上表示单独海损给予赔付。除了平安险的八项保障，它还包括对**自然灾害所引起的部分损失或损坏的赔偿。**

♦ **All Risks 一切险**

"All Risks" is the most comprehensive of the three types of basic coverage under which the insurer is responsible for all total or partial loss of, or damage to the cargo insured either arising from marine perils or general extraneous causes. However, **it does not cover the loss, damage or expenses caused by special extraneous risks such as wars, strikes, riots or civil commotions, etc.** It does not cover the loss of market, or loss or damage caused by delay or inherent vice of the goods, either.

一切险是三个基本险种中责任范围最广的险种。在此险种下，承保人承担不管是由海难还是一般外来原因所造成的被保货物的全损或部分损失的赔偿责任。**但它不负责由战争、罢工、骚乱或民间骚动这样的特殊外来风险等原因造成的损失、损坏或费用的赔偿。**它也不包括市场损失、延误或货物的固有缺陷造成的损失或损害。

8.1.2.2 Additional coverage 附加险

一般附加险包括：偷窃提货不着险、淡水雨淋险、短量险、混杂玷污险、渗漏险、破损破碎险、串味险、受热受潮险、钩损险和生锈险等。一般附加险不能单独投保，只能在**平安险**和**水渍险**的基础上加保，但都包含在一切险之内。

♦ **General additional coverage 一般附加险**

This insurance covers TPND (Theft, Pilferage and Non-Delivery), Fresh Water Rain Damage, Risk of Shortage, Risk of Intermixture and Contamination, Risk of Leakage, Risk of Clash and Breakage, Risk of Odor, Damage Caused by Heating and Sweating, Hook Damage, Risks of Rust, etc. This insurance cannot be purchased independently but should go with **FPA** or **WPA**. Yet they are all covered under All Risks.

特别附加险指战争险、罢工险、交货不到险、进口关税险、舱面险及拒收险等，其中特别附加险中以战争险和罢工险最为普通。这种附加险别通常与平安险、水渍险和一切险一同投保。

♦ **Special additional coverage 特别附加险**

This insurance covers wars, strikes, failure to delivery, import duty, on deck risk, rejection, etc., among which wars and strikes are more common. This insurance is usually purchased together with FPA, WPA and All risks.

To choose a type of coverage that is both economical and effective, you or the importer should be aware of the possible losses to be expected of a particular consignment. Cargoes differ in nature and may need different types of coverage. For example, cargoes like iron ore seldom faces risk of partial loss, so FPA will be sufficient. Most manufactured goods are covered against All Risks, as they are prone to damage caused by sea perils or extraneous risks.

8.2 Insurance Under Other Modes of Transport 其他运输方式下的保险

As air shipping features shorter transit times, lighter packing, quicker clearance and, in most places, stricter theft-pilferage control, a significant number of export cargoes nowadays are shipped by air. While an air disaster is often sensational, air shipping is one of the safest modes of moving goods internationally. Fast delivery and ease with cargo handling help to reduce air shipping risk and lower its premium rate, which has made it increasingly appealing to both the insurer and the insured. Air insurance coverage also comes in two types: **Air Transportation Risks** and **Air Transportation All Risks**. The former is similar to WPA, while the latter to marine All Risks.

航空运输险
航空运输一切险

A large volume of cargoes is now transported by rail and road.

Insurance coverage for land transport also comprises two categories: **Overland Transportation Risks**, which is almost equivalent to WPA for marine insurance, and **Overland All Risks** for land transport, almost equivalent to marine All Risks. 陆运险 陆运一切险

Parcel post insurance covers the losses of or damage to the parcels caused by natural calamities, fortuitous accidents or extraneous risks. It includes **Parcel Post Risks** and **Parcel Post All Risks**. On the basis of these two types of basic coverage, additional coverage may also be added when needed. 邮包险 邮包一切险

8.3 Institute Cargo Clauses 协会货物保险条款

Institute Cargo Clauses drafted by London Insurance Institute, is an influential set of cargo clauses widely adopted in international trade. It was first drafted in 1912 with the most recent revision made in 1982. It has the following subsets: Institute Cargo Clause A, Institute Cargo Clause B, Institute Cargo Clause C, Institute War Clause-Cargo, Institute Strike Clause-Cargo and Malicious Damage Clause. *China Insurance Clauses* were drafted based on the 1936 version of London Insurance *Institute Cargo Clauses*; therefore, they are roughly equivalent to one another. For example, Institute Cargo Clause A is roughly equivalent to All Risks under *CIC* marine cargo insurance, Institute Cargo Clause B to WPA, and Institute Cargo Clause C to FPA. Similarly, Institute War Clause-Cargo and Institute Strike Clause-Cargo are roughly equivalent to War Risk and Strike Risk under *CIC* marine cargo insurance, respectively. However, it should be noted that differences do exist between the two sets of clauses and you are suggested to study them carefully before adopting either one set.

8.4 Procedures in Purchasing Insurance 投保的程序

When purchasing insurance, you need to draft the insurance terms in the contract, and then calculate the premium and insured amount, followed by purchasing the insurance and be aware of the time of commencement and termination of the underwriter's obligations.

8.4.1 Drafting Insurance Terms in the Contract 起草合同中的保险条款

In an international transaction, whoever purchases the insurance depends on the Incoterms rule employed. It could be you or the importer. For example, under CIF or CIP, you are obliged to purchase insurance; under DAP, DPU, DDP, it is optional to you but highly suggested; while under EXW, FCA, FAS, FOB, CFR, CPT, it's optional to the importer, but he/she may also ask you to do it on his/her behalf.

Below is an example of insurance terms in a sales contract when the exporter **is obliged to** obtain insurance, "Insurance to be effected by the exporter for 110% of the invoice value against the WPA and TPND as per Ocean Marine Cargo Insurance Clause of the People's Insurance Company of China dated Jan.1 1981."

有义务

"根据 1981 年 1 月 1 日中国人民保险公司的海洋货物保险条款，卖方对 WPA 和 TPND 的发票价值的 110%进行保险。"

When getting insurance is at the exporter or importer's option, the terms may simply read **"insurance by the exporter"** or **"insurance by the importer".**

"保险由卖方自理"

"保险由买方自理"

8.4.2 Calculating Insured Amount and Premium 计算投保金额和保费

We have discussed this issue in Chapter 5 (5.3.4.2 Insurance 保险). It may help to review it here, but with a different way of calculation. The insured amount is the amount at which the insured cargo is valued, which must be at least the invoice value of the cargo. Under a CIF contract, it is common practice for you to insure the cargo for 10% above the invoice value, an amount considering the cost, the insurance premium, the ocean freight and the expected profit that would otherwise be achieved. The insurance clauses should be expressly stipulated in a sales contract, including the insurer, the insured, the insurance clauses selected, the insured amount, etc. Notably, according to *Incoterms 2020*, CIP now requires an insurance at least with the minimum cover of the Institute Cargo Clause (A) (All Risks, subject to itemized exclusions), instead of the Institute Cargo Clause (C) (Number of listed risks, subject to itemized exclusions) under *Incoterms 2010*.

According to *Incoterms 2020* and *UCP 600*, the insured amount is calculated based on the CIF or CIP value as follows:

$$\text{Insured amount} = \text{CIF or CIP value} \times (1+\text{markup rate})$$

$$\text{insurance premium} = \text{insured amount} \times \text{premium rate}$$

If you are purchasing insurance on behalf of the importer under a CFR or an FOB-based contract, you need to convert the price into a CIF price before you can calculate the insured amount. The formulas for the conversions are as follows:

$$\text{CIF} = \text{CFR}/[1-\text{premium rate}\times(1+\text{markup rate})]$$

$$\because \text{CFR} = \text{CIF} \quad \text{insurance premium}$$

$$= \text{CIF}-\text{CIF}\times(1+\text{markup rate})\times\text{premium rate}$$

$$= \text{CIF}\times[1-\text{premium rate}\times(1+\text{markup rate})]$$

$$\therefore \text{CIF} = \text{CFR}/[1-\text{premium}\times(1+\text{markup rate})]$$

or,

$$\text{CIF} = (\text{FOB}+ \text{sea freight})/[1\text{-premium rate}\times(1+\text{markup rate})]$$

With the conversion complete, you will be able to calculate both the insured amount and the insurance premium. The premium rate charged by the insurance company is a function of the goods, packaging, quantity, mode of transport, the carrying vessel, transit time, scope of coverage, past experience, etc. For specific premium rate, consult the insurance company. In practice, the insurance company normally charges a flat fee for cargoes under a certain value for simplicity.

8.4.3 Purchasing the Insurance 购买保险

Assuming you are obliged to purchase the insurance, you may contact the cargo insurance department of PICC. You may start by inquiring about the right coverage, followed by negotiating on the premium rate. When the negotiation is done, PICC, the insurer, will issue the **insurance policy** to you or the importer, the insured. An insurance policy is essentially a contract, serving as evidence of the agreement between the insurer and the insured. It forms part of the shipping documents and also the basis for filing a claim when a risk does occur.

保险单

8.4.4 Warehouse to Warehouse Clause 仓至仓条款

起讫

When you decide to purchase insurance for your cargo, you may want to know the exact points of **commencement and termination** of the underwriter's liability under your policy. For that purpose, a warehouse-to-warehouse clause is introduced to clarify this issue, which applies to all three types of basic coverage under *CIC* for marine cargo transport insurance. A warehouse-to-warehouse clause extends ocean insurance coverage to include pre-shipment and post-shipment of ocean transportation, specifically, from your warehouse to the importer's warehouse stipulated in the policy. However, notably, the **underwriter's** liability is limited to 60 days and to the designated destination. Beyond 60 days or out of the designated destination, its liability terminates.

承保，保险公司

8.5 Procedures for Filing a Claim 提出索赔的程序

调查员

If a certain risk does occur, resulting in a damage or loss, most underwriters require immediate notice be given to their nearest branch or agency. When notified, the branch or agency appoints a **surveyor** to inspect the cargo and produce a report on the nature and extent of the damage or loss. The surveyor normally sends the report together with his/her findings to the consignee, with the latter paying the fee for inspection. When a claim is filed, the fee is refunded to the **claimants** if the loss is covered under the insurance policy.

索赔人

Under some circumstances, the claim is returned to the place where the insurance is originally arranged and subsequently presented to the underwriter. However, when goods are sold under CIF terms, the insurance policy would be transferred and sent to the consignee and therefore any claim should be indemnified at destination. In such cases, the consignee can contact the agency named in the policy for indemnity. Of course, the procedures may vary by circumstance, but undoubtedly a quicker settlement is necessary if a loss or damage does occur.

The following documents are required for making an insurance claim and should be provided by the importer:

- the commercial invoice issued to the importer,
- the original bill of lading,
- the original policy or certificate of insurance,
- the survey report or other documents detailing the loss or damage incurred,
- **documents supporting claim for extended salvage loss, particular average, or total loss of cargoes,**
- **any exchange of correspondence with the carriers and other parties regarding their liability for the loss or damage, and**
- **any landing account at final destination.**

额外增加的施救损失、单独海损或全损等方面的证明

任何与承运人及其他当事人之间的有关损失责任方面的来往信函

任何有关货物抵达目的地的情况记录

8.6 Principles of Indemnification 保险赔偿的原则

An underwriter normally abides by three fundamental principles in dealing with claims—**principle of indemnity, of good faith, and of insurable interest**.

赔偿原则，诚信原则和可保利益原则

8.6.1 Principle of Indemnity 赔偿原则

A cargo insurance policy is basically a contract of indemnity—an agreement to compensate the insured in the event of a loss. According to this principle, you cannot claim for more than your actual loss, as an indemnity is designed to be a compensation for your loss, not a means to make you rich.

8.6.2 Principle of Good Faith 诚信原则

This principle requires utmost good faith on the part of the insured and the insurer. For example, if you are the insured, you have a duty to disclose to the insurer any relevant information about the cargo that is known before you apply for coverage, such as the nature of the goods and their inherent vice, as this information may influence the insurer's decisions. If either of you fails to **observe** good faith, the other may cancel the contract. For example, the *CIC* clause excludes, among

遵守

others, an underwriter's liability for the "loss or damage arising from the inferior quality or shortage of the insured goods prior to the attachment of this insurance" and "loss or damage arising from normal loss, inherent vice or nature of the insured goods".

8.6.3 Principle of Insurable Interest 可保利益原则

This principle requires the insured have ownership of the goods insured and be the one who suffers financial loss if the risk materializes, otherwise, he/she will have no insurable interest therein and will not be indemnified. An analogy will make this clear. For example, it would be ridiculous if you go to an underwriter and ask to buy insurance against fire on your neighbor's house. You would definitely be rejected. The point is, you have no insurable interest in something that doesn't belong to you. Similarly, under Incoterms rules of FOB and CFR, if the cargo is damaged or lost *en route* from your warehouse to the port of departure, neither you nor the importer can file a claim. You cannot do it because you didn't purchase the insurance; insurance is obligation of the importer under these two terms. But the importer cannot either, because the goods haven't been loaded on board the ship, so that ownership hasn't been transferred to the importer, and so that he/she has no insurable interest therein, either. Therefore, if you export on an FOB or CFR basis, the warehouse-to-warehouse clause of a marine cargo insurance policy is effectively invalid for you. In this case, a CIF term would be better. I'd like to leave it to you to think about why.

Exercises 练习

I. True or False

1. Additional risks can be insured separately. (　　)
2. WPA has the least coverage. (　　)
3. The coverage of All Risks is the broadest, including War Risk and Strike Risk. (　　)
4. In order to save money, exporters usually only insure FPA. (　　)
5. Under the warehouse-to-warehouse clause, the liability of the insurer

terminates if the goods leave the designated destination before the insurance policy expires. (   )

6. Insurance premium rate for air transport is normally lower than that for other modes of transport. (   )
7. Regardless of actual or constructive total loss, the insurance company shall indemnify the insured the total insured amount. (   )
8. For fragile goods, the insured may cover them against All Risks plus Risk of Breakage. (   )
9. Institute Cargo Clause B is roughly equivalent to All Risks of ocean cargo insurance under *CIC*. (   )
10. Insurance against All Risks means that the insurance company is liable for all risks. (   )

II. Multiple Choice Questions

1. If a cargo under a CIF contract is destroyed by fire after being loaded on board, (   ).
   [A] the exporter shall bear the loss
   [B] the exporter should be responsible for making a claim on the insurance company
   [C] the importer should be responsible for making a claim on the insurance company
   [D] the importer shall bear the loss
2. An exporter's cargo ran into a storm halfway and both the vessel and cargo sank into the sea and could not be salvaged. In this incident, the loss of the goods is a kind of (   ).
   [A] partial loss
   [B] total loss
   [C] common loss
   [D] general average
3. According to marine cargo insurance clauses under *CIC*, (   ) can be covered in addition to All Risks.
   [A] **TPND** 偷窃、提货不着险
   [B] **seller's contingent insurance** 卖方利益险
   [C] war risk and strike risk
   [D] **FWRD** 淡水雨淋险

4. The “Warehouse to Warehouse” clause in an insurance contract is one that specifies ( ).
   [A] conditions for the commencement and termination of the carrier’s responsibility for the carriage
   [B] conditions for the commencement and termination of the insurer’s responsibility for insurance
   [C] conditions for the commencement and termination of the exporter’s responsibility for delivery
   [D] conditions for the commencement and termination of the period allowed for the importer to make a claim on the insurance company
5. According to *Incoterms 2020*, which of the following Incoterms rule requires at least an insurance with the minimum cover of Institute Cargo Clause A? ( )
   [A] CIF.
   [B] CFR.
   [C] CIP.
   [D] FOB.
6. The insured under FOB/CIF shall be ( ).
   [A] Importer/Importer
   [B] Exporter/Importer
   [C] Importer/Exporter
   [D] Exporter/Exporter
7. ( ) is not under the coverage of All Risks.
   [A] TPND
   [B] Risk of leakage
   [C] Risk of non-delivery
   [D] Risk of clashing
8. ( ) is not within the coverage of All Risks.

串味险

   [A] **Risk of odor**
   [B] TPND
   [C] Risk of shortage
   [D] War risk

9. In marine cargo insurance, general average loss (　　).
   [A] is a type of partial loss
   [B] is a type of total loss
   [C] is a type of constructive total loss
   [D] sometimes is a type of partial loss, and sometimes a type of total loss
10. In the case of short delivery, a claim can be made on (　　).
   [A] the exporter
   [B] the insurance company
   [C] the carrier
   [D] the exporter, the insurance company or the carrier

III. Case Study

1. A cargo ship sailed from **Dalian** to Singapore. During the voyage, the **cargo hold** caught fire and the fire spread to the engine room. For the common safety of the ship and cargoes, the captain decided to take emergency measures by filling the hold with water in order to put out the fire. Although the fire was put out, the main engine was damaged and unable to continue sailing. So, the captain decided to hire a **tugboat** to **tow** the cargo ship back to Port of Dalian for repair. Then the ship re-sailed to Singapore after maintenance. The investigation showed the losses caused by this incident as follows:
   大连 船舱 拖船 拖
   (1) 1,000 cartons of goods were destroyed by fire;
   (2) 600 cartons of cargo were lost due to water-filling and firefighting;
   (3) the main engine and part of the deck were burned out;
   (4) tugboat costs;
   (5) additional fuel and salaries of captain and the crew for re-sailing to Singapore.
   Please analyze the nature of the losses and determine which were particular average and which were general average.
2. A Chinese manufacturer concluded a deal of exporting a batch of **smart monitoring cameras** under Incoterm CIF. Before shipment, it had the goods insured against FPA for 110% of the total invoice value. The goods were loaded and the vessel sailed on schedule in early June. However, the vessel ran into a storm at sea on June 13, resulting in water damage to some goods, with a loss valued at
   智能监控摄像机

$2,100. A few days later, the vessel hit a reef again, resulting in a partial loss valued at $8,000. Question: Do you think the insurance company will indemnify for the loss of this batch of goods? Why?

便携发电机
名古屋

3. Suppose you quote for a **portable power station** at CFR $300 per unit **Nagoya** to a customer in Japan, but the customer authorizes you to purchase insurance on behalf of him. After consulting PICC, the coverage should be at least 110% of the CIF value, and the premium rate is 0.8%. How much should you pay as insurance premium to cover the cargo on behalf of the customer?

Chapter 9 Methods of Payment (1)

第九章 支付方式（1）

Learning Objectives:

- ◆ Payment methods of cash in advance and open account
- ◆ Telegraphic transfer as a major means to effect the above two payment methods
- ◆ Payment methods of documentary collection—workflow, pros and cons

In international business negotiations, payment terms often become an issue that may **obsess** both you and the importer. You may wonder, "What if I cannot get paid after I ship the goods?" On the other hand, the importer may wonder, "What if I get goods not exactly as I ordered?" These obsessions arise from a lack of trust between you and the importer, which, imaginably, is more **acute** in international transactions than in domestic ones. Consequently, security of the payment method adopted often becomes top concern from your perspective. However, if you require a more conservative payment method, you may lose the deal to a competitor who is willing to accept more **aggressive** payment terms. Therefore, a wise decision regarding payment is to strike a balance between security and market.

困扰 严重的 激进的

Luckily, some useful methods and instruments have been innovated in the history to **approach** this issue, some of which **embodies** great thinking **in retrospect**. In this and the following two chapters, we will be learning about the major methods and instruments of payment adopted in international trade.

应对，解决 体现 回顾起来

9.1 Cash in Advance and Open Account 预付货款和赊账

延迟
理解

As the exporter , you probably want to get paid sooner, preferably by advanced payment. The importer, however, may wish for a **deferred** payment method. Cash in advance and open account represent these two extremes in the timing of payment, with the former most favorable to you, the exporter, and the latter to the importer. There are possibilities in between, but the extremes may help you **appreciate** the crux of international payment.

9.1.1 Cash in Advance 预付货款

低劣的

Cash in advance is a payment method by which you demand payment from the importer before you ship the goods. Obviously, it is most favorable to you, as you have no risk in getting paid. However, it represents utmost risk for the importer and naturally unwelcome to most international buyers, particularly those from developed countries. But when you deal with customers of **shoddy** credit standing or those from high-risk countries or regions, it is surely a better choice. And if your products are in great demand in the target market, you may also request a payment by cash in advance.

9.1.2 Open Account 赊账

由于
在其中

Open account is a payment method by which goods are shipped to the importer before you get paid, which is just the opposite of a cash-in-advance arrangement in terms of the timing of payment and the risk distribution between you and the importer. Exporters are traditionally suggested to avoid it **on account of** the high risk involved **therein**, but as can be expected, it's definitely a welcome method to importers, particularly those from the European Union. Therefore, give it a second thought before you give it up straight away. Two strategies may help you turn it into a marketing tool in the international market. First, conduct a thorough investigation into the importer's credit standing; second, cover the transaction with credit insurance to shift the risk of importer's **default** to **underwriters**. 违约 保险公司

9.1.3 Remittance as Instrument 作为工具的汇款

A cash-in-advance or open-account arrangement is often **effected** via a remittance where the importer may initiate a **mail transfer (M/T)**, a **telegraphic transfer (T/T)** or a **draft remittance** (a remittance by demand draft (D/D)) to your bank account. The three ways of remitting money differ mainly in the means of **communicating the transfer order**, with the first by mail, the second mainly by SWIFT codes and the third by a **bill of exchange**. As telegraphic transfer (T/T) is more popular today than the other two means, "T/T" is used almost **interchangeably** with "remittance" by traders. Its security and efficiency have made it widely adopted as instrument of payment for international transactions. If it is agreed to in the contract, the importer goes to his/her bank, **fills out** a written application form, indicating your full name, address, amount of money to be remitted, your bank account and the corresponding SWIFT code, signs it, and then submits the application form together with the money to his/her bank, instructing it to initiate a T/T in your favor. Then the money will **be credited into** your bank account in two to five workdays. The same process applies if you remit money to the importer, such as in the case of a refund.

实施
信汇
电汇 票汇
转账命令的通信方式
汇票
可互换的
填写
将款项计入某人账户

9.2 Documentary Collection 跟单托收

Another arrangement devised to relieve the concern of exporters is documentary collection.

9.2.1 How Does a Documentary Collection Work? 跟单托收如何进行?

If you are not sure of the importer's creditworthiness, you may entrust somebody who is trustworthy to collect the money for you, instructing it not to release the **title documents** to the goods (bill of lading) among others until the importer satisfies a requirement, most

物权单据

often making the payment or signing a document promising to pay within a given time. The importer needs these documents for clearing customs for import and taking delivery and normally he/she would meet the requirement. But should the importer decide not to pay or take delivery, you retain the option of having the goods shipped back and losing just the **freight** instead of the total value of the goods. Another option is that you may find another customer for the goods.

运费

This arrangement is called a **documentary collection**, or just "**collection**" for short. Under such an arrangement, the party that is entrusted is often a bank in the importer's country, which acts on behalf of you to collect the money from the importer and is called **the collecting bank**. Theoretically, only this one bank is needed for such a service—you send the documents straight to this bank and ask it to represent you. But banks providing such a service normally want to make sure they are dealing with a **legitimate** exporter instead of an unknown foreign business, so, the collecting bank often uses another bank, one that it has dealt with in the past and that it trusts, as a **conduit** for transmitting the documents. This bank is often the **correspondent bank** of the collecting bank in the exporter's country and called the **remitting bank** in a collection service.

跟单托收
托收
代收行
合法正当的
渠道
代理银行
托收行

So, a real-world documentary collection starts with you presenting the documents with a **letter of instruction** to the remitting bank which then **forwards** them to the collecting bank for collecting the money from the importer. The documents involved may roughly fall into two categories: commercial documents and financial documents. Commercial documents mostly relate to the merchandise, such as the commercial invoice, the bill of lading, the insurance policy (if necessary), etc. Of all the commercial documents, the bill of lading is the most critical, because it represents ownership of the goods. Financial documents, possibly a **bill of exchange**, a **promissory note** or a **cheque**, but mostly a bill of exchange—are used as instrument for collecting the money from the importer. A bill of exchange is an unconditional written order drawn by the exporter to the importer requiring the latter to pay immediately or make a firm **commitment** to pay in a fixed or determinable future date.

托收指示信
转交
汇票 本票 支票
承诺

The collecting bank shall release the documents strictly following your letter of instruction, in which you can set forth the conditions for the importer to get hold of the documents, which can be of two types of option to you: "**document against payment (D/P)**" or "**document against acceptance (D/A)**" (see Figure 9-1). 付款交单 承兑交单

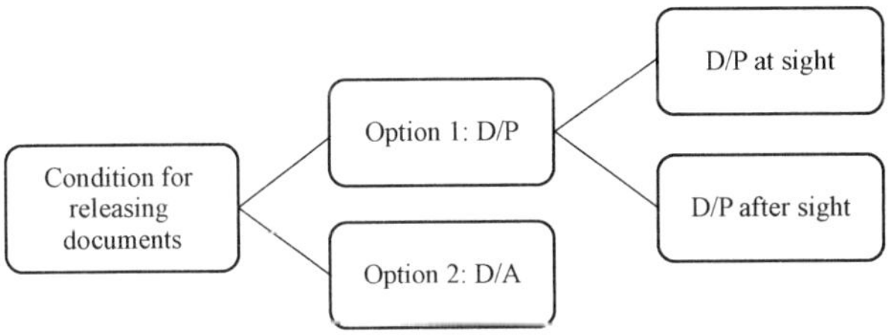

Figure 9-1 Conditions for Releasing Documents

♦ **Option 1—document against payment (D/P) 付款交单**

You instruct the collecting bank NOT to release the documents to the importer until he/she makes cash payment. For this option, you may further choose between a **D/P at sight** or **D/P after sight**—whether you want the importer to pay immediately or **grant him/her some credit terms**. However, notably, D/P at sight is way better than D/P after sight in terms of security of payment. 即期付款交单 远期付款交单 给予他/她一些信用期

♦ **Option 2—document against acceptance (D/A) 承兑交单**

You instruct the collecting bank NOT to release the documents to the importer until he/she promises to pay on a fixed or determinable future date.

So, in effect, you have three options under a collection arrangement—D/P at sight, D/P after sight and D/A, all of which can be achieved by asking the importer to sign a bill of exchange. From your point of view, D/P is better than D/A, and D/P at sight better than D/P after sight in terms of payment security.

In either D/P or D/A, you shall issue an order requesting the importer to pay—a bill of exchange. The importer then pays or promises to pay the bill. The document of title is released to the importer against payment or acceptance of the bill (see Figure 9-2).

The Uniform Rules for Collection (URC) developed by the International Chamber of Commerce (ICC) in Paris, is the internationally recognized **codification of rules** unifying banking practices regarding operations for documentary collections. 《托收统一惯例》 成文规则

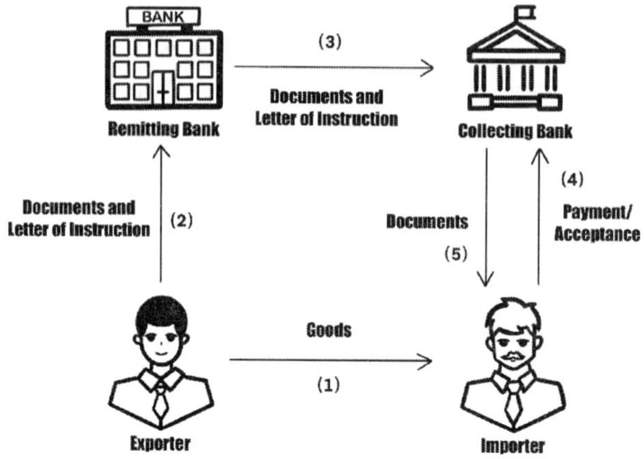

Figure 9-2 Workflow of Documentary Collection

9.2.2 Notes on Documentary Collection 跟单托收注意事项

Success of a documentary collection is largely determined by the importer's credit standing. The banks involved do not guarantee they can acquire the money for you, nor do they assume any credit risk. They merely act as intermediaries to facilitate the collection, strictly following your instructions. They have no obligation to protect the goods, either.

物权

Under the arrangement of D/P, in case the importer refuses to pay, you do keep **title** to the cargo, but you would have to renegotiate with the importer for new terms, find another importer, or have the cargo returned. Whichever is the case may result in additional cost in shipping, insurance, and banking charges. This is particular tricky if the merchandise is perishable so that you must find another importer pretty soon. With D/P after sight, even if the importer promises to pay, as he/she cannot take possession of the goods until he/she pays, the goods have to be warehoused in the port or somewhere else, incurring warehousing fees. The customs of the importing country may even **confiscate** the goods to cover any storage charges incurred.

没收

Under the arrangement of D/P after sight, the importer could be allowed a credit term of 30, 45, 60 or 90 days from the first presentation of the documents. Even if he/she cannot get hold of the documents from the collecting bank until he/she pays, you still need to guard against an **accommodation** practice by which the importer manages to borrow the bill of lading from the collecting bank against a **trust receipt** within the credit term of a time bill of exchange, and then makes payment when the bill of exchange is **due**, normally after he/she has sold the goods. A trust receipt is a notice of the release of merchandise to a buyer from a bank, with the bank retaining the ownership title of the released assets. In an arrangement involving a trust receipt, the bank remains the owner of the merchandise, but the buyer is allowed to **hold the merchandise in trust** for the bank, for manufacturing or sales purposes. The trust receipt serves as a promissory note to the bank that the loan amount will be repaid upon sale of the goods. Companies involved in these arrangements typically include equipment dealers, automotive dealers, or dealers of expensive durable goods. This practice often occurs when the goods arrive at destination before the time bill of exchange is due so that the importer wants to borrow the B/L in case he/she misses business opportunities.

变通
信托收据
到期
保管

Under D/A, in case the importer refuses to accept the bill of exchange, you would be **plunged** in a similarly unfavorable situation with D/P. Even if the importer accepts the bill, it enables him/her to get hold of the shipping documents and take possession of the goods before making payment. As the exporter, you would take great risks as there is still possibility that the importer defaults when the bill is due. Should that occur, you would lose both the money and goods, and have no choice but try to enforce the importer's obligation with the help of the collecting bank or by litigation, both of which would result in additional fees.

置入

It should still be noted that, in some countries or regions, such as South America and Europe, there is no such a thing as "D/P after sight", which would be understood or treated as D/A in practice, meaning that the document of title would be released as long as the importer accepts the time bill of exchange even if a D/P after sight is required, which makes it highly risky to exporters.

Exercises 练习

I. True or False

1. When you deal with an importer with poor credit standing or one from high-risk countries or regions, payment by cash in advance is suggested. (　　)
2. When you sell a product that is high in demand in a certain overseas market, payment by cash in advance can be considered. (　　)
3. Under a documentary collection, there will be no problem with collecting payment as long as we select the remitting bank and the collecting bank with prudence. (　　)
4. From an exporter's point of view, D/P at sight is better than D/P after sight in terms of payment security. (　　)
5. In the case of a payment by D/A, the collecting bank accepts the bill of exchange and releases the documents to the importer. (　　)
6. Under a documentary collection, CIF is a more secure Incoterms rule to the exporter than FOB is. (　　)
7. Cash in advance ensures that the importer gets the goods as he/she has ordered. (　　)
8. Under a documentary collection, both the banks act in strict accordance with the letter of instruction. (　　)
9. Under a documentary collection, the documents should be made in accordance with the contract. (　　)
10. As opposed to D/P, D/A requires payment be made after sight, which is more favorable to the importer. (　　)

II. Multiple Choice Questions

1. Among D/P, D/A and T/T, which of the following group ranks an exporter's risk from large to small? (　　　).
   [A] T/T, D/P, D/A　　　[B] D/A, D/P, T/T
   [C] D/A, T/T, D/P　　　[D] D/P, D/A, T/T
2. Which one of the following payment arrangements involves the greatest risk for the exporter? (　　　)
   [A] Payment by demand draft.

[B] Payment by D/P at sight.

[C] Payment by D/A.

[D] Payment by D/P after sight.

3. The banks involved in a documentary collection act in strict accordance with (   ).

[A] the remitting bank's order

[B] the collecting bank's order

[C] the exporter's letter of instruction

[D] the importer's letter of instruction

4. Which of the following is NOT a method to effect a remittance (   ).

[A] L/C　　[B] M/T

[C] T/T　　[D] D/D

5. Which of the following party normally undertakes to pay under a payment arrangement of D/A? (   )

[A] The importer.　　[B] The payee.

[C] The remitting bank.　　[D] The collecting bank.

6. Which of the following is TRUE about a transaction of documentary collection? (   )

[A] The collecting bank promises to make payment to the exporter.

[B] The collecting bank promises to acquire the payment for the exporter.

[C] The remitting bank promises to acquire the payment for the exporter.

[D] There is a risk of the exporter failing to acquire the payment.

7. Which of the following is NOT a condition for presenting documents under a documentary collection? (   )

[A] D/A.　　[B] D/P at sight.

[C] D/P after sight.　　[D] D/D.

8. Which of the following payment arrangement may incur additional warehousing charges at the port of destination? (   )

[A] D/P at sight　　[B] D/P after sight

[C] D/A　　[D] T/T

9. Which party shall be the owner of the merchandise once it is released against a trust receipt? ( )
   [A] The remitting bank. [B] The collecting bank.
   [C] The exporter. [D] The importer.
10. Which one of the following is NOT an option for the exporter if the importer refuses to pay or take delivery? ( )
   [A] Having the goods shipped back.
   [B] Finding another buyer for the goods.
   [C] Resorting to litigation.
   [D] Asking the remitting bank or the collecting bank to pay.

III. Case Study

沙窝水果萝卜

1. A Tianjin based Chinese exporter of **Shawo Fruit Radish** made a quotation to a Korean merchant at payment terms by D/P at sight. The Korean merchant replied that he could accept payment by D/P 90 days after sight with a collecting bank designated by him. Why do you think the Korean merchant requested such a payment arrangement?

啤酒花

2. Tianshan Agricultural Technology Co., Ltd., a Xinjiang-based Chinese company, once reached a deal of exporting some **hops** to a Polish company Mellow Brewery Co., Ltd. under payment terms of D/P 90 days after sight. After the bill of exchange and the attached documents were sent to the collecting bank through the remitting bank, Mellow Brewery accepted the bill. As World Cup was around the corner, price of hops was rising when the goods arrived at the port of destination and Mellow Brewery was anxious to pick up the goods for production. Therefore, it managed to borrow the documents from the collecting bank against a trust receipt and picked up the goods. When the bill was due, the Polish company went bankrupt due to poor management and was unable to pay. The collecting bank notified the remitting bank that the drawee of the bill refused to pay, and suggested Tianshan Agricultural Technology ask for payment straight from the Polish importer. How do you think the Chinese company should deal with this case?

Chapter 10 Instrument of Payment

第十章 付款工具

Learning Objectives:

◆ Bill of exchange—nature and usage

◆ Promissory note—nature and usage

◆ Cheque/check①—nature and usage

A method of payment is an arrangement for payment. Once it is decided and agreed to between you and the importer, you still need to acquire the money physically, which is often achieved by using a specific instrument, such as a **bill of exchange**, a **promissory note** or a **cheque**. Bills of exchange, also called drafts, are widely used for international transactions, while promissory notes and cheques are more for domestic uses. As they can be transferred, they are also called **negotiable instrument**.

汇票 本票

支票

可转让票据

10.1 Bill of Exchange 汇票

A bill used in domestic trade is a written statement issued by the seller stating the amount of money the buyer owes for the goods or services provided and asking him/her to make payment. We must have been billed by a restaurant where we have dinner. The little piece of paper presented by the waiter or waitress after dinner that shows us how much we have spent on the dinner is a bill. Upon receiving the bill, we have to pay it, either right away or some time later, though the latter is a rare case for a dinner.

---

① cheque: 英式英语; check: 美式英语

A bill used in international trade, likewise, is a written order to pay. It is normally issued and addressed by the exporter to the importer or another party that has the obligation to pay—the payer. When the payer is **presented** the bill and signs it, he/she is legally bound by his/her domestic law to make the payment, then the bill resembles an **IOU (I owe you)** from the payer's perspective, though in a more serious way. He/she has either to **pay on demand** or, when presented the bill again, pay on a fixed or determinable future date.

出示，提示

借条

见票即付

As the exporter, you may also transfer the bill to someone else in order to get payment sooner, **reimburse** your debt, grant discounts in the form of a refund to customers, etc. If you want to get payment sooner, for example, you may sell the bill to anyone interested in buying it, such as a bank, which is called "**negotiation**", but it is mostly sold at a discounted price as the buyer wants to charge a fee for **advancing** the money to you before it is **due**. If you want to reimburse a debt owed to your supplier, you may transfer the bill to him/her. In either case, the bill is **exchangeable** for money, that is why it is called a "bill of exchange". The transfer can be achieved via a behavior called "endorsing" or "endorsement"—you sign at the back of the bill, indicating your intention to transfer it.

偿还

议付

提前给付　到期

可兑换的

This feature of supporting transference enables exporters to collect payment sooner, settle their debts faster and drive sales, which makes the bill of exchange particularly welcome in international trade. In addition, a bill of exchange is also stipulated to be an "unconditional" order to pay, implying that there is no need to ask about the underlying reasons when one deals with transference of a bill, which adds to its **liquidity**.

流动性，即变现能力

Bills of Exchange Act 1882 of Great Britain defines a **bill of exchange (draft)** as an unconditional order to pay in writing, addressed by one person to another, signed by the person drawing it, requiring the person to whom it is addressed to pay on demand or on a fixed or determinable future date a certain sum of money to or to the order of a specified person, or to bearer. China's ***Law on Negotiable Instruments*** defines a bill of exchange as a negotiable instrument, signed and issued by the drawer, who authorizes the drawee to pay unconditionally a sum

汇票，是一个人签发给另一个人的无条件的书面付款命令，由签发人签署，要求受票人根据要求即刻或在一个可确定的将来日期支付一笔资金或根据某人或持有人的指示支付一笔资金。

certain in money to the payee or the holder at sight or on a specified date. 《票据法》
The law also clarifies the jurisdiction issue in Chapter V **Application of Law to Negotiable Instruments Involving Foreign Elements.** 涉外票据的法律适用

10.1.1 Parties Involved 当事人

A bill of exchange usually involves 3 major parties:

Drawer: the party who **issues** the bill. In international trade, normally the exporter draws a bill. 出票人 签发

Drawee (Payer): the party to whom the bill is addressed, or the payer. In international trade, a drawee is often the importer or the importer's bank. 受票人（付款人）

Payee: the party who is to receive the money. In international trade, a payee can be the exporter, or someone nominated by the exporter, or the exporter's bank. 收款人

10.1.2 Indispensable Elements 要素

Even though there is no uniform format for a bill of exchange either domestically or internationally, the following items are generally **indispensable** (see Figure 10-1): 必不可少的

- the term "bill of exchange" or "draft",
- an unconditional order to pay a sum certain in money,
- name of the party who is to pay (drawee or payer),
- time of payment,
- person to whom or to whose order payment is to be made (payee),
- date and place of issue, and
- signature of the party who issues the bill (drawer).

BILL OF EXCHANGE

No. OA_DRGINV01

Exchange For US$120,500.00 GUANGZHOU 15-July-22

(amount in figure) (place and date of issue)

At ******** sight of this FIRST Bill of exchange (SECOND being unpaid)

Pay to BANK OF CHINA, GUANGZHOU BRANCH or order the sum of

SAY U.S. DOLLARS ONE HUNDRED TWENTY THOUSAND AND FIVE HUNDRED ONLY

(amount in words)

Value received for 100 SETS of OAK WARDROBE

(quantity) (name of commodity)

Draw under CITIBANK NEWYORK

LC No. DRG-OKLC01 dated 02-June-22

To: CITYBANK NEWYORK
123 E 86th St,
New York, NY 10028

For and on behalf of
OKART FURNITURE CO., LTD.
蔡欣怡

(Authorized Signature)

Figure 10-1 A Sample Bill of Exchange

10.1.3 Major Acts 主要票据行为

The major acts in dealing with a bill of exchange include: issuance, presentation, payment, acceptance, negotiation, endorsement, dishonor and recourse.

♦ **Issuance 签发**

Issuance is the drawer's act to sign and deliver the bill to the payee. **Crux** of this procedure is **nominating** the **payee**. Generally, the payee is nominated in one of three ways, with different **wordings**.

关键 指定 收款人 措辞

♦ **Restrictive payee 限制性收款人**

A bill may stipulate the payee with wordings like "pay to Tianjin Binhai Import and Export Co., Ltd. **ONLY**", or "pay to Tianjin Binhai Import and Export Co., Ltd., **NOT NEGOTIABLE**". With such wordings, the payee is restrictive as the money can be paid only to the nominated payee and so, the bill is **non-negotiable**.

不可转让

♦ **"To Order" payee 指示性收款人**

A bill may stipulate the payee as "pay to Tianjin Binhai Import and Export Co., Ltd, or order", or "pay to the order of Tianjin Binhai Import and Export Co., Ltd.". The wording of "To Order" indicates that the payer can pay according to the order of the nominated payee, which means, the original payee can further transfer the bill to a third party by endorsement. Negotiation can help an exporter **reimburse debts**, **grant discount**, or **facilitate collection of payment**. 偿还债务 给予折扣 加速收款

♦ **"To Bearer" payee 持票人收款人**

Some bills may be worded as "To Bearer" for nominating the payee. "To Bearer" means the payer can pay to anyone that presents the bill. This indicates that the exporter can transfer the bill to a third party without endorsement. As you can **imagine**, this type of bill can be very risky and are rarely used. And China's *Law on Negotiable Instrument* stipulates that a bill that is **payable to bearer** is invalid. 想象 付给持有人

♦ **Presentation 提示（出示）**

Presentation is the drawer's or any endorsee's act of delivering the bill to the drawee. A bill can be presented with one of two **claims**—"**presentation for payment**" which occurs when a **sight bill** is employed; or "**presentation for acceptance**" which occurs when a **time bill** is employed. In international trade, it is often the exporter or his/her representative who presents the bill to the importer or the importer's bank. 要求 见票付款 即期汇票 承兑付款 远期汇票

♦ **Payment 支付**

Payment is the drawee's (payer's) act of paying the payee. Normally, the importer or the importer's bank makes payment to the exporter. And a bill is often issued in two copies with equal validity, and when any one is paid, the other becomes invalid.

♦ **Acceptance 承兑**

Acceptance is the drawee's act of promising to pay to the payee. The drawee engages himself/herself by stamping "acceptance" and his/her name on the bill, indicating his/her promise to pay when a time bill is due.

♦ **Negotiation 议付**

Negotiation is the drawer's or any endorsee's act of transferring a bill. A sight bill does not need negotiation, as it is paid on demand. In the case of a time bill, you can sell it in the financial market to get payment in advance, but the price is often less than the face value of the bill as the buyer charges a fee for advancing the money to you, which is equivalent to the interest **accrued** from the date of sale to the due date of the bill. This practice is also called **discounting** a bill. Theoretically, a time bill can be discounted for whatever times before it is due. 累计下来 贴现

♦ **Endorsement 背书**

Endorsements is a key step in the process of negotiation, which is achieved by the drawer or any endorsee signing on its back, indicating

转让人
背书人 受让人 被背书人

his/her intention to transfer the bill to a third party. The **transferor** is the **endorser**, and the **transferee** the **endorsee**. Endorsement can be executed in different ways. For example,

♦ **Restrictive endorsement 限制性背书**

A restrictive endorsement contains both the endorser's name and the endorsee's name, without words like "to order", but sometimes with words like "not negotiable", signifying that the bill cannot be further negotiated.

Pay to Singapore Wonka Trading Company Ltd.	→ the endorsee (who cannot further transfer)
李明	→ authorized representative of endorser
For Tianjin Binhai Import & Export Co., Ltd.	→ endorser
Sept. 20, 2022	→ date of endorsing

指示背书不但指名背书人的名称，而且指定按谁的指示来支付

♦ **Order endorsement 指示背书**

An order endorsement specifies not only the endorser's name, but also "to whose order" the bill is to be paid.

Pay to the order of Bank of China, Tianjin Branch	→ the endorsee (who can further transfer)
李明	→ authorized representative of endorser
For Tianjin Binhai Import & Export Co., Ltd.	→ endorser
Sept. 20, 2022	→ date of endorsing

♦ **Blank endorsement 空白背书**

A blank endorsement bears only the endorser's signature but specifies no endorsee.

	→ the endorsee (who can further transfer)
李明	→ authorized representative of endorser
For Tianjin Binhai Import & Export Co., Ltd.	→ endorser
Sept. 20, 2022	→ date of endorsing

♦ **Dishonor and recourse 拒付和追索**

Dishonor is the act of "non-payment" or "non-acceptance" of a bill. Recourse is a right that allows an endorsee of a bill to claim payment from any or all of his/her **prior parties** in the case of a dishonor. Anyone endorsing the bill is a prior party, and any endorsee is a **successor**. If A endorses a bill to B, and B to C, and the bill is due when it comes to C, but is dishonored by the drawee/payer. How could you cope with this if you were C? Generally speaking, you may initiate a recourse to any or all of your prior parties. Should the recourse fail, you may **resort to litigation**.

前手

后手

提出诉讼

10.1.4 Classification of Bills of Exchange 汇票的分类

♦ **Sight (demand) bill & time (usance) bill** 即期付款汇票和远期付款汇票

Depending on the tenor, a bill may be a sight bill or a time bill. If the bill is payable on demand, meaning immediately when asked to pay, it is a sight bill. If it is due to pay at a later but fixed or determinable date, say in 30, 60, or 90 days, it is a time bill.

♦ **Clean bill & documentary bill** 光票汇票和跟单汇票

A clean bill is one without any documents attached, while a documentary bill is one with other documents attached. The documents may include: shipping documents (bill of lading, packing list, etc.), commercial documents (mainly commercial invoice), and sometimes insurance documents. A documentary bill is mostly applied to merchandise trade, while a clean bill to small amount of payment or service trade, etc.

♦ **Commercial bill and banker's bill** 商业汇票和银行汇票

Depending on the drawer, a bill of exchange can be a commercial bill (trader's bill) or a banker's bill. A commercial bill is drawn by a firm to a bank or another firm as the drawee. A banker's bill is drawn by a bank to another bank as the drawee.

♦ **Commercial accepted bill & banker's accepted bill** 商业承兑汇票和银行承兑汇票

If a bill is accepted, depending on the acceptor, it can be a commercial accepted bill or a banker's accepted bill. A bill that is accepted by a firm is a commercial accepted bill and one accepted by a bank is a banker's accepted bill. As bank credit is generally believed to be more trustworthy than a commercial credit, a banker's accepted bill is more popular than a commercial accepted bill.

10.1.5 Payment by Bill of Exchange Under Documentary Collection 跟单托收下通过汇票收款

Parties to a documentary collection include:

♦ **The principal (exporter/drawer)** 委托人 **(**卖方/出票人**)**

As the exporter, you are the principal and prepare the shipping documents and other commercial documents, draw a bill of exchange, and submit them to the remitting bank (often your bank) with a letter of instruction to the collecting bank.

♦ **The remitting bank (the principal's/exporter's bank)** 托收行 **(**受托人/卖方的银行**)**

The remitting bank receives documents from you (principal) and forwards (by remitting) to the importer's bank (collecting/presenting bank) along with the letter of instruction for collecting payment.

♦ **The collecting bank (the presenting bank/importer's bank)** 代收行 **(**提示行/买方的银行**)**

This is the bank that presents the documents to the importer and collects payment (effected by a sight bill) or obtains a promise to pay in the future (effected by a time bill) from the importer (drawee of the bill) in exchange for the documents.

♦ **The payer (drawee/importer)** 付款人 **(**受票人/买方**)**

It is the party that makes payment or signs a bill of exchange according to the terms of the letter of instruction in exchange for the documents from the presenting/collecting bank and takes possession of the goods. The payer (drawee) is the one on whom a bill of exchange is drawn and who owes the indicated amount on the bill.

Figure 10-2 shows a graphic representation of payment by a bill of exchange under the arrangement of a documentary collection.

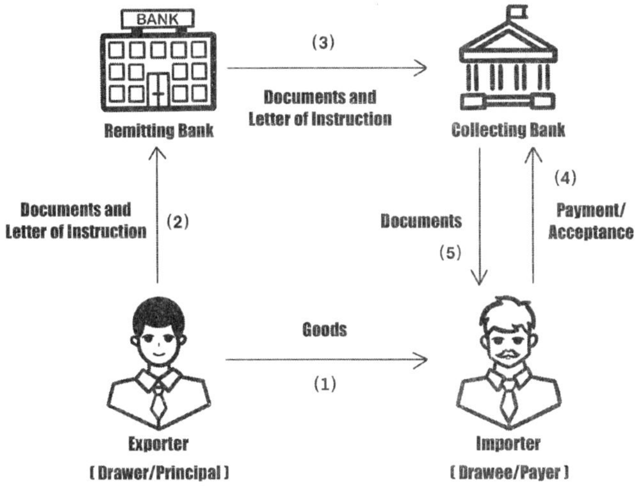

Figure 10-2 Payment by a Bill of Exchange Under Documentary Collection

10.1.6 Filling out a Bill of Exchange 汇票的填写

When a documentary credit or documentary collection is selected as the method of payment, a bill of exchange is usually used as instrument to effect the payment. Generally, your bank provides a blank bill which you fill out and shall be delivered to the drawee for payment or promise to pay. Bills of exchange are generally made in duplicate, and no legal difference exists between the first and the second copy. After one copy is cashed, the other copy will be automatically **voided**. 作废

Now, let's try to figure out how to fill out a bill of exchange (see Figure 10-3 and Table 10-1).

BILL OF EXCHANGE

No. TIA00188

Exchange For USD262,500.00 TIANJIN JUNE 16, 2022

(amount in figure) (place and date of issue)

At ******** sight of this FIRST Bill of exchange (SECOND being unpaid)

Pay to BANK OF CHINA TIANJIN BRANCH or order the sum of

SAY U.S. DOLLARS TWO HUNDRED AND SIXTY TWO THOUSAND FIVE HUNDRED ONLY

(amount in words)

Value received for 3,000 PIECES of SWIMMING SUITS

(quantity) (name of commodity)

Draw under BANK OF CHINA SINGAPORE

L/C No. KOS879 dated MAY 10, 2022

To: BANK OF CHINA SINGAPORE
4 BATTERY ROAD, BANK OF CHINA BUILDING
SINGAPORE 049908

For and on behalf of
TIANJIN BINHAI IMPORT & EXPORT CO., LTD.
李明
(Authorized Signature)

Figure 10-3 A Sample Bill of Exchange

Table 10-1 How to Fill out a Bill of Exchange

1. **No.** fill in the invoice number here (这里填写汇票号码)

   This is your self-made serial number for the bill of exchange. The invoice number could be borrowed to indicate that the bill and the invoice refer to the same transaction. In practice, however, a bank also accepts a bill with this field left blank.

2. **Dated** fill in the date of issue of the bill (这里填写汇票的出票日期)

   This date must be after the date of the contract.

3. **Exchange for** fill in the amount in figures here (这里填写汇票金额小写)

   It should include both the currency code and the figures, such as USD1,234.00

   The amount in figures and in words should be clear, consistent with one another and without alterations. According to China's *Law on Negotiable Instruments*, a bill of exchange is invalid if the amount, date or name of the payee is altered, or if the amount in words and in figures are inconsistent with one another. Besides, for a documentary bill under a letter of credit, unless otherwise specified in the credit, the amount of the bill should not exceed that of the credit, and should be consistent with the invoice amount; and the currency of the bill must be consistent with the one specified in the credit and the invoice.

4. **At** fill in the time limit for payment here (这里填写付款期限)

   For this field, the entry differs depending on whether the bill is a sight bill or a time bill. And for a bill under a documentary collection, the entry for this field is slightly different from one under a documentary credit.

continued

➢ For a **sight bill**, just fill in "sight" in the blank after "at". If "at_____sight" is pre-printed on the bill, just cross the blank out by filling in "******" or "—".

➢ For a **time bill**, there are generally four ways to state the due date of the bill:

- "at ×× days after sight" means the bill is due ×× days after the payer sees the bill.
- "at ×× days after date" means the bill is due ×× days after the bill is issued. In that case, cross out the word "sight" on the bill.
- "at ×× days after B/L" means the bill is due ×× days after the date of the B/L. In that case, cross out the word "sight" on the bill.
- Fill in a designated date as the due date of the bill, such as "On 25th Feb., 2022". In that case, cross out the word "at" and "sight" on the bill. This type of bill is called a bill payable on a stated date ("定期付款汇票" 或 "板期汇票").

➢ Under **a documentary collection**, this field is filled out as follows: "D/P at sight", "D/P at ×× days sight" or "D/A at ×× days sight".

5. **Pay to the Order of** [fill in the payee here (这里填写收款人)]

This entry is also called the title of a bill, which is generally the exporter's bank if under a letter of credit or the exporter if not. There are normally three ways to fill out the payee:

Three Ways of Filling out the Payee

No.	Types of title	Wordings (措辞)	Meaning in Chinese	negotiability
1	Order title (指示性抬头)	Pay to×× Co., or order; Pay to the order of ×× Co.	付给××公司或其指定人	Negotiable with endorsement
2	Restrictive title (限制性抬头)	Pay to×× Co. only	仅付给××公司	Non-negotiable
		Pay to×× Co. Not negotiable	付××公司，不准流通	
3	Bearer title (来人抬头)	Pay to bearer	付给来人	negotiable without endorsement

Note: In China's foreign trade practice, an order title is more common. Under an L/C, it's customary for the exporter to draw a bill of exchange payable to the negotiating bank or its order instead of to the exporter or his/her order if the credit is available by negotiation. Under a documentary collection, the bill is payable to the exporter or order.

6. **The sum of** [fill in the amount in words here (这里填写汇票金额大写)]

This entry should begin with full name of the currency, followed by the amount in words and end with the word "only", such as UNITED STATES DOLLARS ONE THOUSAND TWO HUNDRED AND THIRTY FOUR ONLY.

continued

The amount in figures and in words should be clear, consistent with one another and without alterations. According to China's *Law on Negotiable Instruments*, a bill is invalid if the amount, date or name of the payee is altered, or if the amount in words and in figures are inconsistent with one another.

Besides, unless otherwise specified in the credit, the amount of the bill should not exceed that of the credit, and should be consistent with the invoice amount; and the currency of the bill must be consistent with the one specified in the credit and the invoice.

7. **Value received for** [fill in here the quantity of commodity (这里填写汇票项下商品数量)] **of** [fill in here the name of commodity (这里填写汇票项下商品名称)]

   Sometimes, this information is not necessary.

8. **Draw under L/C No.** [fill in here the L/C number under which the bill is drawn (这里填写作为出票凭证的信用证编号)]

   Leave blank if payment is not by L/C

9. **Dated** [fill in here the opening date of the L/C (这里填写信用证的开证日期)]

   This is not the date of issue of the bill; leave blank under other payment terms than an L/C

10. **Issued by** [fill in here the issuing bank of the L/C (这里填写信用证的开证行)]

    Leave blank if payment is not by L/C

11. **To** [fill in here the name and address of the drawee of the bill (这里填写受票人名称和地址)]

    Under a letter of credit, the drawee is normally the issuing bank, which is also the payer. Both the name and address of the bank in English are needed. Under other terms of payment, fill in the name and address of the importer in English.

    According to *UCP 600*, under an L/C transaction, the drawee (payer) is the issuing bank or its nominated bank and should not be the applicant. If the drawee (payer) is not specified in the credit, please still fill the name and address of the issuing bank in the bill. You may refer to the credit terms "41D"和"42A" for the information about drawee (payer). For example, "… available by bill(s) drawn on us" indicates that the drawee (payer) is the issuing bank while "drawn on yourselves/you" means that the drawee (payer) is the advising bank.

12. **Authorized Signature** [sign and stamp as drawer of the bill here (作为出票人在此签字盖章)]

    Sign as drawer, name of your company in English and stamp at the lower right corner of the bill

10.2 Promissory Note 本票

A promissory note is an unconditional promise in writing made by one person to another and signed by the maker, who promises to pay, on demand or at a fixed or determinable future date, a certain sum of money, to, or to the order of, a specified person or to bearer. As the name indicates, a promissory note is a promise by nature. By promising to pay, the importer also binds himself/herself by his/her domestic law. It differs from a bill of exchange in that it is initiated by the importer.

10.2.1 Parties Involved 当事人

A promissory note normally involves two parties:

Drawer: the party who issues the promissory note. In international trade, the importer, or the importer's representative normally issues a promissory note. 出票人

Payee: the party who is to receive the payment. In international trade, the payee is usually the exporter. 收款人

10.2.2 Indispensable Elements 要素

Like a bill of exchange, there are also items that are indispensable for a promissory note, which are:

- the words "promissory note",
- an unconditional promise to pay,
- name of the payee or his/her order,
- drawer's signature,
- place and date of issue,
- maturity,
- a sum certain in money in words and figures, and
- place of payment

10.2.3 Classification of Promissory Notes 本票的分类

Promissory notes can be a **trader's note** or a **banker's note**. A trader's note is issued by a firm, while a banker's note by a bank. As commercial credit standing is generally believed not as trustworthy as a banker's, a trader's note is rarely used in international trade. The vast majority are banker's notes, which are often payable on demand. 贸易商本票 银行本票

10.3 Cheque 支票

支票是客户向银行所签发的无条件的书面命令，由该客户签署，授权银行按要求支付一定金额给某一特定人员或其指定的人，或持票人。

A cheque is an unconditional order to pay in writing addressed by a customer to a bank and signed by that customer authorizing the bank to pay on demand a certain sum of money to or to the order of a specified person or to bearer.

10.3.1 Parties Involved 当事人

A cheque normally involves three parties:

出票人

Drawer: the party who issues a cheque. If used for international trade, the drawer of a cheque is normally the importer.

付款人

Drawee: the bank on whom the cheque is drawn. It is normally the importer's bank.

收款人

Payee: the party to whom a cheque is stated to be payable. If used for international trade the payee is normally the exporter.

10.3.2 Indispensable Elements 要素

The indispensable items for a cheque include:

- the word "cheque" or "check",
- an unconditional order in writing,
- name and place of the paying bank,
- drawer's signature,
- place and date of issue,
- the word "at sight",
- a certain sum of money in words and figures, and
- name of the payee or his/her order.

10.3.3 Classification of Cheques 支票的分类

A cheque can be classified based on various criteria. Below are some important classifications based on different criteria:

♦ **Cheque payable to order & cheque payable to bearer** 记名支票和来人支票

A cheque payable to order must be signed by the specified person when it is cashed, while a cheque payable to bearer can be cashed without signature of the holder and transferring of the cheque requires no endorsement.

♦ **Crossed cheque & open (uncrossed) cheque 划线支票和开放支票**

Most cheques bear two bold parallel lines on it, which are called "the crossing". A crossing is an instruction to the paying bank that the money should be paid only to another bank that functions as agent of the payee, instead of straight to the payee. Therefore, a crossing restricts payment of a cheque.

♦ **Certified cheque & uncertified cheque 已认证支票和未认证支票**

A "certified" **stamp** on a cheque indicates that the paying bank has collected the corresponding amount of money from the drawer. So, a certified cheque will not be **dishonored**. Without the stamp, a cheque would be uncertified, meaning that the paying bank hasn't collected the money from the drawer. Therefore, an uncertified cheque will be dishonored by the paying bank. It is a **bounced or bad cheque**.

印章

拒付

遭拒付的空头支票

10.4 Bill of Exchange, Promissory Note and Cheque Compared 汇票、本票和支票比较

All of the three are negotiable instruments that can be used for settling international transactions, although promissory notes and cheques are used only in limited regions or countries. Both a bill of exchange and a cheque are orders of payment while a promissory note is a promise of payment. A cheque is a special form of bill of exchange in that its drawee/payer is a bank.

As the exporter, you can draw a bill of exchange, requesting the importer or his/her bank (depending on the payment arrangement) to pay you or your order (such as your bank or supplier). In the case of a time bill that has been **accepted**, you (or other payee specified on the bill) have the option to trade the bill to another party, such as a bank, to get the money sooner.

承兑

On rare occasions, the importer may take the initiative to pay by issuing a promissory note to you. When you get the note, you may also transfer it to another party to get payment sooner.

Alternatively, the importer may write a cheque, instructing his/her bank to pay you or your order, and you can then cash the cheque, deposit it into your bank account or transfer it to another party. See a comparison of bills of exchange, promissory notes and cheques in Table 10-2.

Table 10-2 Bill of Exchange, Promissory Note and Cheque Compared

Item	Bill of exchange	Promissory note	Cheque
Parties involved	drawer, drawee, payee	drawer, drawee	drawer, drawee, payee
Drawer in international trade	exporter	importer	importer
Drawee/payer in international trade	importer/importer's bank	importer	importer's bank
Time of payment	on demand/after sight	on demand/after sight	at sight only
Acceptance	required for time bill	not required	not required
Copies	one set (in duplicate)	one copy	one copy

Exercises 练习

I. True or False

1. In international trade, the drawee of a bill of exchange is usually the exporter or the exporter's bank. (   )
2. A "To Order" bill of exchange is negotiable. (   )
3. A "To Bearer" bill of exchange can be transferred by endorsement. (   )
4. Theoretically, a time bill of exchange can be negotiated countless times before it is due. (   )
5. Blank endorsement means no endorsement. (   )
6. Bankers' accepted bills of exchange are more popular than commercial accepted ones. (   )
7. The date of a bill of exchange shall be prior to that of the contract. (   )
8. A banker's promissory note is usually payable at sight. (   )

9. A crossed cheque is payable directly to the payee. (   )

10. Uncertified cheques will be dishonored by the paying bank. (   )

II. Multiple Choice Questions

1. The payee of a bill of exchange can be filled out in three ways. According to the provisions of the *Law on Negotiable Instruments* of China, a bill that is issued (   ) is invalid.
   [A] payable to a named party only
   [B] payable to order
   [C] payable to bearer
   [D] payable to a named party not negotiable
2. The title of a bill of exchange refers to (   ) of the bill.
   [A] the drawer [B] the drawee
   [C] the payee [D] the time span
3. Among bills of exchange, promissory notes and cheques, (   ) are used most for international transactions.
   [A] bills of exchange [B] promissory notes
   [C] cheques [D] traveler's cheques
4. A bill of exchange is a document issued by (   ) ordering the drawee to pay unconditionally to the payee or bearer a fixed amount at sight or on a specified date.
   [A] the acceptor [B] the payee
   [C] the drawer [D] the drawee
5. Presentation is the act of the payee or holder of a bill of exchange to present it to (   ) for payment or acceptance.
   [A] the drawee [B] the payee
   [C] the exporter [D] the negotiating bank
6. Acceptance is the act of (   ) to accept the liability of payment for a time bill of exchange when it is due.
   [A] the drawee [B] the payee
   [C] the exporter [D] the negotiating bank
7. A promissory note is a document issued by (   ) promising to pay unconditionally at sight to the payee or bearer a fixed amount.
   [A] The drawer himself/herself [B] the acceptor
   [C] the drawee [D] the negotiating bank

8. When issuing a cheque, the drawer should keep a deposit with the paying bank for no less than the face value of the check, otherwise, this check is called (　　).

   [A] a bounced cheque　　[B] a crossed cheque
   [C] a cash cheque　　[D] a transfer cheque

9. The drawee of a bill of exchange under a documentary collection should be (　　).

   [A] the presenting bank　　[B] the remitting bank
   [C] the collecting bank　　[D] the importer

10. If A endorses a bill of exchange to B, and B to C, and the bill is due when it comes to C, but is dishonored by the drawee/payer. How could you cope with this if you were C? (　　)

    [A] I can only initiate a recourse to B.
    [B] I can only initiate a recourse to A.
    [C] I can initiate a recourse to either A or B.
    [D] I can initiate a recourse to neither A nor B.

III. Case Study

1. Discuss in a group of 4 or 5 how to draw a bill of exchange under D/P for a product you want to export and hand in the result of your discussion as group work.
2. In February of a certain year, ERC, a Chinese company, reached an export contract with IML, a French company, under payment terms of D/P 120 days after sight. Bank C of China sent the documents to the French collecting bank F, but did not receive payment even in August. Therefore, at the request of ERC, Bank C instructed Bank F to return the documents. However, it learned that F had released the documents to IML against acceptance and the importer would not pay under various excuses. Bank C believed that Bank F was liable for incorrectly releasing the documents, so it asked the latter to pay instead, but the French bank insisted that it had done nothing wrong. On October 28, Bank F informed Bank C that the importer had declared bankruptcy, with the court's notice attached, which resulted in the exporter's losing of both money and goods. What lesson can we learn from this case?

Chapter 11 Methods of Payment (2)—Letter of Credit

第十一章 支付方式（2）——信用证

Learning Objectives:

◆ An introduction to and a definition of letter of credit
◆ Participants, flowchart and characteristics of a transaction by letter of credit
◆ Exporter's task under a transaction by letter of credit
◆ Major types of letter of credit

As explained in Chapter 9, security of goods and payment in international trade is an issue that **obsessed** both importer and exporter. 困扰 As exporter, you may reason, "If a bank in the importer's country could help me collect the money, that would be better", which is precisely the logic behind a documentary collection. However, under this arrangement, the banks involved do not guarantee to acquire the money for you, but only work as agents and follow your instructions. Then you may wish the banks play a more responsible role. So does the importer. Such thinking leads to the innovation of a letter of credit (L/C), which safeguards both money and merchandise in an ingenious way. In this chapter, we'll be exploring its rationale and workflow—though it is not an intuitive process at first encounter, I will try to make it **accessible** to 容易理解的 beginners like you.

11.1 An Introduction to Letter of Credit 信用证简介

A letter of credit, as the oldest and an extremely successful tool in support of transactions between physically distant parties, can date back to the Renaissance in Europe. However, its relatively recent **predecessor** is a **traveler's letter of credit** in the late 19th and early 20th centuries. In that pre-ATM era, how was a traveler supposed to have cash on hand as he/she moved from country to country? And how was he/she able to keep his/her traveling funds protected from theft and robbery? Before the ATM was the credit card, and before the credit card was the **travelers' check**. Both are still in use today. But before any of these there was the **Circular Letter of Credit**, also known as the traveler's letter of credit, which was issued by the traveler's bank and served as a **letter of introduction**, allowing him/her to withdraw cash from other banks along his/her journey. To obtain such a letter of credit, the traveler normally needed to make a **deposit** as **collateral** and pay a fee to his/her bank.

前任
旅行者信用证
旅行者支票
循环信用证
介绍信
押金　抵押

A documentary credit, a type of **credit** with necessary documents accompanying the collecting process, is now more of a payment mechanism in support of commercial instead of consumptive transactions. It is by nature a conditioned guarantee to pay made by a bank on behalf of the importer, the conditions being terms drafted as per but independent of the sales contract. In a transaction via a documentary credit, a bank, as the entrusted intermediary, will not release the document of title to the goods and other documents until the importer has either paid or **undertaken** to pay; meanwhile, the exporter won't get payment from the bank unless he/she meets requirements in the credit by presenting required documents to the bank. In import and export, a letter of credit mostly refers to a documentary credit.

信用证
承诺

A letter of credit (documentary credit), as the name indicates, is a "letter" written by a bank to the exporter to **testify** the importer's **credit standing** and allow the exporter to **rest assured** in doing business with the importer but also **bind** the exporter to act strictly in accordance with

证明　信用状况
放心
约束

the credit terms. To issue a credit, a bank typically requires a deposit from the importer as collateral and charges a fee at a percentage of the amount covered by the credit.

11.2 Definition in *UCP 600*《跟单信用证统一惯例》中的概念

Most documentary credits are governed by rules **promulgated** by the International Chamber of Commerce known as ***Uniform Customs and Practice for Documentary Credits (UCP)***. *UCP 600,* the latest version of this document, defines a credit as any arrangement, however named or described, that is irrevocable and thereby constitutes a definite undertaking of the issuing bank to **honor** a complying presentation, in which honor means either one of the following three behaviors of the bank:

(1) to pay at sight if the credit is available by sight payment.

(2) to incur a deferred payment undertaking and pay at maturity if the credit is available by deferred payment.

(3) to accept a bill of exchange (draft) drawn by the beneficiary and pay at maturity if the credit is available by acceptance.

颁布

《跟单信用证统一惯例》

信用证不论其名称或描述如何，意指任何不可撤销的安排，因此构成开证行对相符交单予以**兑付**的确定承诺。

对于即期付款信用证即期付款。

对于延期付款信用证，则发出延期付款承诺并在到期日付款。

对于承兑信用证，承兑受益人开出的汇票，并在到期时付款。

11.3 Participants and Flowchart 参与方和流程图

A number of parties might be involved in a credit transaction, each playing a different role. Some of the roles are more basic to the transaction, while other roles are derived from the basic roles in order to facilitate a transaction.

11.3.1 Basic Roles 基本角色

Among the parties engaged in a credit transaction, three of them—the applicant, the issuing bank and the beneficiary play the basic roles. They form the basic bank-intermediated relationship between the importer and the exporter (see Figure 11-1).

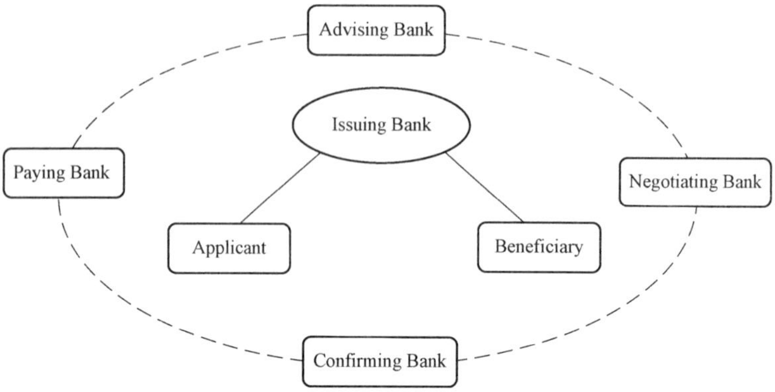

Figure 11-1 Major Parties Involved in a Documentary Credit Transaction

申请人

♦ **The applicant** is normally the importer who applies for a credit to be issued by the issuing bank based on a deposit and a fee.

开证行

♦ **The issuing bank**, based on the deposit made by the applicant and other criteria, issues the credit as requested by the applicant and charges a fee.

受益人

♦ **The beneficiary** is the party entitled to receive the payment, which is normally you, the exporter.

11.3.2 Derivative Roles 衍生角色

通知行 付款行
议付行 保兑行
衍生于

Other parties are also involved in this process, such as **the advising bank**, **the paying bank**, **the negotiating bank**, **the confirming bank**, etc., but their roles are of a derivative nature as they **are derived from** the basic relationship among the applicant, the issuing bank and the beneficiary. And for cost reasons, some roles are often played by the same party.

♦ **The advising bank 通知行**

通知
以你方为受益人
转交
传输
鉴伪 无辜的

The advising bank, located in your country, is the one that **advises**, meaning informs you, that a credit has been issued **in your favor** and **forwards** the credit to you. It has no responsibility to make payment unless it also plays the role of a confirming bank or a negotiating bank. It is needed mainly because the credit has to be **transmitted** through and **authenticated** by the banking system. There were cases where **innocent** exporters suffer losses from **relying on fraudulent** "credits" that are actually sent from post-offices or unknown **credit cooperatives**. Your bank is often nominated by the issuing bank as the advising bank for convenience and for saving cost.

相信欺诈性的
信用合作社

♦ **The paying bank 付款行**

The paying bank is the one nominated by the issuing bank to pay you against your presentation of stipulated documents. In some cases, there is a bank that is willing to accept the nomination, make payment to you and get **reimbursement** from the issuing bank, such as the advising bank. Otherwise, the issuing bank per se shall act as the paying bank.

偿付

♦ **The negotiating bank 议付行**

The negotiating bank is the one that buys the set of **complying documents** at a slightly less value than the face value of the bill of exchange and sells them to the issuing bank at the full amount. It thus makes a profit by buying low and selling high. This role is generally also assumed by the advising bank for convenience. Note that here "negotiate" means "transfer something by selling it". Negotiating the documents to a willing bank enables you to get the money sooner, though at a slightly smaller amount.

相符单据

♦ **The confirming bank 保兑行**

Sometimes, when the issuing bank is small or less known, you may still feel uncomfortable in doing business with the importer even under a documentary credit. In that case, you may wish to obtain a confirmation to pay from a large or well-known bank. The confirming bank is the one that adds its **commitment** to honor the credit. Should the issuing bank refuse to pay under a complying presentation, you may claim payment from the confirming bank, which must pay you **without recourse**. This role could also be played by the advising bank.

承诺
无权追索

As you may have noticed, various derivative roles might exist for a letter of credit—the advising bank, the paying bank, the negotiating bank, the confirming bank and your bank—but in order to speed up transaction and save cost, they all can be assumed by just one party—your bank.

11.3.3 Flowchart of a Credit Transaction 信用证交易的流程图

I've drawn a flowchart to show how a letter of credit works, which can be roughly divided into three stages of issuance, shipment and payment (see Figure 11-2).

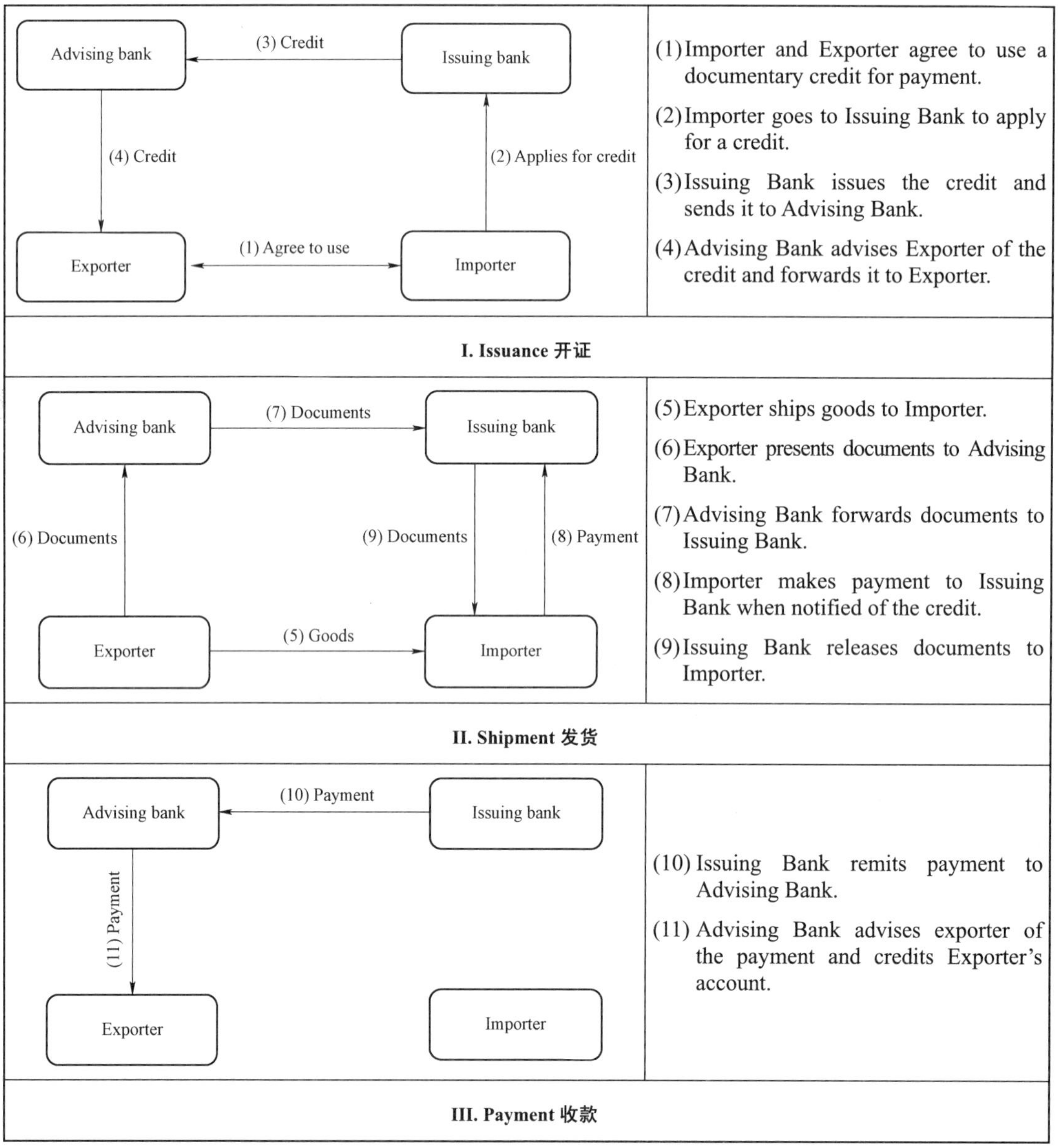

Figure 11-2 Flowchart of a Credit Transaction

11.4 Characteristics of a Letter of Credit 信用证的特征

To make the most of a letter of credit to your advantage, you need to keep in mind the following important features of a credit transaction, which are stipulated in *UCP 600*.

Firstly, a credit transaction is independent of the sales contract. A credit may be issued as per the sales contract, or even contain wordings like "other terms as per contract No. XXX", but once it takes effect, it is a separate transaction from the sales contract that is backed by a banker's credit. The banks are in no way concerned with or bound by such contracts, but only follows instructions in the application submitted by the importer. As long as the documents you have presented comply with the credit, the issuing bank or the confirming bank (if any) should fulfill its own undertaking to pay, regardless of other parties' attitudes or actions.

Secondly, a letter of credit represents a transaction of documents. When a credit is used, all parties concerned deal with documents instead of goods, services or other performances to which the documents may relate. As long as the documents you have presented are in complete compliance with terms of the credit, the issuing bank or the bank nominated by the credit shall fulfill the undertaking to pay, accept or negotiate.

Thirdly, the primary undertaking to make payment rests with the issuing bank. This implies, even if the applicant is bankrupt or in default, the issuing bank still has to pay under a complying presentation. In the case of a confirmed credit, the confirming bank must honor the credit without recourse even when the issuing bank refuses to pay.

These stipulations may seem **counter intuitive** at first sight, but if you put yourself in the shoes of a bank, the logic will be clear—banks are no experts of goods, thus it is just impossible for them to investigate 违反直觉的

every detail of the goods before they can honor a credit. And if they had to reference the sales contract for every decision to pay or not to pay, they would be frequently plunged into dilemmas—which document should they abide by? The credit or the contract? If a bank had to do all these, it may probably **avert** issuing a credit, as this would be too **cumbersome** and inconvenient and too much cost.

避免
麻烦的

11.5 Sample of a Letter of Credit 信用证样本

Traditionally, a letter of credit was transmitted by airmail, telegraph or telex, but beginning in 1973, with the creation of **SWIFT (Society for Worldwide Interbank Financial Telecommunication)**, banks began to **migrate** to **electronic data interchange** as a means for controlling cost. SWIFT has made two important contributions in this endeavor: Firstly, it builds up a secure platform on which financial institutions can communicate with each other in a reliable and efficient manner. It is widely used for sending a **wire transfer**, issuing a letter of credit, **advising a discrepancy**, etc. Secondly, it establishes standard and secure message formats for communication. Each message type has a particular code, called a SWIFT message type. For example, MT 700 is the code for issuing a documentary credit and MT 707 for amending a credit (MT means Message Type). Today, the vast majority of documentary credits are issued in electronic form via SWIFT, making "paperless" credits a standard in the industry. Table 11-1 below is a credit transmitted through SWIFT codes.

全球银行间金融电信协会
转移　电子数据交换
电汇
通知不符点

Table 11-1 A Letter of Credit Transmitted Through SWIFT Codes

FIELD NAME	TAG	TEXT
MESSAGE TYPE	700	ISSUE OF A DOCUMENTARY CREDIT
SENDER		BANK OF CHINA SINGAPORE
RECEIVER		BANK OF CHINA TIANJIN BRANCH, CHINA
SEQUENCE OF TOTAL	27	1/1
FORM OF DOC. CREDIT	40A	IRREVOCABLE
DOC. CREDIT NUMBER	20	KOS879
DATE OF ISSUE	31C	20220510
APPLICABLE RULES	40E	UCP 600
DATE AND PLACE OF EXPIRY	31D	DATE 20220725 PLACE IN CHINA
APPLICANT	50	SINGAPORE WONKA TRADING COMPANY LTD 67 ANG MO KIO AVENUE 8 SINGAPORE 560250
BENEFICIARY	59	TIANJIN BINHAI IMPORT & EXPORT CO., LTD. NO.188 HAIHE ROAD BINHAI DISTRICT TIANJIN
AMOUNT	32B	CURRENCY USD AMOUNT 262,500.00
AVAILABLE WITH/BY	41D	ANY BANK IN CHINA BY NEGOTIATION
DRAFTS AT	42C	AT SIGHT
DRAWEE	42A	BANK OF CHINA SINGAPORE
PARTIAL SHIPMENT	43P	NOT ALLOWED
TRANSSHIPMENT	43T	NOT ALLOWED
LOADING IN...	44A	TIANJIN CHINA
FOR TRANSPORT TO...	44B	SINGAPORE
LATEST DATE OF SHIPMENT	44C	20220615
DESCRIPTION OF GOODS	45A:	3,000 PCS OF SWIMMING SUITS MEN'S SUITS 1,500 PCS IN 3 SIZES AND WOMEN'S SUITS 1,500 PCS IN 3 SIZES ALL DETAILS AS PER SALES CONTRACT NO. TBIM - SWTC - 09.
DOCUMENTS REQUIRED	46A	+ SIGNED COMMERCIAL INVOICE IN TRIPLICATE + PACKING LIST IN TRIPLICATE + CERTIFICATE OF CHINESE ORIGIN CERTIFIED BY CHAMBER OF COMMERCE OR CCPIT + FULL SET OF CLEAN ON BOARD OCEAN BILLS OF LADING MADE OUT TO ORDER MARKED FREIGHT PREPAID AND NOTIFY APPLICANT + FULL SET OF INSURANCE POLICY ISSUED BY PICC + SHIPPING ADVICE PROVIDING FULL DETAILS OF SHIPMENT

continued

FIELD NAME	TAG	TEXT
		+ BENEFICIARY'S CERTIFICATION TO THE EFFECT THAT ALL TERMS AND CONDITIONS OF THIS CREDIT HAVE BEEN COMPLIED WITH
ADDITIONAL CONDITION	47A	+ THE NUMBER AND THE DATE OF THIS CREDIT AND THE NAME OF ISSUING BANK MUST BE QUOTED ON ALL DOCUMENTS EXCEPT INSURANCE POLICY + ALL PRESENTATIONS CONTAINING DISCREPANCIES WILL INCUR A DISCREPANCY FEE OF USD 75.00 PLUS CHARGE WHICH WILL BE DEDUCTED FROM THE BILL AMOUNT WHETHER OR NOT WE SELECT TO CONSULT THE APPLICANT FOR A WAIVER
CHARGES	71B	ALL BANKING CHARGES OUTSIDE THE ISSUING BANK ARE FOR ACCOUNT OF BENEFICIARY
PERIOD FOR PRESENTATION	48	UNTIL THE 21ST DAY AFTER THE DATE OF SHIPMENT, BUT WITHIN THE VALIDITY OF THIS CREDIT
CONFIRMATION INSTRUCTION	49	WITHOUT
INFORMATION TO PRESENTING BANK	78	COURIER TO BANK OF CHINA SINGAPORE 4 BATTERY ROAD, SINGAPORE 049908

11.6 Exporter's Tasks Under a Letter of Credit 信用证下的出口商任务

Take a look at Figure 11-3 for an overview of a transaction under a letter of credit, then you'll have a sense of what you have to do. Your tasks under a letter of credit include the following in succession (see Figure 11-4): agreeing to use a credit for payment, collecting it from the advising bank, examining and amending it (if necessary), shipping the goods and presenting the documents, and obtaining the payment.

11.6.1 Agreeing to Use a Letter of Credit for Payment 同意使用信用证付款

If you want to use a letter of credit as the payment method, you need to negotiate with the importer and have him/her agree to use it for your transaction. If the importer consents, specify it in your sales contract.

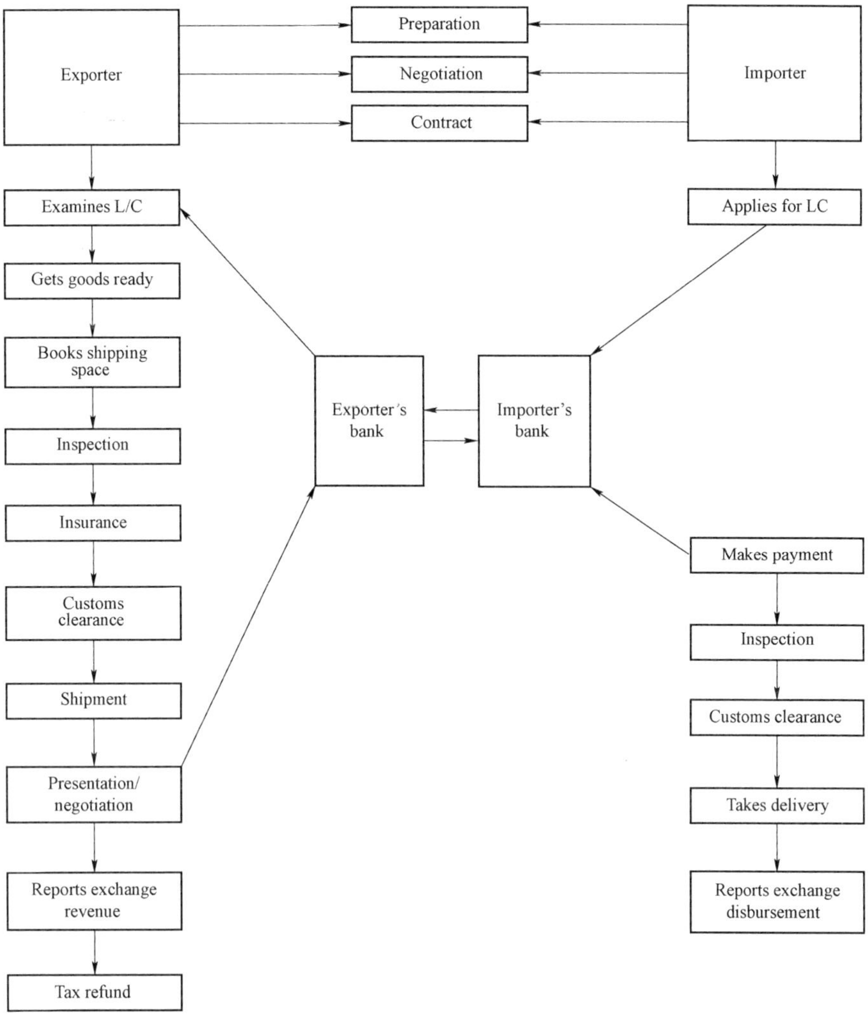

Figure 11-3 An Overview of The Transaction Under a Letter of Credit

(reference: http://www.pocib.com/baike/%E5%B1%A5%E7%BA%A6%E6%B5%81%E7%A8%8B.html)

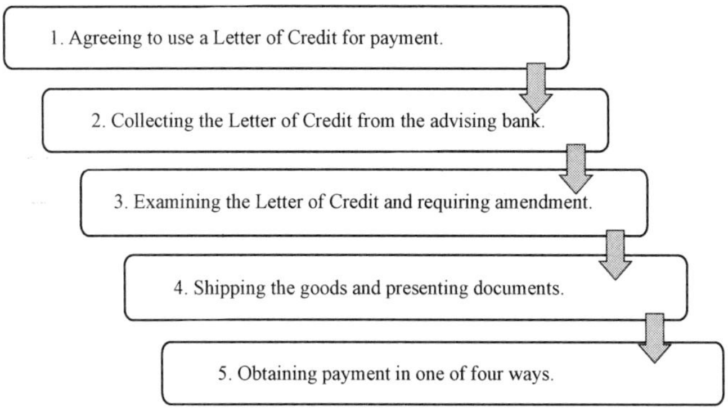

Figure 11-4 An Exporter's Task Under a Letter of Credit Transaction

11.6.2 Collecting the Letter of Credit from the Advising Bank 从通知行处拿回信用证

Once a need for a credit is specified in the contract, the importer requests his/her bank to issue the credit. The issuing bank issues the credit and transmits it to the advising bank which then advises you that the credit has arrived, and you go to the advising bank and collect it. The advising bank is **the correspondent bank** of the issuing bank in your country. Normally your bank is appointed as the advising bank for convenience.

代理银行

11.6.3 Examining the Letter of Credit and Requiring Amendment 审核和修改信用证

Before you sign the sales contract with the importer, remember to examine not only the importer's reputation, but also that of the importer's (issuing) bank before agreeing to rely upon that bank for payment under a letter of credit. Once the credit is received, you must examine all terms of the credit with care to see whether there are errors, discrepancies with the contract or any terms that you are unable to comply with, particularly those that require a document which is dependent on the signature or approval of the importer, *because, by refusing to sign such documents, the importer could refuse to pay.* If you find problems listed above, notify the importer in no time and ask him/her to make an amendment to the credit. To reduce the possibility of amendment and the fees incurred, you'd better add a term in the contract to the effect that "all terms of the L/C must be confirmed by the exporter before the importer opens it".

11.6.3.1 Recommended steps to examine a credit 审核信用证的建议步骤

Step 1: You examine the credit.

Step 2: If you find errors or **discrepancies**, ask the importer to make amendments and inform the advising bank of the request.

不符点

Step 3: The importer requests the issuing bank to issue an **amendment**.

修改书

Step 4: The issuing bank issues the amendment.

Step 5: The advising bank advises the amendment to you (repeat step 1 to 5 until the credit is acceptable to you).

11.6.3.2 Notes on amendment to a credit 修改信用证的注意事项

When it comes to an amendment initiated by the importer, three points need to be highlighted: First, you must notify both the importer and the advising bank of your acceptance or rejection of the amendment. Some exporters may forget to notify the advising bank of their acceptance, then the original credit or the one that incorporates previously accepted amendment shall still be in force. Second, acceptance of an amendment can also be indicated by your act. For example, in case you forget to notify the advising bank of an amendment, but have presented the documents in a manner that they comply with the credit and any not yet accepted amendment, your presentation shall be deemed as your acceptance of this amendment. And as of that moment, the credit is amended. Third, you cannot accept an amendment partially. A partial acceptance shall be deemed to be notification of your rejection of the amendment.

当涉及买方提出的修改条款时，需要强调三点：第一，你必须将你接受或拒绝这项修改的意见通知到买方和通知行。有些出口商会忘记告知通知行他们同意修改的意见，这样原信用证或包含先前已接受修改的信用证仍然有效。第二，如果你忘记告知通知行，但提交的单据符合信用证及任何尚未被接受的修改，那么你提交单据的行为将被视为你接受该修改。从那一刻起，信用证被修改。第三，你不能部分接受一项修改提议，部分接受修改将被视为你拒绝接受修改的通知。

11.6.4 Shipping the Goods and Presenting Documents 发货并提交单据

Once all the credit terms are acceptable to you, you ship the goods, get the shipping document and other documents for presenting them all to the **designated** bank. Presenting the documents is critical as any discrepancy will result in **dishonor** on the part of the bank. Make sure you have noted the following basic principles for presenting documents: You should ship the goods before the date of latest shipment; all the documents should be presented before the **expiry** date of the credit; all the documents should comply with the credit terms; and all the documents should be consistent with each other.

指定的

拒付

失效

11.6.5 Obtaining Payment in One of Four Ways 通过四种方式之一取得款项

A credit must state whether it is available by **sight payment**, **deferred payment**, **acceptance** or **negotiation**. In a SWIFT credit, it appears as one of the following four types of wording.

即期付款

延期付款 承兑 议付

11.6.5.1 "credit available by sight payment" 通过即期付款取得款项

When a credit is available by sight payment, the amount of the credit is available to you as soon as the terms of the credit are met. This

在即期信用证下，如果信用证的条款得到满足，你可立即获得信用证的款项。这是通过付款银行兑付你向其开出的汇票来实现的。一旦付款行对相符的交单进行付款，它就不能对你进行追索。

is achieved by the paying bank's honoring the bill of exchange you have drawn on it. Once the paying bank makes payment against a complying presentation, it cannot take recourse to you.

然而，请注意：当提交单据时，为了方便和省钱，通常只有两家银行参与。在第一种情况下，开证行将你的银行指定为付款行。在第二种情况下，开证行本身充当付款行并付款。两者之间的区别是，在第一种情况下，你可以比在第二种情况下提前获得付款，因为在第二种情况下，你必须等待，直到开证行偿付你的银行。

Please note, however, when you present the documents, normally only two banks are involved for convenience and for saving money. In the first scenario, the issuing bank nominates your bank as the paying bank. In the second, the issuing bank per se acts as the paying bank and makes the payment. The difference between the two is—in the first scenario, you could get payment sooner than in the second, as in the second case, you must wait until the issuing bank reimburses your bank.

11.6.5.2 "credit available by deferred payment" 通过延期付款取得款项

在延期付款信用证下，你无须开出汇票。开证行收到相符单据时，仅仅通过一封承诺书承诺在未来某个日期付款，然后到期时向你付款并在那时获得单据。

When the credit is available by deferred payment, you don't need to draw a bill of exchange. The issuing bank, on receiving complying presentation of documents, merely promises to pay at a future date with a letter of undertaking, and pays when the time is due and gets hold of the documents at that time.

11.6.5.3 "credit available by acceptance" 通过承兑取得款项

对于承兑信用证，付款行承兑你开出的汇票，并在到期时付款，但会在承兑时即获得单据。根据承兑信用证开出的汇票通常有 60 至 180 天的期限。付款行通常是开证行本身

When a credit is available by acceptance, the paying bank accepts the bill of exchange you have drawn on it and pays at maturity, but it gets hold of the documents when it makes the acceptance. Bills drawn under an acceptance credit normally have a term of 60 to 180 days. The paying bank is normally the issuing bank per se.

11.6.5.4 "credit available by negotiation" 通过议付取得款项

当议付方式获得货款时，你可以通过将单据转让（出售）给愿意以低于信用证全部金额的价格购买单据的银行，从而提前获得汇票项下的款项。这家银行被称为议付行，议付行将按照全部汇票金额再将单据转让（出售）给开证行。这种安排能使你更快地拿到钱，同时议付行获取一笔利润。

When a credit is available by negotiation, you can get the money under the bill of exchange in advance by transferring (selling) the documents to a bank which is willing to buy the documents at a lower price than the full amount of the credit. This bank is called the negotiating bank, which will in turn transfer (sell) the documents to the issuing bank at the full amount of the bill. This arrangement enables you to get money sooner and the negotiation bank to make a profit. As you can see, negotiating a credit best exemplifies what a transaction of documents is.

汇票的付款由开证行保证，条件是你提交的单据符合要求。然而，如果开证行基于有效的但未被议

Honoring of the bill of exchange is guaranteed by the issuing bank on condition of a complying presentation. However, what if the issuing bank refuses to reimburse based on valid discrepancies which were not identified by the negotiating bank at the time of negotiation? As there is no saying in *UCP 600* that the negotiating bank can have recourse to the beneficiary in the event the issuing bank fails to reimburse the negotiating bank, a negotiation can be one with or without recourse to you, depending on the agreement between you and the negotiating bank. But if the negotiating bank is also the confirming bank, the negotiation is without recourse to you.

付行发现的不符点拒绝偿付怎么办呢？由于《跟单信用证统一惯例》（2007年修订版）中没有规定在开证行拒绝偿付议付行时议付行对受益人是否具有追索权，因此，议付对你可以是有追索权的，也可以是无追索权的，取决于你和议付行之间的协议。但是如果议付行同时也是保兑行，该议付对你是无追索权的。

A credit is available by negotiation in two cases: by a nominated bank, or by any bank. The most common type of negotiation credit allows negotiation by any bank. Rarely is it limited to specified banks.

可议付信用证可在两种情况下通过议付得到付款：通过指定银行议付，通过任何银行议付。最常见的议付允许任何银行议付。只有很少的情况下议付限于指定银行。

11.7 Types of Letter of Credit 信用证的类型

"Letter of credit" is actually an umbrella term, which covers many different types of credit, including both standard credits with minor variations and special types devised to meet requirements of special use cases.

11.7.1 Sight, Deferred, Acceptance and Negotiation Letter of Credits 即期付款信用证，延期付款信用证，承兑信用证，议付信用证

See discussion above in 11.6.5 Obtaining Payment in One of Four Ways.

11.7.2 Confirmed and Unconfirmed Letters of Credit 保兑和未保兑信用证

Sometimes, even if a letter of credit has been agreed to for payment, you may still feel concerned in doing business with the importer, as you know little about the issuing bank, which in some cases, could be a foreign bank with **shoddy** reputation. In that case, you may wish to request a well-known bank other than the issuing bank to confirm the credit by adding its undertaking to pay to that of the issuing bank. If a certain bank is willing to do this and does confirm, this credit becomes a confirmed credit and this bank is called a confirming bank.

低劣的

The confirming bank is often nominated by the issuing bank and normally is the advising bank. It should be noted that the commitment of the confirming bank is independent of that of the issuing bank, which means, as long as the documents presented comply with the terms of the confirmed credit, the confirming bank has to pay even if the issuing bank cannot or will not honor the bill of exchange for whatever reasons. Therefore, confirmed credits are more expensive than unconfirmed ones because of the additional risk assumed by the confirming bank.

When a credit is unconfirmed, only the issuing bank is obliged to pay. This type of credit is more common and used when traders have no doubt in the reputation and financial strength of the issuing bank or when the transaction is of small volume.

11.7.3 Transferable Letter of Credit 可转让信用证

This type of credit is preferred by trading companies. If you are a trading company and procure goods from a manufacturer (your supplier), but cannot afford to **buy outright** and await payment from the importer, you can request a specific type of credit be opened in your favor which authorizes the advising bank to accept your instructions to transfer the **credit amount** in whole, or in part, to a third party—the manufacturer. This type of credit is called a transferable credit. It simplifies the transaction by avoiding the opening of two or more credits. Under this type of credit, you are **the first beneficiary** and the manufacturer or manufacturers **the second beneficiary**. However, no credit is transferable unless expressly indicated in the credit and notably, a transferable credit can be transferred only once—the second beneficiary cannot transfer it to any subsequent beneficiaries. The transferred credit must accurately reflect the terms and conditions of the original credit, including confirmation, if any, with the exception of: **the amount of the credit**, **any unit price stated therein**, **the expiry date**, **the period for presentation**, or **the latest date of shipment or given period for shipment**, any or all of which may be reduced or **curtailed**.

全部购买，用现金购买

信用证金额

第一受益人

第二收益人

信用证金额

信用证规定的任何单价

到期日　交单期限

最迟装运日期或规定的装运期间　缩短

11.7.4 Back-to-Back Letter of Credit 背对背信用证

When one credit is used as **surety** for the issuance of another, the parties are said to be dealing with a "back-to-back" credit transaction.

担保

Such a transaction, similar to a transferable credit, is also requested by a trading company to provide settlement to a supplier from whom the goods are procured.

11.7.5 Usance Letter of Credit Payable at Sight 即期付款的远期信用证

A **usance** credit payable at sight is a usance credit under which the issuing bank undertakes to pay you at sight against complying documents. When the bill of exchange is due, the applicant reimburses the issuing bank. It is **credit** offered by the issuing bank to the applicant and the interest thereof is normally borne by the applicant.

远期的

信用

11.7.6 Standby Letter of Credit 备用信用证

A standby letter of credit, as the name indicates, is a **standby**, meaning that it is a credit that is ready to be used when needed, but the credit is "called on" only in the worst-case scenario—the importer defaults or delays on payment. It usually has a much longer validity period, sometimes longer than a year to meet the needs of an exporter who makes a series of shipments to a customer. This eliminates the need for opening a new credit for each shipment over a relatively longer period. The usage for standby letter of credit is regulated by the ***International Stand-By Practices (ISP 98)***.

备用品

《国际备用信用证惯例》

11.7.7 Revolving Letter of Credit 循环信用证

A revolving letter of credit is a single letter of credit that covers multiple transactions over a long period of time. Like a standby credit, it is also used when you make regular shipments of the same commodity to the same importer. The credit amount may revolve either in time or in value within the validity of this single credit. If you can draw a fixed amount within each specific period of time (such as a month) as indicated in the credit until it expires, this credit revolves in time. Depending on whether or not any unused portions can be drawn on the subsequent periods, it could further be a cumulative or non-cumulative

补充

credit. If the fixed amount is **replenished** every time just after you utilize it within the overall validity of the credit, this credit revolves in value. Revolving letters of credit also avoid the need for opening a new credit for every transaction.

Exercises 练习

I. True or False

1. As exporter, you are suggested to set a deadline in the contract for the importer to open the L/C. (   )
2. The issuing bank and the paying bank cannot be the same bank. (   )
3. As an L/C is opened in accordance with the contract, it is bound by the contract. (   )
4. The advising bank for an L/C has an obligation to make the payment to the beneficiary. (   )
5. If the applicant of an L/C is bankrupt, the issuing bank can refuse to pay the beneficiary even under a complying presentation of documents. (   )
6. Under a confirmed L/C, both the issuing bank and the confirming bank assume primary undertaking for payment. (   )
7. If the documents presented by the exporter comply with the L/C, but not the sales contract, the issuing bank can refuse to pay. (   )
8. If you agree to an amendment to an L/C, you must inform your agreement both to the importer and the advising bank. (   )
9. An L/C is deemed transferable even if it does not indicate "transferable". (   )
10. If the L/C does not indicate whether "partial shipments are allowed", they are deemed to be allowed. (   )

II. Multiple Choice Questions

1. If the on-board date is July 15, and the L/C is valid till August 15. According to *UCP 600*, the latest date of presentation by the beneficiary to the bank is (   ).

   [A] July 15

   [B] August 5

[C] August 15

[D] August 6

2. When payment is to be made by ( ), a bank undertakes to pay.

[A] a telegraphic transfer

[B] a documentary collection

[C] a documentary credit

[D] a demand draft

3. Which of the following party should NOT be the drawee of a bill of exchange drawn under an L/C? ( )

[A] The issuing bank.

[B] The paying bank.

[C] The confirming bank.

[D] The importer.

4. The drawer of a bill of exchange under an L/C is ( ).

[A] the issuer of the L/C

[B] usually the applicant of the L/C

[C] usually the negotiating bank of the L/C

[D] usually the exporter or beneficiary of the L/C

5. The confirming bank of a confirmed L/C can refuse to pay if ( ).

[A] the product quality does not conform to the contract

[B] the applicant goes bankrupt

[C] the issuing bank goes bankrupt

[D] the documents presented do not comply with the credit

6. Which of the following requirements for documents under an L/C is acceptable to the exporter? ( )

[A] One of the original B/Ls should be airmailed straight to the applicant.

[B] The inspection certificate should be signed by the applicant.

[C] The documents should be presented within 21 days after shipment but prior to the credit's expiry date.

[D] The credit shall not take effect unless the carrying vessel has been approved by the applicant in the form of an amendment to the credit.

7. Which bank's payment could be with recourse to the beneficiary? ( )
   [A] The issuing bank's.
   [B] The confirming bank's.
   [C] The negotiating bank's.
   [D] The nominated paying bank's.
8. From an exporter's view, which of the following facts about an L/C does NOT necessitate an amendment to the credit? ( )
   [A] The total amount of credit in figures are not in consistent with that in words.
   [B] The place of expiry is in the importer's country.
   [C] The documents must be presented 5 days after the time of shipment but within the validity of the credit.
   [D] All banking charges outside the applicant's country are for the account of beneficiary.
9. Which of the two roles cannot be assumed by just one bank? ( )
   [A] The advising bank and the negotiating bank.
   [B] The advising bank and the confirming bank.
   [C] The advising bank and the paying bank.
   [D] The advising bank and the issuing bank.
10. Which type of the following L/C helps the beneficiary get payment sooner? ( )
   [A] An L/C by sight payment.
   [B] An L/C by negotiation with any bank.
   [C] An L/C by deferred payment.
   [D] An L/C by acceptance.

III. Case Study

1. When a deal is concluded under an L/C with the amount available by negotiation, it is customary for the exporter to draw a bill of exchange with the negotiating bank, instead of himself/herself as payee of the bill. Can you explain why? What is the difference if the exporter is filled out as the payee? Discuss in a group of 4 or 5 and try to fill out such a bill in the right way.

2. To prevent a B/L from becoming stale, the importer requires such a clause in a letter of credit that "the beneficiary should post one of the three original B/Ls straight to the applicant of the L/C by express airmail, and the post receipt should be one of the documents required and be presented to the bank with the other two original B/Ls". Is this requirement acceptable to the exporter?
3. A **UAV (unmanned aerial vehicle)** manufacturer in China entered into a deal in November 2021 with an American trading company of exporting 30 UAVs for agricultural use under Incoterm CIF, and payment by L/C at sight. The American company opened an L/C through its bank in early March 2022, which was verified to be consistent with the contract. The insured amount was 110% of the invoice amount. When the exporter was busy with production, the American company advised the exporter an amendment to the L/C through the banks, which changed the insured amount to 130% of the invoice amount. The exporter insured and delivered the goods in accordance with the original L/C, and submitted the full set of shipping documents to the negotiating bank within the validity of the L/C after shipment. After negotiation, the negotiating bank sent the full set of documents to the issuing bank, which refused to pay on the ground that the insurance policy was inconsistent with the amendment to the L/C. Is the issuing bank justified in refusing to honor the L/C? Why? 无人机

Chapter 12 Inspection, Claim, *Force Majeure* and Dispute Resolution

第十二章 检验、索赔、不可抗力和争议解决

Learning Objectives:

- ◆ How to have your goods inspected
- ◆ How to make a claim
- ◆ How to apply the *force majeure* clause
- ◆ How to resolve disputes

Either in domestic or international transactions, no one likes disputes, but they do arise and are **trickier** in international transactions because of different cultures, business conventions, laws or regulations and so forth. Statistics show that most disputes relate to quality, among other things. Therefore, an inspection clause is normally needed for an international sales contract to clarify requirements for how to inspect the goods. Should any **non-conformity** with respect to quality, quantity, packing, etc. occur, the parties could **lodge a claim** against the responsible party for loss, and in order to resolve the claim, some mechanism for **resolving disputes** should be **spelled out** in the contract.

更棘手

不符合

提出索赔

解决争议 规定

12.1 Inspection 检验

An inspection in international trade is an inspection of certain aspects of the goods by the inspection authority or a third-party inspection service of the importing and/or exporting country that aims to protect the health and safety of people, animals, plants, the environment, the interests of both importer and exporter and the security of their countries. An inspection for export can be required out of the following reasons: Firstly, the importer may demand an inspection to make sure the goods delivered conform to contract. Secondly, some countries, including China, **mandate** a **statutory inspection** for export of certain categories of goods before releasing them for overseas market, which makes sure that the merchandise for export is of the right quality, quantity and weight, and that it is safe, **sanitary**, healthy, **authentic** and environmentally friendly. Thirdly, some importing countries may require a pre-shipment inspection of certain imports or imports above a certain value, which could be based on their laws, regulations or **trade conventions**. Fourthly, both the exporting and the importing countries can request an inspection based on **bilateral or multilateral agreements** between the two countries.

要求　法定检验

卫生的　正宗的

贸易惯例

双边或多边协议

An inspection clause in an export contract should generally specify the organization to conduct the inspection, the standard and contents of the inspection and which inspection is taken as final.

Inspections for export are mostly conducted by the **inspection and quarantine authorities** under the General Administration of Customs, or by its authorized inspection services such as **Societe Generale de Surveillance S.A. (SGS)**, the most renowned inspection company based in Geneva, Switzerland. The inspection and quarantine authorities under local **customs district** administer by law all of the statutory inspections for import and export. For a statutory inspection, you can either have the goods inspected in your company's own name or authorize your freight forwarder or a **customer broker** to file an application. Either way, the application should be filed with your local customs district, or any other office designated by the Customs in order

检验检疫部门

瑞士通用公证行

关区

报关行

to speed up clearance. For non-statutory inspections, private inspection services are also available, though your contract with the importer determines which inspection institution is acceptable. The inspections should follow an agreed-upon standard and may cover quality, quantity, weight, package, health, sanitation, origin, etc., and a certificate is issued if the goods pass the inspection. For some products, the container and the trucks that hold or deliver them should also be inspected.

However, it is often not enough to merely have your goods inspected as per the contract, statutes of the government or requirements by the importing country. Sometimes, the goods pass the **pre-shipment inspection**, but fail the re-inspection at destination. This tends to cause a dispute—which inspection is **final**? The pre-shipment inspection at the exporter's side or the destination inspection at the importer's side? And how can we draft the inspection terms in a contract in order to avoid such a dispute?

装运前检验

终局的

Clearly, as either pre-shipment inspection or destination inspection favors one party and disfavors the other, neither is fair enough to both parties. This calls for a more balanced arrangement between the exporter and the importer—a combination of a pre-shipment inspection and a destination re-inspection. With such an arrangement, you may obtain payment sooner by presenting the qualified inspection certificate and other required documents when payment is by letter of credit. The importer, meanwhile, gets to retain the right to re-inspect them and, if supported by valid evidence, to claim for non-conformities as per the contract. Because of the balanced distribution of power between the importer and the exporter, such an arrangement is widely used in import and export.

12.2 Claim 索赔

A claim clause is also necessary for an international contract. It should normally specify which inspection is taken as final, the allowed period for lodging a claim, the type of inspection certificate to support the claim and the institution that is authorized to conduct the inspection and issue the certificate. In case the goods delivered are inconsistent with the contract, this clause allows the importer to lodge a claim against you, the carrier or the insurance company. But it has to be filed within the prescribed time limit and supported by the result of a re-inspection conducted by the agreed-upon inspection institution in the contract. If you are proved to be liable, and the claim is filed within the allowed period, you may consider one of the following ways for a settlement: replacing the faulty goods; giving the importer a discount; or refunding the importer for his/her direct losses or expenses. Please note, however, even though most claims are lodged by the importer against the exporter, the opposite is equally possible. For instance, you may lodge a claim against the importer for late booking of shipping space under Incoterm FOB, or for delayed taking delivery of the goods.

处罚条款 约束 罚款

Sometimes, a **penalty clause** is needed in a contract to further **bind** both parties to perform certain important contractual obligations, preventing certain behaviors such as non-delivery, delayed delivery, delayed opening of L/C, delayed taking delivery of the goods, etc. To sum up, whoever violates the contract must pay a **fine**. Notably, however, this type of clause is invalid and unenforceable under the jurisdiction of common law system.

12.3 *Force Majeure* 不可抗力

国内动乱 禁运 流行病 免除

Every contract contains some sort of a *force majeure* clause. *Force majeure* incidents are unforeseeable circumstances that prevent someone from fulfilling a contract. This term originated from French, which literally means "superior strength". These incidents can neither be anticipated nor reduced or controlled. It could be a natural disaster such as a major storm, a flood, a heavy snow, an earthquake, a volcanic eruption, etc., or a human related incident, such as a fire at the exporter's plant, a **civil unrest**, a strike at a port that delays the delivery of the goods, an **embargo** imposed by one country against another, an outbreak of **epidemic**, etc. A *force majeure* incident often results in termination or postponement of the contract and partial or total **exemption** of the affected party from fulfilling his/her liability under the contract.

However, you cannot claim anything of a nature listed above as a *force majeure* incident. It has to be **attested** to by a certificate issued by a recognized organization. Plus, a **prompt** notice must be sent to the importer in line with trade conventions and contract terms. **China Council for the Promotion of International Trade (CCPIT)** is a recognized organization that can issue such a certificate. When the 2020 COVID-19 pandemic prevented some Chinese plants from performing their contracts, CCPIT issued a certificate of *force majeure* on February 1st, 2020 to a business based in Huzhou, Zhejiang Province, attesting to the pandemic as a *force majeure* incident. This was the first of such certificates in China since the outbreak of the pandemic.

证明
迅速的
中国国际贸易促进委员会，简称贸促会

A *force majeure* clause in a contract should specify the **scope** and consequences of the *force majeure* incident, the allowed period for notifying the other party, the certificate for attesting to such incidents and the organization that issues them.

范围

12.4 Dispute Resolution 争议解决

In international trade, disputes between exporter and importer can be settled through **negotiation**, **mediation**, **arbitration** or **litigation**. Negotiation is always top choice. The majority of disputes are settled through **amicable** negotiations between exporter and importer, and business relations are maintained. If negotiation fails, mediation would be next best, followed by arbitration. Litigation, being costly and time-consuming for cross-national disputes, is never top choice. Compared with negotiation, both mediation and arbitration follow a **structured procedure**, which makes them highly executable and effective and therefore commonly regarded as alternative dispute resolutions to litigation. The International Chamber of Commerce has established frameworks for resolving international trade disputes through mediation and arbitration, which adds to their executability. It has established **the Alternative Dispute Resolution Center** and the **Mediation Rules** and **Arbitration Rules** under its administration.

协商 调解 仲裁 诉讼
友好的
结构化的程序
替代性争端解决中心
调解规则 仲裁规则

For these frameworks to work in case of a dispute, you'd better contain a clause in the contract allowing both parties to refer the case to those rules under ICC or, in the absence of such a clause, to apply for mediation, arbitration or a combination of both to the Alternative Dispute Resolution Center of ICC **unilaterally** or jointly with the importer. If agreed to by the importer, the case can also be submitted for mediation or arbitration to a third country or in China, to **China International Economic and Trade Arbitration Commission (CIETAC)** or **China Maritime Affairs Arbitration Commission**.

单边的
中国国际经济贸易仲裁委员会
中国海事仲裁委员会

In international practice, the place of arbitration is generally set in a third country agreed to by both you and the importer to ensure fairness and impartiality. Sometimes, it is also set in the country where the dispute occurs. Of course, in order to save money, efforts and time, you may try to have the case arbitrated in China, but the importer may also try to have it done in his/her country.

12.4.1 Mediation 调解

Mediation is a structured and **interactive** Alternative Dispute Resolution (ADR) mechanism where an **impartial** third party—the **mediator** works between the **disputants** to find a common ground for both parties. With the mediator **shuttling** between the parties, a mediation is expected to result in an **optimal** agreement satisfying to both parties. Some of the **merits** of mediation compared with arbitration and litigation are summarized in Table 12-1.

互动性的
公正的
调解人　争议者
穿梭
最优的
优点

12.4.2 Arbitration 仲裁

Arbitration is an Alternative Dispute Resolution (ADR) mechanism that aims to resolve disputes outside the **courts**. The dispute will be decided by one or more impartial persons—**the "arbitrators", or the "arbitral tribunal"**, which **renders the "arbitral award"**. An arbitral award is final and **binding** on both sides and enforceable in a court, which implies that neither party can bring up an **appeal** at a **law court** or any other organizations and it is also more enforceable than **a court ruling** awarded by a foreign law court.

法庭
"仲裁员"或"仲裁庭"
作出"仲裁裁决"
有约束力的
上诉　法院
法庭裁决

Table 12-1 A Comparison of Mediation, Arbitration and Litigation

	Mediation	Arbitration	Litigation
Cost	most inexpensive	more inexpensive	expensive
Confidentiality	confidential	confidential	public
Efficiency	most efficient; an agreement can be achieved in days	efficient; an award can be made in weeks	inefficient; a court ruling could take months or years to issue
Enforceability	not binding; not enforceable in a law court	binding; cannot appeal; easily recognized by a foreign law court	binding; can appeal; difficult to be recognized by a foreign law court
Choice of the third party	allowed; jointly selected by both parties	allowed; could be jointly selected by both parties	not allowed, being the judge and/or jury
Choice of language	allowed	allowed	not allowed; by court
Choice of location	allowed; mediator may shuttle between both parties	allowed; could be jointly selected by both parties	decided by court
Skills of the third party	skillful	skillful	limited by law; lack of skill
Experience of the third party	experienced, particularly in communication skills	experienced, particularly in industry specific expertise	less experienced in communication skills or industry specific expertise
Creativity of solutions	creative	creative	less creative, has to be lawful
Allowed participants	all staff of disputing parties	representatives of disputing parties	representatives of disputing parties
Context	informal	formal	most formal
Attitude of disputants	most cooperative	cooperative	may resist to unfavorable rulings
Expected outcome	a win-win solution	a win-win solution	win or lose

Take the ADR center of ICC as an example, the fairness and effectiveness **hinge** highly **on** the procedures followed by the **Arbitration Court** under the Center, particularly the **constitution** of the arbitral tribunal. The Court administers the arbitration including the

取决于
仲裁法庭 构成

首席仲裁员

承诺　公正地

establishment of the arbitral tribunal, which is set up for a particular dispute. According to the Rules, the number of arbitrators could be one or three. In the case of a sole arbitrator, it could be jointly nominated by the disputing parties or in the absence of such agreement, appointed by the Court. In the case of three arbitrators to make an arbitral tribunal, each disputing party can nominate one arbitrator independently. The third arbitrator, serving as **the presiding arbitrator**, shall be jointly nominated by the parties or appointed by the Court. The arbitrator or arbitrators must **undertake** to work **impartially** and independently on the case, which is ensured by certain key procedures, one of which requires the arbitrators to disclose any information that might lead to the questioning of their impartiality and independence; another allows for challenge raised by the disputing parties concerning an arbitrator's impartiality and independence, and if the questioning and challenge is well grounded, the Court may administer a replacement of the arbitrator or arbitrators in question. Some of the merits of arbitration compared with mediation and litigation are summarized in Table 12-1.

《承认及执行外国仲裁裁决公约》

法庭裁决

It should be noted, however, the tricky side about an arbitration lies in the difficulties of enforcing a foreign arbitral award. As an arbitral tribunal doesn't possess the enforcement power, a foreign law court is still needed for executing the award. Even though there is the ***Convention on the Recognition and Enforcement of Foreign Arbitral Awards*** in place and 142 countries have signed the Convention as of 2007, attitudes of member countries toward a foreign award vary. Some countries, such as France, Germany and Greece, treat it as a domestic award and therefore are more supportive in enforcement. Others, such as the UK and US, treat it as a liability under a contract which has to be converted into a domestic award before it can be enforced, but the conversion normally requires a review of not the contents but just procedures of the arbitration. Still others, like Italy, Spain, Portugal, Turkey, Egypt, Iran, the Philippines, Thailand, India, etc., even though are signatory countries to the Convention, treat a foreign arbitral award as a **court ruling**, so, they review not only the procedures but also the contents. Obviously, enforcing a foreign arbitral award is most difficult in the third group of countries. Sometimes, a case resolved by arbitration is even not as good as one by litigation in terms of money, efforts and time required. Therefore, when you draft the arbitration clause of your contract, don't forget to learn about the judicial environment of the importer's country or a third country.

Exercises 练习

I. True or False

1. In international trade, litigation is the preferred way for settling disputes between the importer and the exporter. ( )
2. In international trade, only the importer has the right to require an inspection. ( )
3. A statutory inspection for export ensures that the merchandise for export is of the right quality, quantity and weight, and that it is safe, **sanitary**, healthy, authentic and environmentally-friendly. ( ) 卫生的
4. The legal consequence of invoking a *force majeure* clause is to cancel the contract or delay the execution of the contract. ( )
5. An arbitration agreement must be reached by the parties for signing a contract before a dispute occurs, otherwise the dispute cannot be submitted for arbitration. ( )
6. If there is no claim clause in the contract, the importer has no right to lodge a claim. ( )
7. A claim must be made within the prescribed period of time in the contract with supporting evidence. ( )
8. When an arbitral award is rendered, the disputants can still bring up an appeal to a law court. ( )
9. A mediation agreement is not binding on the disputing parties. ( )
10. All commodities to be exported must be inspected by the commodity inspection authority under the Customs before they are exported. ( )

II. Multiple Choice Questions

1. The common method for inspecting the quality of exported products is that ( ).

   [A] pre-shipment inspection in the exporting country and re-inspection in the importing country are combined as final

[B] inspection at the port of destination is taken as final

[C] inspection at the port of loading is taken as final

[D] weight at the port of loading and quality at the port of destination are taken as final

2. In most cases, claims for short delivery shall be made on (　　).

[A] the buyer

[B] the seller

[C] the carrier

[D] the insurance company

3. In the event of (　　), the defaulting party may invoke the *force majeure* clause to claim exemption of contractual obligations.

[A] a war

[B] international price fluctuations

[C] currency devaluation

[D] mistakes in production

4. Claims in international trade include (　　).

[A] trade claims

[B] transportation claims

[C] insurance claims

[D] all the above

5. When deciding the place of arbitration for an import and export contract, which of the following country do traders generally believe to be fair to both the importer and exporter? (　　)

[A] A third country.

[B] China.

[C] The importer's country.

[D] The exporter's country.

6. Which is the CORRECT statement about "Inspection in the exporting country, re-inspection in the importing country”? (　　)

[A] It is favorable to the importer.

[B] It is favorable to the exporter.

[C] It considers the interests of both the importer and the exporter.

[D] It is favorable to the insurance company.

7. Which one of the following is an INCORRECT statement about the function of the inspection certificate? (　　)
   [A] It determines the standards and methods of inspection.
   [B] It is the certificate required for customs clearance.
   [C] It is one of the documents to be presented by the exporter for negotiation under a letter of credit.
   [D] It is evidence that the goods delivered by the exporter conform. to the provisions of the contract.
8. Which of the methods for resolving disputes has (have) binding force on the disputing parties? (　　)*
   [A] Negotiation.
   [B] Mediation.
   [C] Arbitration.
   [D] Litigation.
9. Which of the following parties may require an inspection? (　　)*
   [A] The importer.
   [B] The exporter.
   [C] The importer's country.
   [D] The exporter's country.
10. Which of the followings is (are) suggested to be specified in the contract for a claim clause? (　　)*
    [A] Which inspection is final.
    [B] The allowed period for making claims.
    [C] The re-inspection certificate.
    [D] The organization that issues the re-inspection certificate.

III. Case Study

1. A Chinese furniture manufacturer Okart Furniture Co., Ltd. concluded an export contract for 200 sets of dining tables and chairs with an American company AllNature Furniture Trading Co., Ltd., under Incoterm CIF New York. The contract stipulated the time of shipment in December 2016. At the end of November, however, Okart's warehouse caught fire, resulting in the burning of about half of the furniture. It asked AllNaure to exempt its responsibility of delivery on the ground of a *force majeure* incident. The US importer disagreed and insisted on it making delivery on time. It had no

choice but managed to deliver the goods in early January 2017, and the importer made a claim for late delivery.

Questions:

(1) Is it reasonable for Okart to ask for exemption from the delivery responsibility? Why?

(2) Is Allnature's claim reasonable? Why?

2. Craftcloth Textile & Garment Co., Ltd., a Chinese textile and garment company exported 50,000 yards of cloth to India through an India trading company Radiance Textile Co., Ltd. The contract had stipulated that the allowed period for claim was 30 days after the arrival of the goods at the port of destination. After the goods were unloaded at the port of destination they were accepted by the importer without problem. Half a year later, however, Radiance made a claim saying that the garments made by the cloth had shrunk after wash and supported it with a certificate issued by the inspection authority of India. What do you think Craftcloth should cope with this issue?

Chapter 13 Documentation

第十三章 制单

Learning Objectives:

◆ How to make or prepare the documents for export

◆ What needs to be noted when you make or prepare the documents

Documentation constitutes the core of an international transaction. While goods change hands in this process, so do documents. The movement of documents is at times even more crucial than that of the goods. Getting acquainted with documentation helps you make connections between steps in the transaction and obtain an overview of the export process.

13.1 Major Documents in the Export Process 出口中的主要单证

The documents in an export transaction might be required as per the contract or by customs authorities of both the exporting country and the importing country. In practice, as exporter, you have to make some of them and apply for others from the Customs of China, the carrier, the insurance company, etc. As documents are crucial in the transaction where one error could be fatal, you must treat them with enough patience and **meticulous** care. You must provide the right documents in the right number and submit them within the right time allowed. 一丝不苟的

13.1.1 Procedures of Export Revisited 出口流程回顾

追踪 重温

Let's learn about the common documents involved in export by roughly **tracing** the process of an export transaction. In this deal, your company—Tianjin Binhai Import & Export Co., Ltd. exports 3,000 swimming suits to Singapore Wonka Trading Company Ltd, including 1,500 men's and women's styles each, with three sizes for each style—X, XL and XXL. Both parties conclude the deal under CIF, and the Singapore company pays by a letter of credit at sight. **Revisiting** the overview of the transaction procedures in Chapter 1 would be helpful.

形式发票

1. At the preliminary stage, you produce the ***proforma* invoice** for making offers, for the importer's reference or for him/her to apply for the import license, foreign exchange or the letter of credit.

2. Once the sales are confirmed, you or the importer make(s) the contract.

商业发票 装箱单 报关单 检验证书

3. In preparing for delivery, produce **the commercial invoice**, **packing list**, **customer clearance form**, and **certificate of inspection** for customs clearance.

4. Obtain insurance.

报关单退税联 出口载货清单

5. After customs clearance, the Customs officially releases the merchandise. The copy of **the customs clearance form for tax refund** will be returned to you if the **export manifest** is clean and shows no problem, indicating that the merchandise has surely left China. You will get the copy a few days later, though the specific number of days varies by case.

6. After delivery you obtain the bill of lading in three originals and three copies.

整理 原产地证 受益人证明

7. For collecting payment, you need to produce, apply for and **sort out** all the documents required by the importer, such as the invoice, packing list, certificate of inspection, **certificate of origin** and **beneficiary certification**.

银行收汇单 清洁舱单

8. Complete tax refund. For this purpose, you normally need the **bank receipt of foreign exchanges**, the copy of customs clearance form for tax refund, **the clean export manifest**, your foreign exchange revenue reported on ASOne maintained by State Administration of

Foreign Exchange, the VAT invoice issued by your supplier and other necessary documents (depending on the transaction).

13.1.2 Major Documents in the Export Process 出口中的主要单据

In this process, the following documents might be involved:

The contract, advice of a documentary credit, a documentary credit, commercial invoice, *proforma* invoice, customs invoice, packing list, application for inspection, inspection certificate, certificate of origin, GSP FORM A, insurance policy, customs clearance form, bill of lading, shipping advice, beneficiary certification, bill of exchange, etc.

出口中的主要单据包括：合同、跟单信用证通知书、跟单信用证、商业发票、形式发票、海关发票、装箱单、检验申请、检验证书、原产地证书、GSP格式A、保险单、报关单、提单、装运通知、受益人证明和汇票等。

13.1.2.1 Contract 合同

A contract is the conclusion of a successful negotiation and the basis for preparing many other documents. Regardless of the form, some terms are common to most import or export contracts. For this reason, exporters tend to draft standardized contract for almost all their customers. However, an oversimplification may **breed** disputes with the importer when things go wrong. As wisely pointed out by an exporter, "problems… are more easily avoided than **rectified** after they occur." Therefore, you need to handle the contract with **discretion**. Some notes are given as follows for each term listed below.

breed 引起，导致

rectified 纠正

discretion 谨慎

- Names and addresses of both parties
- Date and location of signing the contract
- The willingness and guarantee of both parties to conclude this contract and fulfil their respective contractual obligations
- Product description: name, model, quality, quantity, packaging and marking, etc. of the goods
  (1) Remember to distinguish between the brand name and the name of origin of the merchandise. For instance, the commodity name of "Yantai Apple" might be confusing—is "Yantai" the brand name or the place of origin?
  (2) Remember that you can contain a quality tolerance clause in the contract if agreed to by the importer.
  (3) Remember that you can contain a quantity tolerance clause in the contract for bulk cargoes that are prone to shortage in

loading, unloading or storage, such as minerals, foodstuffs and farm produce, but also remember that this clause does not apply to cargoes or packing units that can be counted in numbers, such as computers or printers.

(4) Package the goods properly as claims for damages due to poor packaging is not supported by the **underwriter**.

保险公司

- Unit price and total amount
  (1) Fix the currency with discretion.
  (2) Specify the Incoterms rule employed, following the right syntax for the chosen rule, which requires a precise specification of the point when and where responsibility transfers, and an express indication of the version of the Incoterms Rules, as *Incoterms 2010* and *Incoterms 2020* are currently coexistent and equally valid.
- Terms of payment
  (1) Prepare different versions of the contract by adjusting certain terms, particularly the terms of payment.
  (2) In case a letter of credit is required for payment, don't forget to set a deadline for the opening of L/C in order to guard against the importer's intentional or unintentional delay of such a behavior, which might cause a number of negative consequences to you, such as a tight schedule for shipment and for presenting documents.
  (3) Specify the date and place of expiry of the L/C with discretion. The date must be adequately calculated and the place must be in China. If the place of expiry is not in China, it is beyond your control whether you can make sure that the documents will be presented before the expiry date in a foreign country.

如果到期地点不在中国，您无法确保到期日之前能否在外国交单

- Time of shipment
  It should be adequately calculated.
- Port of loading and port of destination
  Specify a precise port of loading and port of destination. Avoid vague terms such as "European Main Port".
- Partial shipment and transshipment

Specify whether partial shipment or transshipment is allowed.

- Insurance
  (1) When you or the importer is expected to buy insurance at your or his/her option, a simplified insurance clause is enough, such as: insurance to be effected by the exporter/importer.
  (2) When you are obliged to buy insurance, a complete insurance clause is necessary, such as "Insurance to be effected by the exporter for 110% of the invoice value against the **WPA** and **TPND** as per Ocean Marine Cargo Insurance Clause of the People's Insurance Company of China Jan.1, 1981." 水渍险 提货不着险
- Inspection
  You should reach an agreement with the buyer concerning the following aspects:
  (1) inspection institution
  (2) inspection standard
  (3) inspection contents and type of certificate required
  (4) which inspection is taken as final
- Documents required by the importer
  Make sure you can get all the documents needed ready on your own. Do not accept any requirement for a document whose issuance is dependent on the importer, such as the importer's confirmation or signature. By delaying the confirmation or signature, the importer may delay your documentation and presentation of the documents to your bank.
- Complaint or Claim
  You are suggested to reach agreement on the following aspects with the importer：
  (1) The period allowed for lodging a complaint or claim
  (2) The certificate needed as evidence and the institution that has the authority to issue the certificate
  (3) Which inspection is final
- Dispute Resolution
  You are suggested to reach agreement on the following aspects with the importer:

(1) Methods for resolving the dispute: negotiation, mediation, arbitration or litigation
(2) Organization for resolving the dispute
(3) Ways to select the mediator or arbitrator/arbitral tribunal
(4) Location of the hearings or any meetings
(5) Language used for resolving the disputes
(6) Whether or not the resolution is final and binding on both parties
(7) Allocation of fees between the two parties

- *Force majeure*

  You are suggested to reach agreement on the following aspects with the importer:

  (1) Scope of *force majeure*
  (2) The period allowed for notifying the incident to the importer and the importer's rights.
  (3) Certificate to attest to the *force majeure* incident
  (4) Organization that is authorized to issue the certificate

- Remarks

  Other terms such as asking the exporter to confirm all items of an L/C before the importer opens it

- Signature

  Your signature should be in handwriting and specify both your name and position in different lines.

Figure 13-1 is a sample export sales contract.

13.1.2.2 Advice of a letter of credit and a letter of credit 信用证通知书和信用证

In the case that payment is by letter of credit, when the credit is opened and sent to your (the beneficiary's) bank, the bank advises you that a letter of credit in your favor has arrived and transfers it together with the advice to you. Figure 13-2 is a sample advice of a letter of credit and Figure 13-3 the sample letter of credit.

TIANJIN BINHAI IMPORT & EXPORT CO., LTD.
NO. 188 HAIHE ROAD, BINHAI DISTRICT, TIANJIN, P. R. CHINA
TEL No.: 0086-22-8835097X FAX No.: 0086-22-8835099X
WEB: www.tjbhix.com E-MAIL: trade@tjbhix.com

SALES CONTRACT

No.: TBIM-SWTC-09

Date: April 17, 2022
Signed at: Tianjin China

SELLER	BUYER
TIANJIN BINHAI IMPORT & EXPORT CO., LTD. NO. 188 HAIHE ROAD, BINHAI DISTRICT, TIANJIN, P. R. CHINA	SINGAPORE WONKA TRADING COMPANY LTD. 67 ANG MO KIO AVENUE 8, SINGAPORE 560250

The Seller agrees to sell and the Buyer agrees to buy the undermentioned goods on the terms and conditions stated below.

Item	Description	Quantity	Unit Price	Amount
Swimming suits	Swimming suits, polyamide 80%, spandex 20%		CIF Singapore Incoterms 2020	
	Men's suits			
	Size X	500 pcs	USD75 per pc	USD37,500. –
	Size XL	500 pcs	USD85 per pc	USD42,500. –
	Size XXL	500 pcs	USD95 per pc	USD47,500. –
	Women's suits			
	Size X	500 pcs	USD80 per pc	USD40,000. –
	Size XL	500 pcs	USD90 per pc	USD45,000. –
	Size XXL	500 pcs	USD100 per pc	USD50,000. –
total		3,000 pcs		USD262,500. –
total amount in words	SAY USD TWO HUNDRED AND SIXTY-TWO THOUSAND FIVE HUNDRED ONLY			

Terms of Payment

By L/C available by draft at sight to be opened and shall reach the Exporter 30 days before the date of shipment

Packing

To be packed in transparent poly bag, one pc per bag, 100 pcs to one carton

Shipping Marks

SWTC
SINGAPORE
NO.1-30
TBIM-SWTC-09

Delivery Time

June 15, 2022

Port of Loading

Tianjin China

Port of Destination

Singapore

Partial Shipments

Not Allowed

Transshipment

Not Allowed

Insurance

To be covered by the Exporter for 110% of the invoice value against All Risks and War Risk

General Terms and Conditions

(1) The Importer of this Sales Contract shall open the Letter of Credit no later than the time stipulated by this Sales Contract, failing which the Exporter has the right to rescind without prior notice, or to take the whole or any part of this Sales Contract as non-fulfilled by the Importer, or to claim any losses sustained.

(2) For transactions concluded on CIF basis, this insurance coverage will be for 110% of the invoice value against the risks specified in this Sales Contract. If additional coverage is required by the Importer, the Importer must have the consent of the Exporter before shipment, and the additional premium is to be borne by the Importer.

(3) Quality/Quantity Discrepancy: In case of quality discrepancy, the Importer may, within 60 days after the arrival of goods at the Port of Destination, lodge a claim against the Exporter. In case of quantity discrepancy, the Importer may, within 15 days after the arrival of the goods at the Port of Destination, lodge a claim against the Exporter. The claim(s) should be supported by reports issued by a recognized public surveyor appointed by the Exporter, and the Exporter shall not be liable for any discrepancies attributable to the insurance company, shipping company, other transportation organization or post office.

(4) All disputes arising from the execution of this contract shall be settled through friendly negotiation. If no settlement can be reached through negotiation, the case shall be submitted to Hong Kong International Arbitration Centre for arbitration in accordance with its rules of procedure. The arbitral award is final and binding upon both parties.

(5) The Exporter shall not be held liable for failure or delay in the delivery of the entire lot or a portion of the goods under this Sales Contract in consequence of any Force Majeure incidents.

(6) The Importer is requested to quote the number of this Sales Contract in the Letter of Credit opened in favor of the Exporter.

(7) Upon receipt of this Sales Contract, the Importer is requested to sign and return one copy of the Contract immediately. Objection, if any, should be raised by the Importer within five days after the receipt of this Sales Contract, otherwise, it is assumed that the Importer has accepted all the terms and conditions of this Sales Contract.

(8) The above General Terms and Conditions of this Sales Contract are integral parts of this Sales Contract.

THE SELLER	**THE BUYER**
李明	Willy Wonka
Authorized Representative	Authorized Representative

Figure 13-1 A Sample Export Sales Contract

中国银行
BANK OF CHINA

TIANJIN BRANCH

EB02

ADDREES: NO. 8, NORTH YOUYI ROAD, TIANJIN, CHINA

CABLE: 689X

TELEX: 3501X BOCHZ CN

SWIFT: BKCHCNBJ200

FAX: 022 –2710777X

信用证通知书

NOTIFICATION OF DOCUMENTARY CREDIT

2022/05/11

TO 致：209953X TIANJIN BINHAI IMPORT & EXPORT CO., LTD. NO.188 HAIHE ROAD, BINHAI DISTRICT, TIANJIN, CHINA TEL No.: 0086-22-8835097X FAX No.: 0086-22-8835099X		**WHEN CORRESPONDING PLEASE QUOTE OUR REF NO.**	AD91009103334
ISSUING BANK 开证行 80009876 BANK OF CHINA SINGAPORE		**TRANSMITTED TO US THROUGH 转通行** **REF. NO.** **REIM. BANK**	
LC NO. 信用证号 KOS879	**DATED 开证日期** 20220510	**AMOUNT 金额** USD262,500.00	**EXPIRY PLACE 有效地** CHINA
EXPIRY DATE 有效期 20220725	**TENOR 期限** AT SIGHT	**CHARGE 未付费用** RMB200.00	**CHARGE BY 费用承担人** BENEFICIARY
RECEIVED VIA 来证方式 SWIFT	**AVAILABLE 是否生效** VALID	**TEST/SIGN 印押是否相符** YES	**CONFIRM 我行是否保兑** NO

DEAR SIRS, 敬启者：
WE HAVE PLEAUSRE IN ADVISING YOU THAT WE HAVE RECEIVED FROM THE A/M BANK A(N) LETTER OF CREDIT, CONTENTS OF WHICH ARE AS PER ATTACHED SHEET(S).

THIS ADVICE AND THE ATTACHED SHEET(S) MUST ACCOMPANY THE RELATIVE DOCUMENTS WHEN PRESENTING FOR NEGOTIATION.
兹通知贵司，我行自上述银行收到信用证一份，现随附通知，贵司交单时，请将本通知书及信用证一并提示。

REMARKS 备注：
PLEASE NOTE THAT THIS ADVICE DOES NOT CONSTITUTE OUR CONFIRMATION OF THE ABOVE LC NOR DOES IT CONVEY ANY ENGAGEMENT OR OBLIGATION ON OUR PART.
本通知书不构成我行对此信用证之保兑及其他任何责任。

THIS LC CONSISTS OF 2 SHEET(S), INCLUDING THE COVERING LETTER AND ATTACHMENT(S).
本信用证连同面函及附件共 2 张。

IF YOU FIND ANY TERMS AND CONDITIONS IN THE LC WHICH YOU ARE UNABLE TO COMPLY WITH AND OR ANY ERROR(S), IT IS SUGGESTED THAT YOU CONTACT APPLICANT DIRECTLY FOR NECESSARY AMENDMENT(S) SO AS TO AVOID ANY DIFFICULTIES WHICH MAY ARISE WHEN DOCUMENTS ARE PRESENTED.
如本信用证中有无法办到的条款及/或错误，请迳与开证申请人联系，进行必要的修改，以排除交单时可能发生的问题。

THIS LC IS ADVISED SUBJECT TO ICC UCP PUBLICATION NO. 600.
本信用证之通知系遵循国际商会跟单信用证统一惯例第 600 号出版物办理。

IF YOU HAVE ANY QUESTION OR DOUBT ABOUT THIS CREDIT, PLEASE CONTACT THE REVIEW SECTION OF THE SETTLEMENT DEPARTMENT. TEL: 86-22-5289658X.
此证如有任何问题及疑虑，请与结算业务部审证科联络，电话：86-22-5289658X。

YOURS FAITHFULLY,
FOR BANK OF CHINA TIANJIN BRANCH

Figure 13-2 A Sample Advice of a Letter of Credit

FIELD NAME	TAG	TEXT
MESSAGE TYPE	700	ISSUE OF A DOCUMENTARY CREDIT
SENDER		BANK OF CHINA SINGAPORE
RECEIVER		BANK OF CHINA TIANJIN BRANCH, CHINA
SEQUENCE OF TOTAL	27	1/1
FORM OF DOC. CREDIT	40A	IRREVOCABLE
DOC. CREDIT NUMBER	20	KOS879
DATE OF ISSUE	31C	20220510
APPLICABLE RULES	40E	UCP 600
DATE AND PLACE OF EXPIRY	31D	DATE 20220725 PLACE IN CHINA
APPLICANT	50	SINGAPORE WONKA TRADING COMPANY LTD 67 ANG MO KIO AVENUE 8 SINGAPORE 560250
BENEFICIARY	59	TIANJIN BINHAI IMPORT & EXPORT CO., LTD. NO. 188 HAIHE ROAD BINHAI DISTRICT TIANJIN
AMOUNT	32B	CURRENCY USD AMOUNT 262,500.00
AVAILABLE WITH/BY	41D	ANY BANK IN CHINA BY NEGOTIATION
DRAFTS AT…	42C	AT SIGHT
DRAWEE	42A	BANK OF CHINA SINGAPORE
PARTIAL SHIPMENT	43P	NOT ALLOWED
TRANSSHIPMENT	43T	NOT ALLOWED
LOADING IN…	44A	TIANJIN CHINA
FOR TRANSPORT TO…	44B	SINGAPORE
LATEST DATE OF SHIPMENT	44C	20220615
DESCRIPTION OF GOODS	45A:	3,000 PCS OF SWIMMING SUITS MEN'S SUITS 1,500 PCS IN 3 SIZES AND WOMEN'S SUITS 1,500 PCS IN 3 SIZES ALL DETAILS AS PER SALES CONTRACT NO. TBIM - SWTC - 09.
DOCUMENTS REQUIRED	46A	+ SIGNED COMMERCIAL INVOICE IN TRIPLICATE + PACKING LIST IN TRIPLICATE + CERTIFICATE OF CHINESE ORIGIN CERTIFIED BY CHAMBER OF COMMERCE OR CCPIT + FULL SET OF CLEAN ON BOARD OCEAN BILLS OF LADING MADE OUT TO ORDER MARKED FREIGHT PREPAID AND NOTIFY APPLICANT + FULL SET OF INSURANCE POLICY ISSUED BY PICC + SHIPPING ADVICE PROVIDING FULL DETAILS OF SHIPMENT + BENEFICIARY'S CERTIFICATION TO THE EFFECT THAT ALL TERMS AND CONDITIONS OF THIS CREDIT HAVE BEEN COMPLIED WITH

continued

FIELD NAME	TAG	TEXT
ADDITIONAL CONDITIONS	47A	+ THE NUMBER AND THE DATE OF THIS CREDIT AND THE NAME OF ISSUING BANK MUST BE QUOTED ON ALL DOCUMENTS EXCEPT INSURANCE POLICY. + ALL PRESENTATIONS CONTAINING DISCREPANCIES WILL INCUR A DISCREPANCY FEE OF USD 75.00 PLUS CHARGE WHICH WILL BE DEDUCTED FROM THE BILL AMOUNT WHETHER OR NOT WE SELECT TO CONSULT THE APPLICANT FOR A WAIVER
CHARGES	71B	ALL BANKING CHARGES OUTSIDE THE ISSUING BANK ARE FOR ACCOUNT OF BENEFICIARY
PERIOD FOR PRESENTATION	48	UNTIL THE 21ST DAY AFTER THE DATE OF SHIPMENT, BUT WITHIN THE VALIDITY OF THIS CREDIT
CONFIRMATION INSTRUCTION	49	WITHOUT
INFORMATION TO PRESENTING BANK	78	COURIER TO BANK OF CHINA SINGAPORE 4 BATTERY ROAD, SINGAPORE 049908

Figure 13-3 A Sample Letter of Credit

13.1.2.3 Commercial invoice 商业发票

A commercial invoice (or invoice for short), is a **bill** issued by the exporter to the importer listing the goods or services the exporter has provided, stating how much the importer owes and requesting payment. An invoice is sometimes (when mandated by the importing or exporting countries) though not necessarily in a standardized format, but normally includes the following information for an international sale: the invoice number, a date, basic contact information, descriptions of goods or services (commodity name, unit price, quantity, total amount, packaging), time of shipment and terms of payment. And notably, an invoice in international trade should not be mistaken for a "**fapiao**" in China's domestic trade. The latter is printed in a standard format under the supervision of the tax authority of China and is often used both as a tax record and a **voucher** for **reimbursement**.

账单 发票 票券 报销

As important evidence of the authenticity of a cross-border deal, a commercial invoice is the most basic document in export and the starting point for many other procedures. As an exporter, you need it in applying for inspection and the certificate of origin, obtaining insurance, clearing customs for export, collecting payment from the bank and preparing for these and other relevant documents. The importer needs the invoice mainly for the purpose of clearing customs for import. The import duty is normally calculated based on the invoice. The importer may also need to see it before making payment, or to make claims when things go wrong. A well-prepared invoice safeguards your interests and is also an indicator of good customer service. Therefore, please note the following tips when you prepare it:

- The commercial invoice should be in consistency with the contract and the letter of credit if any.
- Describe the goods clearly and accurately to assist the importer's customs clearance. **As the import tariff may be a function of a number of factors**, including the category of goods determined by their HS code and the weight and measurement of the goods, please provide this information when you are required and do it right.

由于进口关税取决于多个因素

- Specify the Incoterms rule employed, with an express indication of the version of the Incoterms rules—2010 or 2020.
- Provide a detailed list of what you have prepaid for the importer, as some countries may exclude insurance premium, **stevedore charges**, or domestic transport when tariff is calculated. For instance, the US Customs exclude insurance premium when calculating tariff for goods imported on a CIF or CIP basis.

装卸费

- Don't forget to provide the shipping marks, the currency code for the unit price and the total amount and to write the total amount both in numbers and in words.

Figure13-4 is a sample commercial invoice.

13.1.2.4 *Proforma* invoice 形式发票

Despite the name, a *proforma* invoice is not an invoice, but a "preview" provided by the exporter to the importer of what the actual invoice would be like. As **parameters abound** for international transactions, it is often difficult for an importer to visualize what his/her final cost will be like. A *proforma* invoice, literally an invoice **"as a matter of form"**, helps the importer see in advance what the actual

参数很多

"作为一种形式的发票"

invoice would be like if the transaction were to take place.

As an invoice "in form", it also enables the importer to **set about** a number of things that he/she could not without such a device, such as applying for the import license, the import quota, foreign exchanges or opening a letter of credit, which are often **granted** on condition of a commercial invoice.

着手

给予，授予

Thanks to the customer-friendly feature, *proforma* invoices are widely used as quotes or sales confirmations as clients from certain countries prefer to use a confirmed *proforma* invoice as the contract. When it is used this way, however, a **term of validity** should be specified, as in the case of an offer. And it should be noted that an unconfirmed *proforma* invoice should never be allowed in applying for a letter of credit! This may result in serious problems as the actual commercial invoice has to be precisely consistent with the *proforma* invoice, otherwise, it constitutes discrepancies with the letter of credit and the bank shall refuse to pay!

有效期

请注意，在申请信用证时，不应允许使用未经确认的形式发票！这可能会导致严重的问题，因为实际的商业发票必须与形式发票完全一致，否则，它将构成信用证项下单据的不符点，银行将拒绝付款！

The format of a *proforma* invoice is quite similar to that of a commercial invoice so that you can almost substitute a commercial invoice for a *proforma* invoice merely by changing the title of the former into "*Proforma* Invoice". Figure 13-5 is a sample *proforma* invoice.

13.1.2.5 Customs invoice 海关发票

A customs invoice is an invoice in a standard format required by the customs of some importing countries for import clearance. The blank form can be downloaded from the website of the importing country. It contains almost the same elements with a commercial invoice and is used for the similar purposes in clearance—compiling customs statistics, verifying country of origin, examining components of the import price, calculating duties and taxes, etc., but with a standard format, it relieves the workload of customs officers and speeds up clearance. Figure 13-6 is a sample customs invoice of Canada.

TIANJIN BINHAI IMPORT & EXPORT CO., LTD.
NO. 188 HAIHE ROAD, BINHAI DISTRICT, TIANJIN, P. R. CHINA
TEL No.: 0086-22-8835097X FAX No.: 0086-22-8835099X
WEB: www.tjbhix.com E-MAIL:trade@tjbhix.com

COMMERCIAL INVOICE

INVOICE NO.: TBIM-SWTC-09 S/C NO.: TBIM-SWTC-09
DATE: JUNE 10, 2022 DATE: April 17, 2022

SHIPPED FROM TIANJIN CHINA BY SEA TO SINGAPORE
FOR ACCOUNT AND RISKS OF MESSRS.: SINGAPORE WONKA TRADING COMPANY LTD 67 ANG MO KIO AVENUE 8 SINGAPORE 560250

MARKS & NO.	DESCRIPTION	UNIT PRICE	AMOUNT
SWTC SINGAPORE NO.1-30 TBIM-SWTC-09	30 CARTONS = 3,000 PCS SWIMMING SUITS, Polyamide 80%, spandex 20%	CIF SINGAPORE Incoterms 2020	
	MEN'S SUITS 1,500 PCS IN 3 SIZES		
	Size X 500 PCS	USD75 per pc	USD37,500. –
	Size XL 500 PCS	USD85 per pc	USD42,500. –
	Size XXL 500 PCS	USD95 per pc	USD47,500. –
	WOMEN'S SUITS 1,500 PCS IN 3 SIZES		
	Size X 500 PCS	USD80 per pc	USD40,000. –
	Size XL 500 PCS	USD90 per pc	USD45,000. –
	Size XXL 500 PCS	USD100 per pc	USD50,000. –
	TOTAL: 3,000 PCS		TOTAL AMOUNT: USD262,500. –
	CREDIT NUMBER: KOS879 DATE OF CREDIT: 20220510 THE NAME OF ISSUING BANK: BANK OF CHINA SINGAPORE		TOTAL AMOUNT TWO HUNDRED AND SIXTY-TWO THOUSAND FIVE HUNDRED U.S. DOLLARS ONLY.

李明

Legal Representative or Authorized Signature

Figure13-4 A Sample Commercial Invoice

TIANJIN BINHAI IMPORT & EXPORT CO., LTD

NO. 188 HAIHE ROAD, BINHAI DISTRICT, TIANJIN, P. R. CHINA

TEL No.: 0086-22-8835097X FAX No.: 0086-22-8835099X

WEB: www.tjbhix.com E-MAIL: trade@tjbhix.com

Proforma Invoice	Number: TBIM - SWTC - 09
	Date: April 12, 2022

For Account and Risk of Messrs.: SINGAPORE WONKA TRADING COMPANY LTD
67 ANG MO KIO AVENUE 8 SINGAPORE 560250

Item	**Description**	**Quantity**	**Unit Price**	**Amount**
	Swimming suits Polyamide 80%, spandex 20%		CIF Singapore Incoterms 2020	
	Men's Suits			
	Size X	500 pcs	USD75 per pc	USD37,500. –
Swimming suits	Size XL	500 pcs	USD85 per pc	USD42,500. –
	Size XXL	500 pcs	USD95 per pc	USD47,500. –
	Women's Suits			
	Size X	500 pcs	USD80 per pc	USD40,000. –
	Size XL	500 pcs	USD90 per pc	USD45,000. –
	Size XXL	500 pcs	USD100 per pc	USD50,000. –
Total		3,000 pcs		USD262,500.-

Terms of Payment: By L/C available by draft at sight

Packing: To be packed in transparent poly bag, one pc per bag, 100 pcs to one carton

Delivery Time: June 15, 2022

Port of Loading: Tianjin China

Port of Destination: Singapore

Insurance: To be covered by the Exporter for 110% of the invoice value against All Risks & War Risk

Price Valid By: April 18, 2022

Special Requirement: L/C to be opened and shall reach the Exporter 30 days before date of shipment

李明

Authorized Representative Signature

Figure13-5 A Sample *Proforma* Invoice

Canada border Services Agency	Agence des services frontalier du Canada	CANADA CUSTOMS INVOICE FACTURES DES DOUANES CANADIENNES	Page of de

1. Vendor (name and address) - Vendeur (nom et adresse)	2. Date of direct shipment to Canada - Date d'expédition directe vers le Canada yyyy/mm/dd 3. Other references (include purchaser's order No.) Autres références (inclure le nº de commande de l'acheteur)
4. Consignee (name and address) - Destinataire (nom et adresse)	5. Purchaser's name and address (if other than consignee) Nom et adresse de l'acheteur (s'il diffère du destinataire) 6. Country of transshipment - Pays de transbordement 7. Country of origin of goods Pays d'origine des marchandises IF SHIPMENT INCLUDES GOODS OF DIFFERENT ORIGINS ENTER ORIGINS AGAINST ITEMS IN SI L'EXPÉDITION COMPREND DES MARCHANDISES D'ORIGINES DIFFÉRENTES, PRÉCISEZ LEUR PROVENANCE EN.
8. Transportation: Give mode and place of direct shipment to Canada Transport: Précisez mode et point d'expédition directe vers le Canada	9. Conditions of sale and terms of payment (i.e. sale, consignment shipment, leased goods, etc.) Conditions de vente et modalités de paiement (p. ex. vente, expédition en consignation, location de marchandises, etc.) 10. Currency of settlement - Devises du paiement

11. Number of packages Nombre de colis	12. Specification of commodities (kind of packages, marks and numbers, general description and characteristics, i.e., grade, quality) Désignation des articles (nature des colis, marques et numéros, description générale et caractéristiques, p. ex. classe, qualité)	13. Quantity (state unit) Quantité (précisez l'unité)	Selling price - Prix de vente 14. Unit price Prix unitaire	15. Total Total
18. If any of fields 1 to 17 are included on an attached commercial invoice, check this box ☐ Si tout renseignement relativement aux zones 1 à 17 figure sur une ou des factures commerciales ci-attachées, cochez cette case Commercial Invoice No. - Nº de la facture commerciale		16. Total weight - Poids total Net- Réseau	Gross - Brut	17. Invoice total Total de la facture

19. Exporter's name and address (if other than vendor) Nom et adresse de l'exportateur (s'il diffère du vendeur)	20. Originator (name and address) - Expéditeur d'origine (nom et adresse)
21. Agency ruling (if applicable) - Décision de l'Agence (s'il y a lieu)	22. If fields 23 to 25 are not applicable, check this box Si les zones 23 à 25 sont sans objet, cochez cette case ☐

23. If included in field 17 indicate amount: Si compris dans le total à la zone 17, précisez:	24. If not included in field 17 indicate amount: Si non compris dans le total à la zone 17, précisez:	25. Check (if applicable): Cochez (s'il y a lieu) :
(i) Transportation charges, expenses and insurance from the place of direct shipment to Canada Les frais de transport, dépenses et assurances à partir du point d'expédition directe vers le Canada	(i) Transportation charges, expenses and insurance to the place of direct shipment to Canada Les frais de transport, dépenses et assurances jusqu'au point d'expedition directe vers le Canada	(i) Royalty payments or subsequent proceeds are paid or payable by the purchaser Des redevances ou produits ont été ou seront versés par l'acheteur ☐
(ii) Costs for construction, erection and assembly incurred after importation into Canada Les coûts de construction, d'érection et d'assemblage après importation au Canada	(ii) Amounts for commissions other than buying commissions Les commissions autres que celles versées pour l'achat	(ii) The purchaser has supplied goods or services for use in the production of these goods L'acheteur a fourni des marchandises ou des services pour la production de ces marchandises ☐
(iii) Export packing Le coût de l'emballage d'exportation	(iii) Export packing Le coût de l'emballage d'exportation	

In this form, all references to individuals refer to men and women.
Dans ce formulaire, toutes les expressions désignant des personnes visent à la fois les hommes et les femmes.

CI1 (08/09) If you require more space, please attach another sheet. - Si vous avez besoin de plus d'espace, veuillez joindre une autre feuille. BSF189

Figure 13-6 A Sample Customs Invoice of Canada

13.1.2.6 Packing list 装箱单

A packing list is a supplement to the commercial invoice, which shows a detailed list of the goods and their packing, such as the quantity, package, weight and measurement. It is needed by the customs of the importing country for **ascertaining** the contents and quantity, etc. of a shipment and determining the applicable tariff rate. The importer also needs it for checking the goods on arrival against the contract. Should any non-conformity to the contract occur, the packing list constitutes one of the documents supporting a claim. It also provides information that is necessary to the carrier for moving the cargo and loading the container or vessel in the proper way.

确定

The format is similar to that of a commercial invoice except that the unit price and the total amount are not listed. Listed items include the name, quantity, packages, gross weight, net weight and measurement of the commodity. But a signature is optional, depending on the requirement of the importing country. Several originals and copies are also needed for different purposes. And in most cases, the packing list and the invoice bear the same date. Figure13-7 is a sample packing list.

13.1.2.7 Application form for inspection and certificates of inspection 检验申请和检验证书

To obtain a certificate of inspection, you need to file an application to the Customs, stating your needed certificates. When the goods pass the inspection, the needed certificates are issued. Common inspection certificates for export may include a quality certificate, a certificate of quantity and weight, a veterinary (health) certificate, a health certificate, **a sanitary certificate**, an animal health certificate, a **phytosanitary certificate**, and **a fumigation/disinfection certificate**. Figure 13-8 is a sample application form for inspection and Figure 13-9 a sample quality inspection certificate.

卫生证书
植物检疫证书
熏蒸/消毒证

TIANJIN BINHAI IMPORT & EXPORT CO., LTD

NO. 188 HAIHE ROAD, BINHAI DISTRICT, TIANJIN, P. R. CHINA

TEL No.: 0086-22-8835097X FAX No.: 0086-22-8835099X

WEB: www.tjbhix.com E-MAIL: trade@tjbhix.com

PACKING LIST

INVOICE NO.: TBIM-SWTC-09 S/C NO. : TBIM-SWTC-09

DATE: JUNE 10, 2022 DATE: April 17, 2022

MARKS & NO.	NUMBER AND KIND OF PACKAGES DESCRIPTION OF GOODS	QUANTITY	PACKAGE	GROSS WEIGHT	NET WEIGHT	MEAS.
	30 CARTONS = 3,000. – PCS		ONE POLY BAG PER PC			
	SWIMMING SUITS Polyamide 80%, spandex 20%		100 PCS TO ONE CARTON			
	MEN'S SUITS 1,500 PCS IN 3 SIZES					
SWTC SINGAPORE NO.1-30 TBIM-SWTC-09	Size X	500 PCS	15 CARTONS NO. 1 – 15	630 KGS.	600 KGS.	150 cm *80 cm *70 cm
	Size XL	500 PCS				
	Size XXL	500 PCS				
	Subtotal	1,500 PCS				12.6 M^3
	WOMEN'S SUITS 1,500 PCS IN 3 SIZES					
	Size X	500 PCS	15 CARTONS NO. 16 – 30	630 KGS.	600 KGS.	150 cm *80 cm *70 cm
	Size XL	500 PCS				
	Size XXL	500 PCS				
	Subtotal	1,500 PCS				12.6 M^3
Total		3,000 PCS	30 CARTONS	1,260 KGS.	1,200 KGS.	25.2 M^3

李明

Legal Representative or Authorized Signature

Figure13-7 A Sample Packing List

出境货物检验检疫申请

申请单位（加盖公章）： *编号

申请单位登记号： 联系人： 电话： 申请日期：

<table>
<tr><td rowspan="2">发货人</td><td colspan="5">（中文）</td></tr>
<tr><td colspan="5">（外文）</td></tr>
<tr><td rowspan="2">收货人</td><td colspan="5">（中文）</td></tr>
<tr><td colspan="5">（外文）</td></tr>
<tr><td>货物名称（中/外文）</td><td>H.S. 编码</td><td>产地</td><td>数/重量</td><td>货物总值</td><td>包装种类及数量</td></tr>
<tr><td></td><td></td><td></td><td></td><td></td><td></td></tr>
<tr><td>运输工具名称号码</td><td></td><td>贸易方式</td><td>一般贸易</td><td>货物存放地点</td><td></td></tr>
<tr><td>合同号</td><td></td><td>信用证号</td><td></td><td>用途</td><td></td></tr>
<tr><td>发货日期</td><td></td><td>输往国家（地区）</td><td></td><td>许可证/审批号</td><td></td></tr>
<tr><td>启运地</td><td>上海</td><td>到达口岸</td><td></td><td>生产单位注册号</td><td></td></tr>
<tr><td colspan="2">集装箱规格、数量及号码</td><td colspan="4"></td></tr>
<tr><td colspan="2">合同、信用证订立的检验检疫条款或特殊要求</td><td colspan="2">标记及号码</td><td colspan="2">随附单据（划“ √ ”或补填）</td></tr>
<tr><td colspan="2"></td><td colspan="2"></td><td>□合同
□信用证
□发票
□装箱单
□厂检单
□包装性能结果单</td><td>□许可/审批文件
□报检委托书
□其他单据
□
□
□</td></tr>
<tr><td colspan="4">需要证单名称（划“ √ ”或补填）</td><td colspan="2">*检验检疫费</td></tr>
<tr><td colspan="2" rowspan="3">□品质证书 正 副
□重量证书 正 副
□数量证书 正 副
□兽医卫生证书 正 副
□健康证书 正 副
□卫生证书 正 副
□动物卫生证书 正 副</td><td colspan="2" rowspan="3">□植物检疫证书 正 副
□熏蒸/消毒证书 正 副
□
□
□
□</td><td>总金额（人民币元</td><td></td></tr>
<tr><td>计费人</td><td></td></tr>
<tr><td>收费人</td><td></td></tr>
<tr><td colspan="3" rowspan="3">申请人郑重声明：
1. 本人被授权申请检验检疫。
2. 上列填写内容正确属实，货物无伪造或冒用他人的厂名、标志、认证标志，并承担质量责任。
签名：________</td><td colspan="3">领取证单</td></tr>
<tr><td>日期</td><td colspan="2"></td></tr>
<tr><td>签名</td><td colspan="2"></td></tr>
<tr><td colspan="6">注：有“*”栏由海关填写</td></tr>
</table>

Figure 13-8 A Sample Application Form for Inspection

ENTRY-EXIT INSPECTION AND QUARANTINE

正 本
ORIGINAL

编号 No.: XXX

QUALITY INSPECTION CERTIFICATE

发货人 Consignor	TIANJIN BINHAI IMPORT & EXPORT CO., LTD.
收货人 Consignee	SINGAPORE WONKA TRADING COMPANY LTD.

品名 Description of Goods	SWIMMING SUITS	标记及号码 Marks & No.
报检数量/重量 Quantity/Weight Declared	-3,000- PIECES/1,200 KGS（N.W.）	SWTC SINGAPORE NO.1-30 TBIM-SWTC-09
包装数量及种类 Number and type of packages	-30-CARTONS	
运输工具 Means of Conveyance	S. S. DONG FENG V.133	

检验结果：

RESULTS OF INSPECTION:

IN ACCORDANCE WITH THE RELEVANT STANDARD, THE REPRESENTATIVE SAMPLE WERE DRAWN AT RANDOM AND INSPECTED WITH RESULTS

AS FOLLOWS:

OF NORMAL QUALITY

THE QUALITY OF THE GOODS IS IN CONFORMITY WITH THE RELEVANT REQUIREMENTS.

印章 Official Stamp

签证地点 Place of Issue	TIANJIN, CHINA	签证日期 Date of Issue	JUNE 13, 2022
授权签字人 Authorized Officer	GUO SIRAN	签名 Signature	

中华人民共和国检验检疫机关及其官员或代表不承担签发本证书的任何财经责任。No financial liability with respect to this certificate shall attach to the entry-exit inspection and quarantine authorities of P. R. of China or to any of its officers or representatives.

Figure 13-9 A Sample Quality Inspection Certificate

13.1.2.8 Certificate of Origin and GSP FORM A 一般原产地证和普惠制产地证

Two types of certificates of origin exist in export—a general certificate of origin and a Generalized System of Preference Form A.

Like an identity card, the certificate of origin is a document **attesting** to the origin or place of manufacture of the goods when they enter the international market. It is used mainly for the customs of the importing country to adopt differentiated trade policies and treatments toward different countries. In countries where customs or consular invoices are not used, certificates of origin are often required for determining the tariff rates applicable to the imported goods. Countries that restrict the import of goods from a certain country or region also require the document to verify the origin of the goods. It can be issued by **notary firms,** chamber of commerce in the place of export, **the Entry-Exit of Inspection and Quarantine (EEIQ)** under the Customs or China Council for the Promotion of International Trade (CCPIT). As for who shall issue the document or what kind of certificates shall be issued, it should be handled in accordance with the provisions of the contract or the letter of credit if any.

证明

公证行

出入境检验检疫局

The Generalized System of Preferences is a universal, non-discriminate and non-reciprocal preferential tariff system provided by developed countries to developing countries on the latter's export of finished and semi-finished products, aiming to help the latter increase export and foreign exchanges, promoting their industrialization and economic growth. The certificate of origin under GSP, also known as G.S.P FORM A, is a document required by the preference granting countries that attests to the beneficiary country as the origin of manufacture and entitles the goods to preferential tariffs in the preference-granting country.

普惠制是发达国家给予发展中国家出口制成品和半制成品普遍的、非歧视的、非互惠的一种关税优惠制度。普惠制产地证，又称 GSP 证书或格式 A 证书，是依据给惠国要求而出具的能证明出口货物原产自受惠国的证明文件，并能使货物在给惠国享受普遍优惠的关税待遇。

For a commodity to enjoy the GSP treatment, it must meet the following conditions:

(1) Condition of origin: for the goods exported by the beneficiary country to obtain the preferential treatment of GSP tariff, the goods must be produced or manufactured in the beneficiary country, and the imported raw materials or parts used must be fully processed, so that these imported raw materials or parts have undergone **substantial changes,**

实质性改变

or meet other conditions proposed by the preference granting country.

(2) Condition of direct transport: The export commodity must not only be produced or manufactured in the beneficiary country, but also be transported directly from the beneficiary country to the preference granting country. Those passing through a third country must be under the supervision of the customs of the third country and cannot be sold or delivered to the local market of the third country, let alone be reprocessed there.

(3) Condition of valid certification: To enjoy GSP treatment, one must hold the GSP certificate of origin issued by the government or a qualified institution of the beneficiary country, namely the GSP certificate FORM A, which legally certifies that the goods of the beneficiary country may enjoy preferential treatment of tariff reduction and exemption when exported to the preference granting country.

40 regions or countries had given GSP treatment to China: 27 EU countries, Britain, Japan, Canada, Switzerland, Australia, Norway, Russia, Belarus, New Zealand, Turkey, Ukraine, Kazakhstan, and Liechtenstein. However, as of December 1st, 2021, 36 of them have successively canceled this treatment, leaving only 4 countries—Switzerland, Australia, Norway and New Zealand—maintaining this policy.

Similarly, it can be issued by the chamber of commerce, EEIQ under the Customs or CCPIT. When it is to be issued by the Customs, you need to fill out an application and a blank Form A and send them together with a copy of the commercial invoice to the Customs for verification. it takes effect after being verified and certified by the Customs. It is usually issued in one original and two copies, with the original acceptable to a bank for negotiation. Figure13-10 is a sample certificate of origin. Form A looks remarkably similar to the ordinary certificate of origin. So, no sample is provided here.

13.1.2.9 Application for cargo insurance and insurance policy 投保单和保险单

When you go about purchasing cargo insurance, you start by submitting an application for insurance, providing information about the insured, the cargo, the voyage, the needed coverage, etc. Once the insurance premium is determined for your shipment, the insurance

<table>
<tr><td>1. Exporter (full name and address)
TIANJIN IMPORT AND EXPORT CORPORATION NO.188 HAIHE ROAD, BINHAI DISTRICT, TIANJIN, P. R. CHINA</td><td colspan="3" rowspan="2">CERTIFICATE NO.

CERTIFICATE OF ORIGIN
OF
THE PEOPLE'S REPUBLIC OF CHINA</td></tr>
<tr><td>2. Consignee (full name and address)
SINGAPORE WONKA TRADING COMPANY LTD 67 ANG MO KIO AVENUE 8 SINGAPORE 560250</td></tr>
<tr><td>3. Means of Transport and Route
FROM TIANJIN CHINA TO SINGAPORE BY SEA</td><td colspan="3" rowspan="2">5. For Certifying Authority Use Only</td></tr>
<tr><td>4.Country/Region of Destination
SINGAPORE</td></tr>
</table>

6. Marks and Numbers	7. Number and Kind of Packages: Description of Goods	8. H.S. Code	9. Quantity or Weight	10. Number and Date of Invoices
SWTC SINGAPORE NO.1-30 TBIM-SWTC-09	30 CARTONS = 3,000. – PCS SWIMMING SUITS MEN'S SUITS WOMEN'S SUITS CREDIT NUMBER: KOS879 DATE OF CREDIT: 20220510 THE NAME OF ISSUING BANK: BANK OF CHINA SINGAPORE	62111100 62111200	15 CARTONS=1,500 PCS 15 CARTONS=1,500 PCS	INVOICE NO. TBIM-SWTC-09 April 17, 2022

11. Declaration by the Exporter	12. Certification
The undersigned hereby declare that the above details and statements are correct; that all the goods were produced in China and that they comply with the Rules of Origin of the People's Republic of China [Stamp: TIANJIN BINHAI IMPORT & EXPORT CO., LTD. 天津滨海进出口有限公司] 李明 TIANJIN, CHINA, JUNE 10, 2022 Place and date, signature and stamp of authorized signatory	It is hereby certified that the declaration by the exporter is correct. [Stamp: TIANJIN CUSTOMS 中华人民共和国 天津 ORIGIN 海关 THE PEOPLE'S REPUBLIC OF CHINA] TIANJIN, CHINA, JUNE 13, 2022 刘星辰 Place and date, signature and stamp of authorized signatory

Figure 13-10 A Sample Certificate of Origin

company issues the insurance policy based on information and documents you have supplied. Insurance can be arranged as soon as you get goods ready or after you have learned of the vessel name. Either way, make sure your insurance policy takes effect at a time no later than the date of shipment, namely, the on-board date of the bill of lading, otherwise, a gap on the voyage exists when the cargo is not covered by insurance. Should anything happen in that gap, you are liable for the damages to or losses of the cargo. Figure 13-11 is a sample application form for cargo transportation insurance and Figure 13-12 shows a sample insurance policy.

13.1.2.10 Customs clearance form for export 出口货物报关单

This is the form you need to fill out for customs clearance based on your export license (if any) and commercial invoice. It has certain legal effect after being checked and verified by the Customs. It not only evidences the customs clearance and departure of the goods from China, but also serves as an important certificate for applying for tax refund. However, most exporters, with the exception of large trading companies or manufacturers, authorize their freight forwarder or a licensed customer broker to do that. Figure 13-13 is a sample customs clearance form. For a detailed guidance on how to fill it out, see the following website for reference.

http://www.pocib.com/baike/%E5%87%BA%E5%8F%A3%E8%B4%A7%E7%89%A9%E6%8A%A5%E5%85%B3%E5%8D%95.html

13.1.2.11 Instruction for shipment and bill of lading 托运单和提单

When you plan to ship the goods, normally you contact a freight forwarder to book the shipping space on a ship, or charter an entire ship when necessary. The freight forwarder then gives you a form to fill out as your **instruction for the shipment**, which might include basic information about the shipment and your requirement for shipping, such as the number and size of containers you need. Most of the information shall be used for issuing the bill of lading later on, so you must treat it with care when you fill out this form, especially with the consignee box and the freight box. Once the cargo is loaded on board the ship, you shall be issued the bill of lading. Figure 13-14 is a sample instruction for cargo transport by sea and Figure 13-15 a sample bill of lading. For a detailed introduction to a bill of lading, see Chapter 7.

装运指示，托运单

中国人民保险集团公司天津分公司

THE PEOPLE'S INSURANCE COMPANY OF CHINA TIANJIN BRANCH

货物运输险投保单

APPLICATION FOR CARGO TRANSPORTATION INSURANCE

投保单号：

注意：请您在保险人明确说明本投保单及适用保险条款后，如实填写本投保单，您所填写的材料将构成保险合同的要约，成为保险人核保及签发保险单的依据。除双方另有约定外，保险人签发保险单且投保人向保险人缴清保险费后，保险人开始按约定的险种承保货物运输保险。

投保人 Applicant					
投保人地址 Applicant's Add.				邮编 zip code	
联系人 Contact		电话 Tel.		电子邮箱 E-mail	
被保险人 The Insured				电话 Tel.	
贸易合同号 Contract No.		信用证号 LC No.		发票号 Invoice No.	

标记 Marks & Nos.	包装及数量 Packing & quantity	保险货物项目 Description of goods

装载运输工具 Name of the carrier			
启运日期 Departure date		赔付地点 Claims payable at	

航行路线 Route　自 From ________ 经 via ________ 到达（目的地）To (destination) ________

包装方式 ________ 运输方式 ________

承保条件 投保人可根据意向选择投保险别及条款，并划√确认，但保险人承保的险别及适用条款以保险人最终确定并在保险单上列明的险种、条款为准。

Conditions:

进出口海洋运输	□ 一切险　□ 水渍险　□ 平安险　（《海洋运输货物保险条款》） □ ICC （A）　□ ICC （B）　□ ICC （C）　（《伦敦协会条款》）
进出口航空运输	□ 航空运输险　□ 航空运输一切险　（《航空运输货物保险条款》）
进出口陆上运输	□ 陆运险　□ 陆运一切险　（《陆上运输货物保险条款》）
特殊附加险	□ 战争险　□ 罢工险

特别约定 Special conditions：

1. Value Plus About ________%
2. CIF 金额 CIF Value________　3. 保险金额 Insured value ________
4. 费率（%）Rate ________　5. 保险费 premium ________

投保人声明；

1. 本人填写投保单之前，保险人已经就本投保单及适用的保险条款内容，尤其是关于保险人免除责任的条款及投保人和被保险人义务条款向本人作了明确说明，本人对该保险条款和条件已完全了解，同意接受本保险条款的约束。
2. 本投保单所填各项内容均属事实。同意以本投保单作为保险人签发保险单的依据。
3. 保险合同自保险单签发之日起成立。

投保人签字（盖章）　　　　日期：

Figure 13-11 A Sample Application Form for Cargo Transportation Insurance

中国人民保险集团公司天津分公司

THE PEOPLE'S INSURANCE COMPANY OF CHINA TIANJIN BRANCH

海洋货物运输保险单

第一正本

THE FIRST ORIGINAL

发票号码 保险单号码

INVOICE NO. **POLICY NO.**

TBIM-SWTC-09 PICCSHA0345688

中 国 人 民 保 险 公 司 （ 以 下 简 称 本 公 司 ）

This Policy of Insurance witnesses that People's Insurance Company of China (hereinafter called "the company")

根 据

at the request of TIANJIN BINHAI IMPORT AND EXPORT CORPORATION

（ 以 下 简 称 被 保 险 人 ） 的 要 求，由 被 保 险 人 向 本 公 司 缴 付 的 约 定

（hereinafter called the "Insured"） and in consideration of the agreed premium paid to the Company by the

的 保 险 费 ，按 照 本 保 险 单 承 保 险 别 和 背 面 所 载 条 款 与 下 列

Insured, undertakes to insure the undermentioned goods in transportation subject to the condition of this

特 殊 条 款 承 保 下 述 货 物 运 输 保 险 ，特 立 本 保 险 单

Policy as per the Clauses printed overleaf and other special clauses attached hereon.

标记 **MARKS & NOS.**	包装及数量 **PACKING AND QUANTITY**	货物描述 **DESCRIPTION OF GOODS**	保险金额 **AMOUNT INSURED**
AS PER INVOICE	PACKED IN TOTAL 30 CARTONS	SWIMMING SUITS	USD288,750.00

总保险金额

Total Amount Insured USD288,750.00

保费 费率 装载运输工具

Premium AS ARRANGED **Rate AS ARRANGED** **Per Conveyance S.S. DONG FENG V.133**

开航日期 自 至

Slg. on or abt. JUNE 15, 2022 **From TIANJIN CHINA** **To SINGAPORE**

承保险别

Conditions ALL RISKS AND WAR RISKS

所 保 货 物 ，如 遇 出 险 ，本 公 司 凭 第 一 正 本 保 险 单 及 其 有 关 证 件 给 付 赔 款

Claims, if any, payable on surrender of the first original of the Policy together with other relevant documents

所 保 货 物 ，如 发 生 本 保 险 单 项 下 可 能 引 起 索 赔 的 损 失 或 损 坏 ，应 立 即

In the event of accident whereby loss or damage may result in a claim under this Policy, immediate notice applying

通 知 本 公 司 下 述 代 理 人 查 勘。

for survey must be given to the Company's Agent as mentioned hereunder:

中国人民保险公司天津分公司

THE PEOPLE'S INSURANCE COMPANY OF CHINA TIANJIN BRANCH

赔款偿付地点

CLAIM PAYABLE AT **SINGAPORE**

出单日期

ISSUING DATE: **JUNE 13, 2022**

Figure 13-12 A Sample Insurance Policy

出口货物报关单

预录入编号　　海关编号：　　页码/页数：

境内发货人	出境关别	出口日期	申报日期	备案号
境外收货人	运输方式	运输工具名称及航次号	提运单号	
	江海运输			
生产销售单位	监管方式	征免性质	许可证号	
	一般贸易（0110）	一般征税（101）		
合同协议号	贸易国（地区）	运抵国（地区）	指运港	离境口岸

包装种类	件数	毛重（千克）	净重（千克）	成交方式	运费	保费	杂费

随附单据及编码
标记唛码及备注

项号	商品编号	商品名称及规格型号	数量及单位	单价	总价	币制	原产国（地区）	最终目的国（地区）	境内货源地	征免

报关人员	报关人员证号	电话	兹申明对以上内容承担如实申报、依法纳税之法律责任	海关批注及签章
申报单位			申报单位（签章）	

Figure 13-13 A Sample Customs Clearance Form

INSTRUCTION FOR CARGO TRANSPORT BY SEA						
国际海运货物委托书						
SHIPPER（发货人）:					TEL	
ADDRESS（地址）:						
DATE（日期）:						
CONSIGNEE（收货人）					TEL	
ADDRESS（地址）:						
ALSO NOTIFY（通知人）					TEL	
ADDRESS（地址）:						
PORT OF LOADING(装运港):			POFT OF DESTINATION（目的港）:			
OCEAN VESSEL（船名）:						
CHOICE	DESCRIPTION OF GOODS	MARKS & NUMBERS	NO. OF PACKAGE	GROSS WEIGHT/KG	NET WEIGHT/KG	MEAS.
		TOTAL:				
RATE AGREED（运费协议）			SPECIAL INSTRUCTION（特别附注）			
☐ 货柜						
☐ 拼箱						
柜型及数量	☐ 20' CONTAINER ×		☐ 40' CONTAINER ×		☐ 40’ HQ ×	
	☐ 20' REEFER ×		☐ 40' REEFER ×		☐ 40‘ REEFER HIGH×	
	☐ 20' PLATFORM ×		☐ 40' PLATFORM ×			
	☐ 20' CAR ×		☐ 40' CAR ×			
IMPORTANT-Please indicate which party pays for freight			FREIGHT（运费）		☐	PREPAID
					☐	COLLECT
DOCUMENTS（单证）	INVOICE（发票号码#）:					
	PACKING LIST（装箱单号#）:					
CONSIGNOR’S DETAIL（委托人资料）						
CONSIGNOR’S NAME & ADDERSS（公司名称及地址）			INSTRUCTION BY:（经手人） SIGNED & SEALED: 签字及盖章			

Figure 13-14 A Sample Instruction for Cargo Transport by Sea

1. Shipper
TIANJIN BINHAI IMPORT & EXPORT CO., LTD.
NO.188 HAIHE ROAD BINHAI DISTRICT TIANJIN

2. BL No. SINOTRANS-CAS-20056

中国对外贸易运输总公司
CHINA NATIONAL FOREIGN TRADE TRANSPORTATION GROUP

3. Consignee or order
TO ORDER

4. Notify Party
SINGAPORE WONKA TRADING COMPANY LTD 67 ANG MO/
KIO AVENUE 8 SINGAPORE 560250

OCEAN BILL OF LADING

SHIPPED on board in apparent good order and condition (unless otherwise indicated) the goods or packages specified herein and to be discharged at the mentioned port of discharge or as near thereto as the vessel may safely get and be always afloat.

The weight, measure, marks and numbers, quality, contents and value, being particulars furnished by the Shipper, are not checked by the Carrier on loading.

The Shipper, Consignee and the Holder of the bill of lading hereby expressly accept and agree to all printed, written or stamped provisions, exceptions and conditions of this bill of lading, including those on the back hereof.

IN WITNESS WHEREOF the number of original BLs stated below have been signed, one of which being accomplished the other(s) to be void.

5. Pre-carriage by

6. Port of Loading TIANJIN CHINA

7. Vessel and Voy. No. DONG FENG V.133

8. Port of Transshipment

9. Port of Discharge SINGAPORE

10. Final Destination SINGAPORE

11. For arrival info & release of cargo contact

12. Marks & Nos.	13. No. of cont. or pkgs.	14. Description of packages and goods	15. Gross weight (kgs.)	16. Measurement (cbm)
SWTC SINGAPORE NO.1-30 TBIM-SWTC-09	30 CARTONS	SWIMMING SUITS 30 CARTONS CREDIT NUMBER: KOS879 DATE OF CREDIT: 20220510 THE NAME OF ISSUING BANK: BANK OF CHINA SINGAPORE	1,260 KGS.	25.20 M^3

17. Total number of Containers or other Packages or units received by the Carrier (in words) SAY TOTAL THIRTY CARTONS ONLY

18. Freight and charges | **19. Revenue tons** | **20. Rate** | **21. Per** | **22. Prepaid** | **23. Collect**

24. Exchange rate

25. Prepaid at TIANJIN CHINA

27. Payable at

28. Place and date of issue JUNE 15, 2022 TIANJIN CHINA

26. Total prepaid in national currency

29. No. of original B(s) /L Three (3)

32. Signature
Signed for or on behalf of the Master
张楠
as Agent

30. LADEN ON BOARD THE VESSEL
Date June 16, 2022 **By**

31. CONTAINER/SEAL NO. MBLU4459040/771126/CY-CY

Figure 13-15 A Sample Bill of Lading

13.1.2.12 Shipping advice 装船通知

Shipping advice is the notice you send to the consignee that the cargo has been "on board" the ship before or no later than the date of departure. There is no uniform format, but the following elements should be included: consignee, consignor, name of goods, B/L number, container/**seal number**, vessel name, voyage, port of loading, port of destination, estimated time of departure and estimated time of arrival. It has particular significance under Incoterms FOB and CFR, as the importer depends on the shipping advice to purchase insurance. Therefore, don't forget to send the shipping advice to the importer under these terms. Figure13-16 is a sample shipping advice.

集装箱封箱号

13.1.2.13 Beneficiary certification 受益人证明

The beneficiary certification is a document under a letter of credit, as the exporter is normally referred to as the "beneficiary" under an L/C. With other payment arrangements, however, the similar document is called a "supplier declaration". It is used mainly on occasions where the importer has certain special requirements that are difficult or unable to be attested to with official documents which necessitates the exporter's guarantee to take on some or some possible obligations. When used this way, it functions sort of like a **letter of guarantee**.

保函

The format is not in uniform. You need only to entitle the letter, "beneficial certification", and start the main body with "We hereby certify that…", followed by what the customer requires , and end it with a signature and a stamp. Figure 13-17 is a sample beneficiary certification.

13.1.2.14 Bill of exchange 汇票

See Chapter 10. Figure 13-18 is a sample bill of exchange.

TIANJIN BINHAI IMPORT & EXPORT CO., LTD.

NO. 188 HAIHE ROAD, BINHAI DISTRICT, TIANJIN, P. R. CHINA

TEL No.: 0086-22-8835097X FAX No.: 0086-22-8835099X

WEB: www.tjbhix.com E-MAIL: trade@tjbhix.com

SHIPPING ADVICE

INVOICE NO.: TBIM-SWTC-09

DATE: JUNE 10, 2022

S/C NO.: TBIM-SWTC-09

DATE: April 17, 2022

CREDIT NUMBER: KOS879

DATE OF CREDIT: May 10, 2022

THE NAME OF ISSUING BANK: BANK OF CHINA SINGAPORE

WE HEREBY INFORM YOU THAT THE GOODS UNDER THE ABOVE-MENTIONED CREDIT HAVE BEEN SHIPPED. THE DETAILS OF SHIPMENT ARE STATED BELOW.

COMMODITY: SWIMMING SUITS

QUANTITY: TOTAL 3,000 PCS IN 30 CARTONS

INVOICE VALUE: USD262,500.00

OCEAN VESSEL/SHIPPED PER S.S.: DONG FENG V.133

BILL OF LADING NO.: SINOTRANS-CAS-20056

DATE OF SHIPMENT: JUNE 15, 2022

PORT OF LOADING: TIANJIN CHINA

PORT OF DESTINATION: SINGAPORE

ETA: JUNE 30, 2022

CONTAINER/SEAL NO.: MBLU4459040/771126/CY-CY

MARKS:

SWTC

SINGAPORE

NO. 1-30

TBIM-SWTC-09

李明

Legal Representative or Authorized Signature

Figure 13-16 A Sample Shipping Advice

TIANJIN BINHAI IMPORT & EXPORT CO., LTD.

NO. 188 HAIHE ROAD, BINHAI DISTRICT, TIANJIN, P. R. CHINA

TEL No.: 0086-22-8835097X FAX No.: 0086-22-8835099X

WEB: www.tjbhix.com E-MAIL: trade@tjbhix.com

BENEFICIARY CERTIFICATION

CREDIT NUMBER: KOS879

DATE OF CREDIT: May 10, 2022

THE NAME OF ISSUING BANK: BANK OF CHINA SINGAPORE

INVOICE NO.: TBIM-SWTC-09

DATE: JUNE 10, 2022

S/C NO.: TBIM-SWTC-09

DATE: April 17, 2022

WE HEREBY CERTIFY THAT ALL TERMS AND CONDITIONS OF DOCUMENTARY CREDIT NO. KOS879 HAVE BEEN COMPLIED WITH.

李明

Legal Representative or Authorized Signature

Figure 13-17 A Sample Beneficiary Certification

BILL OF EXCHANGE

No. TIA00188

Exchange For USD262,500.00 TIANJIN JUNE 16, 2022

(amount in figure) (place and date of issue)

At ******** sight of this FIRST Bill of exchange (SECOND being unpaid)

Pay to BANK OF CHINA TIANJIN BRANCH or order the sum of

SAY U.S. DOLLARS TWO HUNDRED AND SIXTY-TWO THOUSAND FIVE HUNDRED ONLY

(amount in words)

Value received for 3,000 PIECES of SWIMMING SUITS

(quantity) (name of commodity)

Draw under BANK OF CHINA SINGAPORE

LC No. KOS879 dated MAY 10, 2022

To: BANK OF CHINA SINGAPORE
4 BATTERY ROAD, BANK OF CHINA BUILDING
SINGAPORE 049908

For and on behalf of
TIANJIN BINHAI IMPORT & EXPORT CO., LTD.

李明

(Authorized Signature)

Figure 13-18 A Sample Bill of Exchange

13.2 Notes on Documentation 制单中的注意事项

The documents involved in an export transaction normally constitute **a full set**, used for presentation, negotiation and collecting payment. Documents are important for a transaction regardless of the payment method, but more so under a letter of credit. Principles of documentation under an L/C transaction are generally summarized as "two consistencies"—all other documents should be consistent with the L/C terms, and any one document should be consistent with other documents. For example, the entry for quantity as well as its unit should be consistent in the invoice, the packing list, and any other

一整套

documents. And if the bill of lading specifies a shipping mark, the invoice should not indicate "N/M (no marking)". Furthermore, every document has an issuing date, and these dates should be logical and in compliance with international trade conventions.

Documentation is critical for a transaction. A simple error with documents is likely to result in significant losses. Particularly when the market fluctuates dramatically or when business disputes arise, an error with documents makes a good excuse for the importer to break the contract. However, normally, not every error is fatal. So, neither should you take it lightly nor **make a fuss about everything**. A reasonable assessment of the impact might be a proper attitude toward an error. Hopefully, now you may have obtained a deeper understanding of the export process by grasping the key points with documentation.

大惊小怪

Exercises 练习

I. True or False

1. Under an L/C, all the documents must comply with the credit. ( )
2. The documents must be consistent with each other. ( )
3. The date of invoice should be prior to that of any other document. ( )
4. The date of the packing list is normally the same with that of the invoice. ( )
5. The date of packing list is normally no prior to that of the B/L. ( )
6. The on-board date should be no earlier than the latest date of shipment specified in the L/C. ( )
7. The date of the insurance policy should be later than that of the B/L. ( )
8. The date of the insurance policy could be prior to that of the invoice. ( )
9. The date of the certificate of origin should be prior to that of the invoice. ( )
10. The date of the inspection certificate should be no later than that of the B/L. ( )
11. The date of the inspection certificate could be half a year prior to that of the B/L. ( )

12. The date of the beneficiary certification should be no earlier than that of the B/L. (   )
13. The date of the bill of exchange should be earlier than that of the B/L, invoice and other documents. (   )
14. The date of the bill of exchange should be later than the expiry date of the L/C. (   )
15. The bill of exchange is the latest of all documents. (   )

II. Multiple Choice Questions

1. Which of the following documents can be used as a quotation? (   )
   [A] The commercial invoice.
   [B] The *proforma* invoice.
   [C] The customs invoice.
   [D] The consular invoice.
2. Which of the following documents is always in a standard format for the importing country that requires it? (   )
   [A] The commercial invoice.
   [B] The *proforma* invoice.
   [C] The customs invoice.
   [D] The consular invoice.
3. Which of the following term of the contract or L/C is unacceptable to the exporter? (   )
   [A] A contract term that requires a deadline for the importer to open the L/C.
   [B] A contract term that allows a quantity tolerance.
   [C] A credit term that requires an inspection certificate signed by the importer.
   [D] A credit term that requires a shipping advice.
4. Which of the following statement is INCORRECT about a *proforma* invoice? (   )
   [A] It can be used as an offer to the importer.
   [B] It has to fix a validity period when used as an offer.
   [C] It must be confirmed by both the exporter and importer before used as an offer.
   [D] It can be used the same way as a commercial invoice.

5. Which of the following term for a letter of credit is unacceptable to the exporter? (　　)
   [A] The credit requires the B/L be "MADE OUT TO APPLICANT".
   [B] The credit requires the B/L be "MADE OUT TO ORDER".
   [C] The credit requires the B/L be "MADE OUT TO ISSUING BANK".
   [D] The credit requires the inspection certificate be signed by the importer.

III. Documentation

Fill in the application forms for applying for inspection, cargo transport, cargo transportation insurance and customs clearance.

Chapter 14 An Overview of the Import Process

第十四章 进口流程概述

Learning Objectives:

◆ An overview of the import process
◆ Procedures of the import process

2021 marks the 20th **anniversary** of China's accession to the World Trade Organization. Data from the **WTO's Research and Statistics Division** show that while world trade in goods has nearly doubled in the past 20 years, China's total export of goods has grown more than **sevenfold**, and its total imports nearly **sixfold**. In 2020, China accounted for an **astonishing** 12% of the world's total import of goods.[①] And beginning in 2018, China International Import Expo, which was held in Shanghai, has given a further boost to China's import. As of 2021, the Expo has held four sessions (see Figure 14-1).

周年
WTO 研究和统计司
7 倍　6 倍
惊人的

Figure 14-1 The 4th China International Import Expo

① http://chinawto.mofcom.gov.cn/article/ap/p/202105/20210503063176.shtml.

14.1 Overview 概述

有利可图的

Suppose you are still working for that Tianjin Binhai Import & Export Co., Ltd. and are sourcing online for a **lucrative** product to sell in the Chinese market. If the searching turns out promising, how do you set about importing the desired product? What procedures do you follow? And what formalities must be completed? The following instruction may help you answer these questions.

进出口经营权
进口许可证
进口免税证明
进料加工或来料加工
补偿贸易

First of all, it doesn't hurt to repeat that you must obtain the **right for import and export** before you can import in the name of your company. Refer to Chapter 1 in case you forget the formalities. Sometimes, an **import license** or a **duty-exemption certificate for import** is necessary before you sign the contract. If you are in the businesses of **processing with imported or customer-supplied materials**, or of **compensation trade**, approval should also be obtained from certain government departments beforehand. Once approved, your company name will be put on record by the Customs.

Secondly, it's good to know that Incoterm FOB is preferred by many importers and thus advisable to you as a beginner. It saves you the sea freight, the insurance premium and outgoings of foreign exchange, as you can arrange for shipping and insurance on your own.

授信额度　单笔授信
洗钱
制裁
业务合规审查要求
业务资料

Thirdly, if payment is by letter of credit, the following requirements should be satisfied before you can apply to a bank for the opening of a credit: (1) You have the right for import and export; (2) You have a good credit standing and no bad financial record; (3) You have the **credit line** or **a single credit** required for opening the L/C; (4) The transaction is real; you are not involved in any sort of money **laundering** or other illegal activities; the exporter's bank has no record of being **sanctioned** by any international financial organizations; and the transaction complies with the **compliance review requirements** of the issuing bank; (5) You have a full and valid set of **transaction documents**.

If the deal is the first between you and the exporter, a letter of credit is mostly required for payment. Assuming that the deal is concluded under FOB and the payment is by L/C at the request of the exporter. After signing the sales contract, you need to complete a number of tasks—opening the L/C, booking the shipping space, purchasing ocean cargo insurance, having the cargo shipped, examining the documents, making the payment, receiving the cargo at the port of destination, inspecting the commodity, clearing the goods for import, taking delivery, and making claims on the responsible party (parties) if problems arise with the delivery, the commodity or any other aspects of the deal (see Figure 14-2).

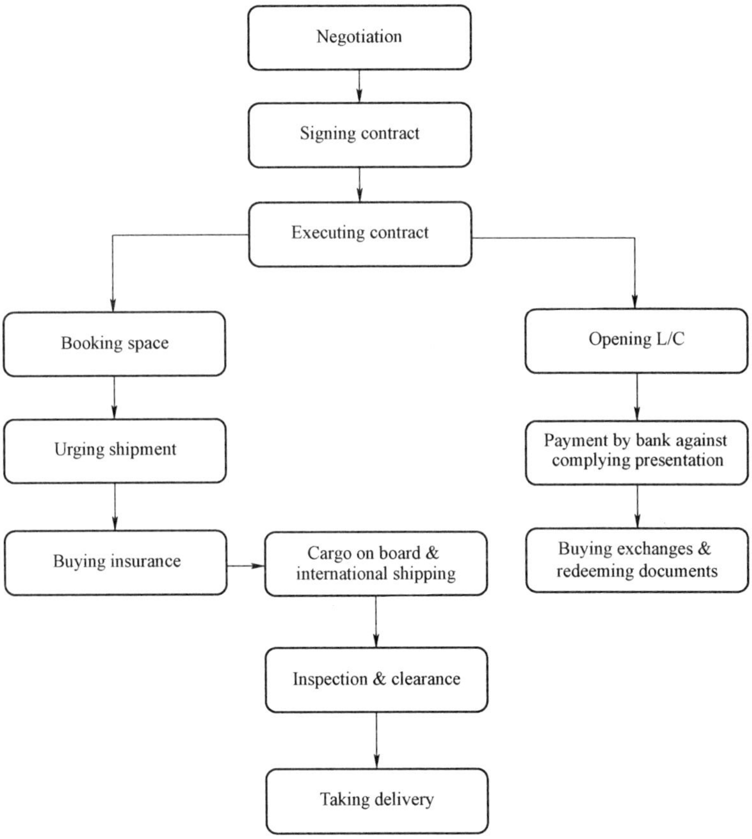

Figure 14-2 An Overview of the Import Process

If the import contract is concluded under other Incoterms rules or terms of payment, the procedures may have some differences. For example, a CFR contract shifts the task of booking shipping space to the exporter, and a CIF contract shifts both responsibilities for transportation and insurance to the exporter. And when the deal is paid by T/T or collection, you are relieved of the trouble of opening an L/C. Therefore, your duties in an import transaction vary by the contract terms, particularly the Incoterms rule and the payment terms adopted.

14.2 The Import Process 进口流程

Suppose you have concluded an import contract based on Incoterm FOB and payment by L/C, let's see how you should perform your duties under this contract.

14.2.1 Opening the L/C 开立信用证

As the importer, you must open the L/C if so required by the contract. A deadline for opening the L/C is normally stipulated in the contract, which is generally a date that allows the exporter enough time for shipment, such as 30 days before the time of shipment. As the deadline is set forth in the contract, this should be complied with.

营业执照
进口许可证 进口配额证
审批文件

Applying to a bank for an L/C normally requires a copy of your **business license**, the contract and other necessary attachments, such as the **import license**, a **certificate for import quota**, **approval documents** from certain government departments, etc.

开证申请人承诺书
在此不可撤销地受约束

You need to fill out an application form for a letter of credit, which requires such information as business name and address of the beneficiary and contract number, expiry date and place of the credit, latest time of shipment, nature of the credit, description of goods, documents required, amount and type of the credit, special terms and conditions and other terms and conditions, etc. Finally, sign and stamp the **letter of undertaking**, declaring that you have "completed all formalities before import, and are **hereby irrevocably bound** by the credit to be opened by the issuing bank in accordance with the application form". The credit shall be issued and forwarded to the exporter after being examined by the bank. Should the exporter ask to extend the time of shipment or expiry date of the credit, change the port of destination or other terms of the credit, you need to apply to the issuing bank for an amendment if you agree to the changes proposed by the exporter.

Finally, transfer the foreign exchange or **foreign exchange quota** to the issuing bank. And in line with international trade conventions, make a **deposit** and pay a **fee** for the bank's service. The amount of deposit varies depending on your credit standing and the financial strength of the bank, such as 50%~70% of the total amount of the credit.

外汇额度

保证金 手续费

14.2.2 Arranging for Shipment 办理运输

As the contract is under FOB, you are responsible for arranging for shipment. You may book the shipping space on your own or authorize it to a freight forwarding company or to the exporter. Upon receiving the expected shipping date advised from the exporter, you book the shipping space via the forwarder by filling out a form detailing your shipping instructions. After that, inform the exporter of the name of the vessel and its estimated time of arrival at the loading port, and urge the exporter to dispatch the goods.

14.2.3 Purchasing Insurance 购买保险

As the contract is under FOB, you are also responsible for covering the goods with insurance. On receiving the exporter's shipping advice, you should waste no time in purchasing insurance from an underwriter such as the People's Insurance Company of China. Cargo insurance for import is normally arranged in one of two ways: a **specific cover** or an **open cover**. A specific cover is an insurance cover for a specific shipment while an open cover is one for more than one shipment. For imports that **spread** over several shipments over a relatively longer period, an open cover simplifies the formalities and avoids the possibility that you forget to cover a certain shipment, as you do not need to take out a new cover for each shipment. Instead, you merely notify the underwriter of the vessel name, B/L No., date of

逐笔投保 预约保险

摊开

departure, commodity name and quantity, port of delivery, port of destination, etc. upon receiving the shipping advice sent from the exporter.

14.2.4 Making Payment 付款赎单

As the contract is settled by an L/C, once the goods are loaded on board the ship, the exporter may negotiate payment with one of his/her local banks against a complying presentation of documents you require. The documents are subsequently transferred by the negotiating bank to the issuing bank (sometimes a paying bank nominated by the issuing bank) which then examines them. If no discrepancy is found, the issuing bank reimburses the negotiating bank. Finally, you will be asked to pay the issuing bank in order to obtain the documents.

When payment is by collection, the documents are forwarded to you by the banks against payment or acceptance, but neither the remitting bank on the exporter's side nor the collecting bank on your side is responsible for examining the documents—you must examine them on your own, with special care. If the documents turn out to be not in conformity with the contract, your options available may include postponing the payment or refusing to pay for or accept the cargo. Whichever your decision is, you must have sound reasons and evidences and inform the exporter through the banks without delay.

14.2.5 Clearing Customs for Import 进口清关

When the cargo arrives at the port of destination, it must be cleared for import. Customs clearance requires a **Customs Entry Form** together with copies of the contract, invoice, packing list and bill of lading. The Customs shall verify the consistency of cargo with the documents, collect the import duty and other taxes and inspect the cargo (discussed in 14.2.6 in detail). Once these are done, it **releases the cargo** by signing and **stamping** the B/L. After that, you may take delivery of the goods.

进口货物报关单

放行货物

盖章

14.2.6 Inspecting the Cargo 进口检验

Once picking up the goods, you must check and inspect them carefully. If any problems should be found with the quality, quantity, packing, etc., you must have them reinspected by a mutually agreed-upon or reputable inspection authority or service, obtain the inspection certificates in time, and make a claim or claims within the prescribed period as per the contract. Don't forget that goods subject to a statutory inspection must be inspected by the inspection and quarantine authority under the Customs at the port of discharge or the final destination, otherwise they are not allowed to be sold or used. Goods not in the list for statutory inspection might be **spot checked** by the inspection authority as well, and must be **rectified**, returned or destroyed if problems are found, depending on the seriousness of the problems. 抽检 纠正

In order to make a claim within the prescribed period, goods under the following circumstances must be inspected at the port of discharge: The contract requires so; you are obliged to make payment on condition that the goods pass the inspection; the contract allows a short valid period for making claims; or the cargo is found damaged, short-delivered or abnormal upon discharge. In the absence of the above circumstances and in case your company is far from the port, the goods can be transferred to your company's premise for **checking and acceptance**. In so doing, if you should find any problems with the goods, ask your local inspection authority for reinspection immediately so that the claim can be made within the valid period. 验收

14.2.7 Claim 索赔

If a delayed delivery causes you a loss or the goods are found defective upon arrival, you may make a claim against the party or parties that you believe to be responsible. Here are some tips for doing that:

- Find out the cause and determine the responsible party for the damage or loss. The responsible party could be the exporter, the carrier, or the insurance company, etc., depending on the nature and cause of the damage or loss.

• Claim against the responsible party with sound evidence, such as records of accident, necessary certificates and reports, physical evidence and photos, etc.

• Watch for the allowed period for claims. The claim against the responsible party should be submitted within the prescribed period and would be invalid after expiration. The valid period for claims is usually stipulated in the contract.

• The amount of claim should be determined taking consideration of the specific circumstances, which normally include the value of the damaged goods and related expenses such as the inspection fees.

Exercises 练习

I. True or False

1. You have to obtain the right for import and export before you can import in your companies' own name. (　　)
2. You cannot open an L/C with a bank if the underlying transaction is not real. (　　)
3. When you agree to an amendment to the L/C advised from the exporter, you should notify your consent both to the exporter and the issuing bank. (　　)
4. For import, we need to arrange for a ship to pick up the goods at a foreign port if the deal is concluded under FOB. However, under CIF, the exporter shall book the space and ship the goods to a Chinese port. Therefore, the cargo risk we assume under FOB is greater than that under CIF. (　　)
5. The procurement cost of imported goods includes the procurement price, the import duty and other taxes. (　　)
6. The CIF price includes the sea freight and insurance premium which covers the distance till the named port of destination, but the exporter is under no obligation to make sure the goods reach the port of destination. (　　)
7. Among the methods of payment, L/C is more reliable to exporters, while D/P and D/A are more popular with importers. (　　)
8. An inspection for import could only be conducted at the port of destination. (　　)

9. Quality is an integral part of a sales contract. If the merchandise does not conform to the agreed upon quality, the importer has the right to make a claim or even reject the goods. ( )
10. The Customs has no governing power over import of goods that are not subject to statutory inspection. ( )

II. Multiple Choice Questions

1. Which of the following documents grants you the fundamental right for import and export? ( )
   [A] The import license.
   [B] The import quota.
   [C] The Form for Registration as a Foreign Trade Dealer.
   [D] The duty exemption certificate for import.
2. Which of the following quotations is a CORRECT syntax of Incoterms rule for import to China? ( )
   [A] $55 per carton FOB Shanghai
   [B] $90 per carton CIF Tianjin
   [C] $55 per carton FCA Zhengzhou
   [D] $90 per carton FAS Ningbo
3. Which of the following is NOT a possible reason for the wide adoption of FOB for import to China? ( )
   [A] The exporter doesn't want to bear the risk of the freight rate rising.
   [B] The exporter doesn't want to bear the trouble of international transport.
   [C] It helps the importer save on foreign exchange.
   [D] It helps the exporter save on foreign exchange.
4. Which one of the following practices regarding the time of opening an L/C is NOT appropriate? ( )
   [A] The L/C should be opened within the deadline if any such deadline is stipulated in the contract.
   [B] The L/C should be opened when the exporter notifies his/her readiness for shipment.
   [C] The L/C should be opened when the exporter confirms the time of shipment.
   [D] The L/C should be opened at the importer's convenience.

5. When a shipment for import is covered All Risks as per *CIC* under Incoterms CIF, ( ).
   [A] the exporter bears all risks when the cargo is *en route*
   [B] the importer bears all risks when the cargo is *en route*
   [C] the insurance company bears all risks after the cargo is loaded on board the vessel
   [D] responsibility for the cargo transfers from the exporter to the importer when the cargo is loaded on board the vessel
6. An inspection term of a contract reads "Shipping weight, landed quality", which means ( ).
   [A] inspection at the port of destination is final
   [B] inspection in the exporting country and re-inspection in the importing country are combined as criteria for acceptance of the goods
   [C] inspection at the loading port is final
   [D] inspection of weight at the loading port and of quality at the destination port are combined as criteria for acceptance of the goods
7. Which is (are) the possible outcome(s) when a batch of imported goods subject to a statutory inspection doesn't pass the inspection? ( )*
   [A] It may be returned to the exporting country.
   [B] It may be destroyed under the supervision of the Customs.
   [C] It may be rectified and resold in China.
   [D] It may still be sold in the Chinese market.
8. Under an import transaction by L/C, the exporter has presented complying documents for negotiation, but the importer finds the goods defective upon arrival at the port of destination, then, ( ).
   [A] the importer can instruct the issuing bank not to reimburse the negotiating bank
   [B] the issuing bank should be responsible for the discrepancy between the goods and documents
   [C] the importer should not make payment to the issuing bank
   [D] the importer should make payment to the issuing bank but make a claim on the exporter as per the contract

9. Which of the following payment term is most favorable from an importer's perspective? ( )
   [A] Cash in advance.
   [B] Open account.
   [C] Documentary collection.
   [D] Documentary credit.
10. Which one of the following statements is TRUE about making a claim upon receiving the goods? ( )
   [A] You can make a claim any time after the goods arrive at destination.
   [B] The claim must be supported with necessary evidence, such as a certificate of re-investigation issued by an agreed upon or recognized inspection authority or institution.
   [C] You may only make a claim on the exporter.
   [D] You may only make a claim on the carrier.

III. Case Study

1. Suppose you are a seafood importer, and now considering importing a batch of frozen **white shrimp** from **Ecuador**. How would you negotiate terms of quality and inspection with the exporter to make sure the shrimp is safe and not contaminated by the new corona virus? Discuss in groups, draft your contract terms and submit them as group work.

   白虾　厄瓜多尔

2. A Chinese company imported coca beans from a Brazil merchant. The goods were to be delivered in two shipments. The payment method was by L/C at sight issued by Bank of China, with one L/C for each shipment. After each shipment, the exporter presented the documents within the validity period to his bank for negotiation. Once having examined the documents for the first shipment and finding no discrepancies, the bank negotiated the payment to the exporter and Bank of China reimbursed the negotiating bank. However, when the first shipment arrived, the importer found the quality of the goods was not in conformity with the contract, so she asked Bank of China not to pay for the second shipment, but the Bank refused. Do you think Bank of China did the right thing?

牙科的

3. Jyemey Dental Co., Ltd., a **dental** hospital group in China, imported a medical equipment through an agency for the opening of a new hospital. The contract had stipulated that the allowed period for claim should be within 30 days after the arrival of the goods at the port of destination. After the goods were unloaded at the port of destination, the agency transferred the goods to the hospital without delay. As Jyemey's new **outpatient** building had not been built up, the equipment could not be installed and tested. Half a year later, the building was completed, the equipment was installed and tested, and it was found that the equipment could not work properly. Re-inspection by the commodity inspection authority of China proved that the equipment was second-hand, so Jyemey asked the agency to make a claim, but the exporter refused to compensate Jyemey for the loss, and Jyemey suffered a great loss. What lesson should we learn from this case?

门诊

IV. Calculations

原奶

1. A Chinese company is going to import **raw milk** from Rotterdam. The exporter's offer is €500 per M/T CIF Shanghai (for 110% of the CIF value). If the sea freight from Rotterdam to the Chinese port is €110, and the insurance premium rate is 2%, what is the FOB price of this transaction?

杏仁，扁桃仁

2. We are making an enquiry about **almonds** to an American exporter, and it quotes us $155 per case CIF Shenzhen. If the FOB price of the American company is $140, the sea freight is $10 per case, and the insurance premium rate is 0.5%, will the exporter accept our counteroffer at $145 per case CIF Shenzhen?

Chapter 15 Cross-Border E-Commerce

第十五章 跨境电商

Learning Objectives:

- ◆ An overview of cross-border e-commerce
- ◆ Basics about cross-border e-commerce for import
- ◆ Basics about cross-border e-commerce for export

Cross-border e-commerce (CBEC) is online trade that crosses national or customs borders. It is becoming a new development trend in international trade and China is the driving force. Over the past two decades, China's CBEC has emerged and evolved into a new accelerator of economy, particularly at a time when the wide adoption of online consumption patterns during the Covid-19 pandemic has fueled the rapid growth of worldwide e-commerce. According to China Customs Statistics, from 2016 to 2020, China's CBEC import and export scale has increased nearly 10 times, reaching 1.92 **trillion** yuan (万亿) in 2020. And an average annual growth rate of transaction value at about 20% is much higher than that of traditional international trade. The landscape of international business has never been the same. No **practitioner** (从业者) of import and export could afford to turn a blind eye to the development in this field.

15.1 Overview 概述

Over the past two decades, e-commerce has revolutionized both business models and our life. The same also occurs in the international marketplace. Cross-border e-commerce meets our **aspirations** for better life and provides businesses **immense** opportunities to expand worldwide. In this chapter, we shall begin with an overview of this sector in China and then discuss major business models, platforms and key issues for running a cross-border e-commerce business, etc. Let's start with the overview by tracing its development in China and comparing its features with traditional import and export.

渴望
巨大的

15.1.1 Development of Cross-Border E-Commerce in China 跨境电商在中国的发展历程

It is generally agreed that CBEC in China has gone through three stages of beginning, development and maturity:

♦ **1999—2003 : beginning**

The launch of Alibaba in 1999 started China's exploration for cross-border e-commerce. This marked the beginning of Chinese traders to establish business relations with overseas buyers via the Internet, and of transformation from a traditional mode of trade to an ever more Internet-based one. However, at this initial stage, CBEC platforms mainly played the role of an advertising media—displaying products, introducing factories, publicizing businesses, etc. Constrained by technology and national policies, the transaction function had not been realized. The platforms targeted primarily at small and medium-sized enterprises, aiming to help them develop global market.

♦ **2004—2012 : development**

敦煌网

In 2004, **DHgate.com** was launched, marking the beginning of an era of integration. In addition to advertising, offline payment and logistics were integrated to complete the entire transaction process. The B2B model familiar to us was pioneered at this stage. This model reduced links in the transaction, saved cost for commodity inspection and customs clearance, shortened the supply chain, **slashed** the overall

大幅削减

cost for import and export, which all translated into improved bargaining power of Chinese businesses in the international market. For platforms, the initial business model based on membership fees gradually gave way to a commission-based model—the platforms charged a commission from sellers at a percentage of their sales for the service provided.

♦ **2013—present : maturity**

Since 2013, CBEC in China has entered a stage of growing maturity. This stage is no longer marked by the establishment of one or two platforms, but by three features. First, the user base of CBEC platform has expanded from small and medium-sized enterprises to include large businesses and factories, which **propels** a constant improvement in product quality and technology and has paved the way for a switch of competitive edge from price to technology. Second, more and more big Internet service providers have got involved, boosting the capability of platforms in processing transactions. Third, the addition of mobile terminals has **skyrocketed** the user base. Previously, CBEC was conducted merely on computers or laptops. Beginning from this stage, more users have been able to engage in CBEC via their smartphones, thanks to the wide coverage of 4G network.

驱动

使……剧增

15.1.2 Features of Cross-Border E-Commerce in China 中国跨境电商的特征

You may engage in CBEC for import, export or both; but no matter which one, you often rely on a CBEC platform. Popular platforms include: Alibaba, AliExpress, Amazon, eBay, Tmall Global, JD Worldwide, Wish, Shopee, Lazada, **KaolaHaigou**, **Xiaohongshu**, **SHEIN**, to name just a few. Some of them have a global reach, such as AliExpress and Amazon, others are rising stars locally, such as Shopee and Lazada for Southeast Asian market. They may focus on export, import or both, and may be comprehensive or specialized in terms of product categories.

考拉海购 小红书

希音

Your basic business model on a certain platform, depending on the platform you choose, could be B2B (business to business), B2C (business to consumer) or C2C (consumer to consumer) based on your identity as the seller and your customer's identity. However, in recent years, platforms tend to diverge in their admission policies. Some still allow both businesses and individuals to register, such as eBay, Amazon and Wish. Others have ceased to accept application from individual sellers, such as AliExpress. Still others have always been business-only platforms, such as Lazada.

CBEC also differs significantly from traditional import and export. In comparison, it's not difficult to find the following features that are unique to CBEC:

Firstly, the consumer side of CBEC is more striking than that of traditional import and export. In the past, global trade was dominated by large corporations, but digital platforms have empowered entrepreneurs and small businesses to become "micro cross-border businesses". Most of them now engage in retailing instead of wholesaling and serve the needs of end users instead of businesses. Meanwhile, the strengthening of network security and supervision of the platforms has boosted consumer confidence in online shopping, resulting in a surge of both domestic and foreign consumer base for CBEC. Therefore, in many cases, "CBEC" is used predominantly to refer to B2C or C2C selling, though B2B should not be neglected.

Secondly, the obvious lean towards the consumer side also makes transactions exhibit some striking features which are different from traditional import and export. For example, orders for CBEC are mostly in much smaller quantities of shorter intervals. They are distributed within a year and have a much shorter fulfillment period, which requires both new operation strategies on the part of businesses and new supervision policies on the part of the government.

Thirdly, the industry is drastically matured in recent years. A full spectrum of B2B, B2C and C2C platforms for both import and export is formed, though with a heavy **dose** of the latter two models in terms of user base. To serve the booming industry and unique needs, both commercial and public service providers have got involved and **refined** their services. Logistics, payment, customs clearance, etc. are becoming more and more speedy and convenient. The supply chain is maturing and a CBEC ecosystem is gradually coming into being.

剂量

改进，改善

Notably, however, in this textbook, we shall only focus on CBEC for B2C and C2C transactions, as CBEC for B2B transactions shares a lot with what has already been discussed in the previous chapters.

15.2 Cross-Border E-Commerce for Import 进口跨境电商

In recent years, "**haitao** (buying from overseas)" has become increasingly popular among some Chinese consumers. "Haitao" via an online platform is essentially CBEC for import. Statistics from **IResearch** in 2016 and 2017 shows 84% of the consumers are women aged 19 to 40, and 30% of them have a monthly income between 5000 and 8000 RMB. The driving force are married women with babies or kids, who look for brand or quality products such as cosmetics, garments, handbags, watches, diapers, milk powder and other baby products. However, sometimes the buying process is frustrating. The major pain points for consumers include: possibility of receiving **counterfeit** or inferior products, **prolonged** or expensive logistics, and difficulties in **return and replacement** of goods.

海淘

艾瑞咨询

假冒的 拖长的

退换货

Businesses and government alike have been working hard to resolve these issues. Over nearly a decade's development, China's CBEC for import has achieved significant advancement in maturity. The supply chain has been completed and refined. Overseas brands or individual sellers and Chinese consumers are connected by B2B intermediaries and/or B2C retailers, supported by logistics, payment, customs clearance services and local **CBEC comprehensive pilot zones** and associations. **Peripheral** services also develop to facilitate transactions. Some businesses provide shopping guidance and **rebates** on their websites to customers; others serve as agent for foreign brands or sellers, running their Chinese-version websites; still others provide system integration services to CBEC businesses. So basically, some of the above issues now can be resolved to customers and businesses. Getting to know the following business models of CBEC firms may help you obtain a deeper understanding of this sector.

跨境电商综合试验区

外围的，周边的

返利

15.2.1 Business Models 商业模式

The business models of Chinese CBEC firms for import has been innovated and flourished, with the following typical types emerging on the market:

♦ **The buyer model 买手模式**

The CBEC platform recruits overseas buyers to set up accounts on the platform and source quality products around the world for consumers. Quality control may be a weakness under this model. Representatives include **ymatou.com**; **g.taobao.com.**

洋码头　淘宝全球购

♦ **The self-running model 自营模式**

The business runs its own CBEC platform and primarily sources and imports products directly from overseas sellers. Even if the platform offers the opportunity for other companies to set up **flagship stores**, it's not the main service of the platform. Representatives include: **mia.com**; **kaola.com.**

旗舰店

蜜芽　考拉海购

♦ **The platform model 平台模式**

Businesses set up stores on the CBEC platform and sell to consumers, relying on the services provided by the platform, but the platform does not sell to consumers. Representative: **tmall.hk.**

天猫国际

♦ **The self-running+ platform model 自营＋平台模式**

The platform both provides services to platform users and sells to consumers. Representatives include: **jd.hk**; **g.suning.com.**

京东国际　苏宁国际

♦ **The social media guided model 社交媒体导流模式**

Businesses create high quality and engaging contents and leverage on such social media behaviors of people as liking, following, commenting and sharing, etc. to gain traffic and achieve sales. Representative: **xiaohongshu.com**.

小红书

♦ **The live streaming model 直播模式**

Businesses on a live streaming platform invites **influencers/key opinion leaders** and present a sponsored live show and achieve publicity and/or sales via the platform's transaction functions. Representative: TikTok Shop.

高影响力者（网红）/意见领袖

♦ **The shopping guide and rebate model 导购和返利模式**

The business runs its own platform which offers shopping guide service and rebates to customers by selecting quality products and/or discount information of international brand name products. It achieves this by automatically grabbing product links directly from other e-commerce platforms or cooperating with them. Consumers place orders from its website instead of the original platforms and the order is fulfilled by the business. Representatives include: **55haitao.com**; **momoso.com** 55海淘 么么搜

As to payment method selected by consumers, about 55% pay by Visa, 47% by **China UnionPay**, 40% by PayPal and 40% by MasterCard. 中国银联

15.2.2 Logistics and Customs Clearance 物流和清关

Three models for logistics and customs clearance are commonly adopted for CBEC import, which are:

Direct mail model: The product is displayed on a CBEC platform for sale. When ordered, it is directly mailed to consumers from abroad and cleared and taxed as personal luggage or postal packages. 直邮模式

Bonded warehouse model: The product is shipped in bulk to a bonded warehouse located in China in advance, and displayed on a CBEC platform for sale. When ordered, it is mailed to the consumer from the bonded warehouse, and cleared and taxed as personal luggage or postal packages. 保税仓模式

Direct sale with duty paid: The product is imported and cleared in bulk with duty paid like traditional import, and then displayed on a CBEC platform for sale to consumers. 直邮完税模式

15.2.3 Return and Replacement 退换货

Return and replacement of goods is the trickiest issue for CBEC import. Three common models also exist to resolve this:

The bonded warehouse model: Return and replacement is most convenient and speedy under this model, as the purchased product shall be returned to the domestic bonded warehouse or CBEC platform. It normally applies to seller-related return and replacement or to products with a money back guarantee. 保税仓库模式

直邮模式 情况

The direct mail model: Under this model, return and replacement is processed differently in two **scenarios**. In the first, the foreign seller has a bonded warehouse or physical entity in China, so that the purchased product can be returned to the warehouse or the seller's branch or office in China. In the second, the foreign seller does not have any bonded warehouse or physical entity in China, then the purchased product has to be mailed directly back to the seller, with the distribution of freight, duty and fees decided by the platform. However, as this incurs high cost, foreign sellers generally do not offer such an option for problems other than product quality.

转运模式 名义上的

The transshipment model: Return and replacement is the most difficult under this model. As the product is transshipped to China, with the trans-shipper as the **nominal** recipient of the package. This makes the way back highly difficult and costly. Considering the expected obstacles ahead, most buyers tend to give up return or replacement.

15.3 Cross-Border E-Commerce for Export 出口跨境电商

CBEC for export provides a fast track for businesses to expand international market. If you want to pursue a career in this sector, the following questions may be of concern to you: Q1: What platform shall I choose? Q2: What product shall I sell? Q3: How shall I price my product? Q4: How shall I operate my online store? Q5: What payment options shall I offer? Q6: How shall I make international delivery? Let's explore how to run a CBEC business for export guided by these questions.

15.3.1 Choose the Right Platform 选择恰当的平台

Major B2C or C2C CBEC platforms include AliExpress, eBay, Amazon, Wish, Shopee, Lazada, etc. However, consumers from different regions may prefer different platforms, use different devices and have different browsing habits. For example, while European and

American consumers mostly buy on eBay; Russia and Brazil customers favor AliExpress; Shopee and Lazada are popular in Southeast Asian countries; Wish focuses on mobile end and is favored by American youths. Considering such diversity, you must decide your target market, do your homework on their consumption habits before you choose the platform.

15.3.2 Choose the Right Product 选择恰当的产品

Consumer demands vary by country, region and time, so that it is necessary to keep track of what's hot and trending in order to run a successful CBEC business. Choosing a product intuitively is not suggested. You'd better collect and analyze data using data analysis tools both on and outside the platform, which will facilitate your job a lot! Nowadays almost every CBEC platform provides powerful tools on the platform to assist your decision making. Outside tools include Google AdWords, Google Analytics, Google Trending, Google shopping, etc. Small items with higher value to weight may be a good start, such as wedding dresses, as transportation, customs clearance and after-sales service are not complicated. Consumables with higher repeat purchase rate can be another consideration, which help you build customer base and stabilize sales volume. But delicate and perishable products should be avoided.

15.3.3 Price Your Product Properly 合理制定价格

Once you've decided on the platform and the product to sell, you need to price your product. To do that, first you need to research and track the international market of your category to get a sense of expected price and profit. Then, set your pricing goal and choose among one or a combination of several basic pricing strategies: a cost-plus strategy prices the goods by adding a desired margin to the cost. This is the most straightforward way of setting prices, but it ignores competition and consumers' perception; a prevailing pricing strategy prices the goods in line with the market price for similar products, which applies when you do not enjoy significant competitive advantage; a perception pricing strategy prices the goods based on consumers' perception or recognition of the product, which often applies to expensive products with unique selling points. Adopt the basic strategy and make adjustments to achieve your goal. Sometimes, you may also need to consider whether you would offer free shipping, and if not, the ratio between the price and the freight. Statistics from some platforms show that, for some categories of product, an 8:2 or 7:3 ratio drives sales better than more extreme ratios.

15.3.4 Operate Your Online Store 经营你的线上店铺

Operating your online store involves aiming for a high store performance score and keeping improving, and promoting your products with the tools on the platform and conducting marketing campaigns or advertising outside the platform. Your store performance score may reflect such aspects as your product descriptions, customer reviews, store services, logistics performances, honesty in operation, etc., among which customer review is king. Many studies have shown that customer review is a strong predictor of sales. Promotional tools may vary by platform, but mostly include paid advertising or various discounts on the platform. Outside your platform, exposure of products can be improved by search engine optimization or paid advertising relying on Google AdWords, Google Analytics, Google Trending, Google Shopping, etc. Social media marketing or advertising should also be considered, which requires you to set up your business account on mainstream social media networks such as Facebook, Twitter and LinkedIn or video or picture platforms such as YouTube, Instagram and Pinterest. Customers from certain regions may prefer their local social media networks. So, do your homework before you choose the social media platform and then create engaging contents to pose a professional image for your business.

15.3.5 Offer Flexible Payment Options 提供灵活的支付方式

Different from B2B orders, most B2C orders for CBEC are in small amount with high frequency, so that online payment becomes top choice, which further leads to the flourishing of a wide range of small-amount payment methods or tools, including but not limited to credit card, debit card, third-party payment, bank transfer, e-check, e-wallet, gift card, and even **bitcoin** and cash, among which third-party payment is the most preferred option by both businesses and customers, such as PayPal, Alipay, Escrow (an international version of Alipay), Payoneer and PingPong, which are followed by credit card, such as Visa, MasterCard and American Express. Third-party payment service like Escrow is a financial and legal agreement designed to protect both buyer and seller in a transaction. For a fee, Escrow holds payment until both parties fulfill their responsibilities in the transaction. With an Escrow payment, the seller receives the funds only when the buyer has received and accepted the products and/or services that are part of the transaction. However, the seller knows they will receive payment because Escrow.com is holding the funds on his/her behalf.

比特币

As a CBEC seller, you should be aware of the payment options supported by the platform and consider local preferences for payment. As most CBEC platforms expand worldwide, they normally support both mainstream and localized payment methods. It will surely drive sales if you offer your customers the most favored method available on the platform and also diversify the payment options to accommodate varied needs. For instance, though PayPal and Visa dominate the online payment market in Europe with market share of 72% and 54% respectively, iDeal, a similar service to China UnionPay, is the most widely used method in Netherlands, with 82% market share in the country. Clearly, offering this option is a must if you target the Netherlands market.

15.3.6 Make International Delivery 发送货物

Fulfilling the order makes the biggest difference between cross-border and domestic e-commerce. Different from the significant advancing of domestic logistics and the continuous reduction of shipping cost in recent years, international logistics remains weak in terms of safety, timeliness and cost. Thus, it is essential that you select a logistics partner in a **prudent** and reasonable way. Common logistics options include making delivery by:

谨慎的

♦ **Postal package service 邮政包裹服务**

The postal service of a country is generally owned and subsidized by the state, particularly if the country is a developed economy and a member of the **Universal Postal Union**, which makes it the most cost-effective way for fulfilling CBEC orders. However, it is less timely and has a strict restriction with regard to size and weight of the package.

万国邮联

♦ **International couriers 国际快递**

Foreign couriers such as DHL (Germany), TNT (the Netherlands), FEDEX(US), UPS (US) fulfill orders faster, yet are more expensive and have less insights into the pain points of the latest development of CBEC in China. Against such a background, domestic couriers have emerged to be an important force. Representatives include **SF EXPRESS**, **EMS**, **JD Logistics, Cainiao Network,** etc.

顺丰速递　特快专递
京东物流　菜鸟网络

♦ **Special line logistics service 专线物流**

By specializing in shipping to a certain country or region, such as America, Europe, Australia, the Middle East, etc., this type of service can reduce costs through **economies of scale**.

规模效应

♦ **Overseas warehousing 海外仓储**

By warehousing goods in the target country in advance, you can make delivery of the order upon placement from the warehouse like a local business, which dramatically shortens the delivery time and speeds up fulfillment.

15.4 Conclusion 结论

E-commerce has drastically changed our life and commerce, both domestically and internationally. And it keeps innovating, with new platforms and business models constantly popping up. No one can predicate the future, but the only thing for sure is that it will keep powering ahead globally in the foreseeable future. Therefore, keeping a close eye on it is imperative if you want to pursue a career in international business.

Exercises 练习

I. True or False

1. Cross-border e-commerce is a good way for every product to go global. (　　)
2. Most international buyers use PayPal or Alipay for cross-border e-commerce. (　　)
3. Overseas warehouse is applicable for every product for export through cross-border e-commerce. (　　)
4. Lazada and Shopee are popular platforms for South East Asian countries. (　　)
5. Some cross-border e-commerce platforms acquire traffic and sales through livestreaming, such as TikTok Shop. (　　)
6. Managing customer review of your online store requires you to achieve enough sales and positive reviews to your store. (　　)
7. Analyzing data about your online store is mostly done manually and very exhausting. (　　)
8. When you conduct social media marketing, posting engaging content is critical. (　　)
9. Online marketing campaign can be conducted both on and outside a platform for cross-border e-commerce. (　　)
10. When you buy foreign products from online, your order is probably fulfilled in one of the following ways: directly mailed to you, mailed from a bonded warehouse located in China, or directly sold to you with duty paid. (　　)

II. Multiple Choice Questions

1. Which one of the following mainly adopts a buyer model for cross-border e-import? (　　)
   [A] Ymatou.com.
   [B] Jd.hk.
   [C] Xiaohongshu.
   [D] Tmall.hk.
2. Which one of the following platforms mainly adopts a self-running model for cross-border e-import? (　　)
   [A] Ymatou.com.
   [B] Tmall.hk.
   [C] Jd.hk.
   [D] Kaola.com.
3. Which one of the following platforms for cross-border e-import acquires traffic and sales through shared contents of social media influencers and online word of mouth? (　　)
   [A] Ymatou.com.
   [B] Tmall.hk.
   [C] Xiaohongshu.
   [D] TikTok Shop.
4. Which one of the following platforms for cross-border e-import offers shopping guide and rebates to customers? (　　)
   [A] Mia.com.
   [B] 55haitao.com.
   [C] Xiaohongshu.
   [D] Tmall.hk.
5. Under which model is return and replacement most difficult for cross-border e-import? (　　)
   [A] The direct sale model.
   [B] The bonded warehouse model.
   [C] The transshipment model.
   [D] The direct sale with duty paid model.
6. Which of the following factor(s) should be considered when you run a cross-border e-business? (　　)*
   [A] Product.
   [B] Price.

[C] Promotion.

[D] Place.

7. Which one of the following is the correct order of preferred payment services for cross-border e-commerce by most European buyers? (   )

[A] Visa, PayPal, Mastercard.

[B] PayPal, Alipay, Visa.

[C] PayPal, Visa, Mastercard.

[D] PayPal, Visa, Alipay.

8. Which of the following factor(s) influence (s) how much you price your product online? (   ) *

[A] Your pricing goal.

[B] Your target market.

[C] Your cost.

[D] Your competitors' prices.

9. According to the textbook, which of the following online platforms are preferred by Russia and Brazil customers respectively? (   )

[A] Ebay and Amazon.

[B] Ebay and Alibaba.

[C] Amazon and AliExpress.

[D] AliExpress and AliExpress.

10. If you do not consider overseas warehouse, what logistics option(s) do you have for cross-border e-export? (   )*

[A] Postal package service.

[B] Foreign couriers.

[C] Domestic couriers.

[D] Special line logistics.

III. Case Study

1. Log onto the listed platforms for cross-border e-commerce, find out which one you like, clip a web page and talk about why.
2. Select one product and compare it across the platforms and comment on your findings.

附录1：国际贸易相关机构

国际贸易的主角为进出口商，二者在行使其权利与完成义务的过程中，各有不同的相关机构或行业管理监督或介入协助，有助于整个交易过程顺利完成。主要包括贸易主管机关、相关政府机构、相关地方机构和相关民间机构。

一、贸易主管机关

中华人民共和国商务部（Ministry of Commerce of the People's Republic of China）：是目前主管我国国内外贸易和国际经济合作的国务院组成部门，**对外贸易司（Department of Foreign Trade）**则为商务部下设办公机构，直接管理进出口贸易，其主要职能包括拟订进出口商品管理办法和进出口商品目录，拟订进出口配额、关税配额管理制度以及贸易推广、制定发展战略等事项。

二、相关政府机构

与贸易有关的政府机构繁多，仅选择较具代表性者，概述如下。

1. 中华人民共和国海关总署（General Administration of Customs, People's Republic of China，GACC）：负责进出境监管及法定检验检疫、征收关税和其他税、查缉走私以及编制海关统计等事项。关于商品法定检验检疫职能，原本由质检总局领导下的国家出入境检验检疫局（China Entry-Exit Inspection and Quarantine，CIQ）负责，主要实施进出口商品、动植物产品的法定检验，办理进出口商品鉴定业务，对进出口商品的质量和检验工作实施监督管理。2018年4月20日起，中国出入境检验检疫局正式并入中国海关，分设以下部门：

（1）商品检验司（Department of Commodity Inspection）：拟订进出口商品法定检验和监督管理工作制度的实施细则，承担进口商品安全风险评估、风险预警和快速反应工作。承担国家实行许可制度的进口商品验证工作，监督管理法定检验商品的数量、重量鉴定。依据多双边协议承担出口商品检验相关工作。

（2）进出口食品安全局（Bureau of Import and Export Food Safety）：拟订进出口食品、化妆品安全和检验检疫工作制度的实施细则，依法承担进口食品、化妆品的检验检疫、监督管理工作，按分工组织实施风险分析和紧急预防措施工作。依据多边协议承担出口食品相关工作。

（3）卫生检疫司（Department of Health Quarantine）：拟订出入境卫生检疫监管工作制度的实施细则及口岸突发公共卫生事件处置预案措施，承担出入境卫生检疫、传染病及境外疫情监测、卫生监督、卫生处理以及口岸突发公共卫生事件应对工作。

（4）动植物检疫司（Department of Animal and Plant Quarantine）：拟订出入境动植物及其产品检验检疫工作制度的实施细则，承担出入境动植物及其产品的检验检疫、监督管理工作，按分工组织实施风险分析和紧急预防措施，承担出入境转基因生物及其产品、生物物种资源的检验检疫工作。

2. 国家税务总局（State Taxation Administration，STA）：统筹规划管理全国的税务工作，办理进出口商品的税收及出口退税业务。

3. 国家知识产权局（China National Intellectual Property Administration，CNIPA）：主管专利工作和统筹协调涉外知识产权事宜。

4. 国家外汇管理局（State Administration of Foreign Exchange，SAFE）：主管外汇流向，并统计贸易金额。

5. 中华人民共和国教育部（Ministry of Education of the People's Republic of China，MOE）：审理教育文化用品的进出口。

三、相关地方机构

主要包括各地分支机构，如各省(自治区、直辖市)海关。

四、相关民间机构

1. 中国国际贸易促进委员会（China Council for the Promotion of International Trade，CCPIT）：

由中国经济贸易界有代表性的人士、企业和团体组成的全国民间对外经贸组织。其宗旨为：遵循国家的法律政策，开展促进对外贸易、利用外资、引进外国先进技术及各种形式的中外经济技术合作等活动，促进中国同世界各国、各地区之间的贸易和经济关系的发展，增进中国同世界各国人民以及经贸界之间的了解与友谊。

2. 中国国际经济贸易仲裁委员会（China International Economic and Trade Arbitration Commission，CIETAC）：

是以仲裁的方式，独立、公正地解决合同性或非合同性的经济贸易等争议的常设商事仲裁机构，同时也受理当事人提交的国内仲裁案件。

3. 中国海事仲裁委员会（China Maritime Arbitration Commission，CMAC）：

设在中国国际贸易促进委员会内，以仲裁的方式，独立公正地解决产生于远洋、沿海和与海相通的水域的运输、生产和航行过程中的合同性或非合同性的海事争议，以保护当事人的合法权益。

4. 中国海商法协会（China Maritime Law Association，CMLA）：

是由全国从事海商、海事、经贸、保险及法律工作的个人和单位组成的专业性民间团体，其主要任务是：组织会员对海商法律、国际公约、海运惯例和习惯做法进行调查和研究；向政府及有关主管机关就海商法立法、司法和行政管理方面的问题提出建议或报告；组织会员收集、整理和编译出版国内外海商法规、案例和有关的文献资料；开展对外交流活动，加强同各国和国际海商法组织、人士的联系，研究国外海商法的发展动向，积极参加国际海事委员会和其他有关国际组织的活动。

5. 中国检验认证集团（China Certification & Inspection Group，CCIC）：

其主要职能是接受对外贸易关系人的委托，办理各项进出口商品检验鉴定及认证等业务，为之提供顺利交接结算、合理解决索赔争议等方面的服务。

6. 各行业进出口商会（Chamber of Import and Export Trade）：

其目的在于借组织力量帮助会员收集资料，促进贸易。例如中国医药保健品进出口商会（www.cccmhpie.org.cn）、中国纺织品进出口商会（www.ccct.org.cn）等。

7. 进出口银行（The Export-Import Bank of China, EXIMBC）：

办理各种进出口融资、担保等业务，为中国企业提供政策性金融服务。

8. 邮局（post office）：

负责进出口邮件的传递工作。

9. 电信局（telecommunications offices）：

提供电话、电报和传真等信息的传递。

10. 保险公司（insurance company）：

承办进出口货物运输保险业务。

11. 运输公司（transportation company）：

从事出口货物的运载工作。

12. 公证处（public surveyor）：

对进出口货品质、量、包装或价值进行公证报告。

13. 报关行（customs broker）：

受进出口商委托代办报关、报检、冲退税、代订舱位、仓库及提领货物等事宜。

（参考资料：POCIB 百科 http://www.pocib.com/baike/%E8%B4%B8%E6%98%93%E5%9F% BA% E7%A1%80%E7%9F%A5%E8%AF%86.html）

附录 2：国际贸易法律法规、惯例和公约

- **国内外法律法规 domestic and foreign laws or regulations：**

《中华人民共和国对外贸易法》*Foreign Trade Law of the People's Republic of China*

《中华人民共和国海关法》*Customs Law of the People's Republic of China*

《中华人民共和国海商法》*Maritime Code of the People's Republic of China*

《中华人民共和国进出口商品检验法》*Law of the People's Republic of China on Import and Export Commodity Inspection*

《中华人民共和国进出境动植物检疫法》*Law of the People's Republic of China on the Entry and Exit Animal and Plant Quarantine*

《中华人民共和国国境卫生检疫法》*Frontier Health and Quarantine Law of the People's Republic of China*

《中华人民共和国食品安全法》*Food Safety Law of the People's Republic of China*

《中华人民共和国票据法》*Law of the People's Republic of China on Negotiable Instruments*

《中华人民共和国企业所得税法》*Law of the People's Republic of China on Enterprise Income Tax*

《中华人民共和国外汇管理条例》*Regulations on Foreign Exchange System of the People's Republic of China*

《中华人民共和国民法典》*Civil Code of the People's Republic of China*

（英国）1882 年《票据法》*Bills of Exchange Act* 1882 (Great Britain)

（美国）《统一商法典》*Uniform Commercial Code* (United States of America)

- **国际贸易惯例 International trade customs：**

➢ 买卖双方权利义务方面：

《国际贸易术语解释通则》*International Rules for the Interpretation of Trade Terms*

《1932 年华沙牛津规则》*Warsaw-Oxford Rules 1932*

《美国对外贸易定义 1941 年修正本》*Revised American Foreign Trade Definitions 1941*

《国际统一私法协会国际商事合同通则》*UNIDROIT Principles of International Commercial Contracts (UPICC)*

➢ **国际货物运输及保险方面：**

《统一杂货租船合同》*Uniform General Charter*

《贸发会议/国际多式联运单证规则》*UNCTAD/ICC Rules for Multimodal Transport Documents*

《协会货物条款》*Institute Cargo Clauses (I.C.C.)*

（中国人民保险公司）《海洋运输货物保险条款》*Ocean Marine Insurance Clauses (P.I.C.C.)*

（中国人民保险公司）《航空运输货物保险条款》*Air Transportation Cargo Insurance Clauses (P.I.C.C.)*

（中国人民保险公司）《陆上运输货物保险条款（火车、汽车）》*Overland Transportation Insurance Clauses (P.I.C.C.)*

➢ **国际贸易结算方面：**

《托收统一规则》*The Uniform Rules for Collections (URC522)*

《跟单信用证统一惯例》*Uniform Customs and Practice for Documentary Credits (UCP 600)*

《关于审核跟单信用证项下单据的国际标准银行实务》*International Standard Banking Practice for the Examination of Documents under Documentary Credits Subject to UCP 600 (ISBP)*

《国际备用信用证惯例》*The International Standby Practices (ISP98)*

➢ **国际商事调解、仲裁方面：**

《国际商会调解规则》*Mediation Rules of the International Chamber of Commerce*

《国际商会仲裁规则》*Rules of Arbitration of the International Chamber of Commerce*

《中国国际经济贸易仲裁委员会仲裁规则》*Arbitration Rules of China International Economic and Trade Arbitration Commission*

《中国海事仲裁委员会仲裁规则》*Arbitration Rules of China Maritime Arbitration Commission*

《中国海事仲裁委员会网上仲裁规则》*Online Arbitration Rules of China Maritime Arbitration Commission*

- **国际公约 International Conventions：**

➢ **国际货物买卖合同方面：**

《国际货物买卖统一法公约》（1964 年）*Convention on Uniform Law for the International Sale of Goods*

《国际货物买卖合同成立统一法公约》（1964 年）*Convention on Uniform Law for the Formation of Contracts for the International Sale of Goods*

《联合国国际货物买卖合同公约》（1980 年）*United Nations Convention on Contracts for the International Sale of Goods*

《联合国国际货物买卖时效期限公约》（1974 年）*United Nations Convention on the Limitation Period in the International Sale of Goods*

➢ **国际货物运输方面：**

《统一提单的若干法律规则的国际公约》（1924 年）*International Convention for the Unification of Certain Rules of Law Relating to Bills of Lading*

《修改统一提单若干法律规则的国际公约的议定书》（1968 年）*Protocol to Amend the International Convention for the Unification of Certain Rules of Law Relating to Bills of Lading*

《联合国海上货物运输公约》（1978 年）*United Nations Convention on the Carriage Goods by Sea*

《统一国际航空运输某些规则的公约》（华沙 1929 年公约）*Convention for the Unification of Certain Rules for International Carriage by Air (Warsaw Convention 1929)*

《修改华沙公约的议定书》（海牙议定书，1955 年）*Protocol to Amend the Convention on the Unification of Certain Rules Relating to International Carriage by Air Signed in Warsaw on 12 October 1929 (Hague Protocol, 1955)*

《统一非缔约承运人所办国际航空运输某些规则以补充华沙公约的公约》（1961 年）*Convention Supplementary to the Warsaw Convention for the Unification of Certain Rules Relating to International Carriage by Air Performed by a Person Other Than the Contracting Carrier*

《国际铁路货物联运协定》（国际货协）*Agreement on International Railway Freight Transport (SMGS)*

《关于铁路货物运输的国际公约》（国际货约）*Uniform Rules Concerning the Contract of International Carriage of Goods by Rail (CIM)*

《联合国国际货物多式联运公约》（1980 年）*United Nations Convention on International Multimodal Transport of Goods*

➢ **国际支付方面：**

《统一汇票本票法公约》（1930 年）*Convention on the Unification of the Law Relating to Bills of Exchange and Promissory Notes*

《统一支票法公约》（1931 年）*Convention Providing a Uniform Law of Cheques*

《联合国国际汇票和国际本票公约》（1988 年，未生效）*Convention on International Bill of Exchange and International Promissory Note of the United Nations*

➢ **国际商事仲裁方面：**

《承认及执行外国仲裁裁决公约》（1958 年）*Convention on the Recognition and Enforcement of Foreign Arbitral Awards*

➢ **税收方面：**

《关税与贸易总协定》*General Agreement on Tariffs and Trade (GATT)*

参考文献

[1] August, Ray. International Business Law—Text, Cases, and Readings (6th Edition)[M]. 北京：机械工业出版社，2018.

[2] Pierre A. David. 国际物流——国际贸易中的运作管理（第 4 版）[M]. 北京：清华大学出版社，2014.

[3] 傅龙海，丛晓明，邵李津. 国际贸易实务双语教程（第二版）[M]. 北京：对外经济贸易大学出版社，2015.

[4] Hinkelman, Edward G. 国际支付简明教程 [M]. 上海：上海外语教育出版社，2017.

[5] 黄海涛. 外贸七日通 [M]. 北京：中国海关出版社，2008.

[6] 姜宏. 出口业务操作——习题与实训 [M]. 北京：清华大学出版社，2015.

[7] 姜宏. 进口业务操作——习题与实训 [M]. 北京：清华大学出版社，2015.

[8] Carl A. Nelson. 进出口业务——带领企业走出国门（第 4 版 • 双语教学版）[M]. 北京：人民邮电出版社，2011.

[9] 李博婵. 新编国际贸易实务双语教程 [M]. 北京：中国人民大学出版社，2015.

[10] 刘德标，吴珊红，董芳，韩猛. 外贸实务案例精华 80 篇 [M]. 北京：中国海关出版社，2009.

[11] 苏宗祥，徐捷. 国际结算（第五版）[M]. 北京：中国金融出版社，2010.

[12] 王斌义，顾永才. 进口贸易操作 15 步 [M]. 北京：首都经济贸易大学出版社，2006.

[13] 王陶（波锅涅）. 实用外贸技巧助你轻松拿订单（第二版）[M]. 北京：中国海关出版社，2015.

[14] 杨雪雁. 跨境电子商务实践 [M]. 北京：电子工业出版社，2018.

[15] 易露霞，陈新华，尤彧聪. 国际贸易实务案例教程（双语）（第 2 版）[M]. 北京：清华大学出版社，2016.

[16] 易露霞，陈新华，尤彧聪. 国际贸易实务双语教程（第 4 版）[M]. 北京：清华大学出版社，2016.

[17] 毅冰. 十天搞定外贸函电 [M]. 北京：中国海关出版社，2012.

[18] 毅冰. 外贸高手客户成交技巧 [M]. 北京：中国海关出版社，2012.

[19] 张近松. 金牌外贸业务员找客户（第三版）[M]. 北京：中国海关出版社，2016.

[20] 中国进口网. 进口实务操作指南 [M]. 北京：中国海关出版社，2008.

[21] http://www.difference.wiki/

[22] http://www.letterofcredit.biz/
[23] https://www.usa.gov/import-export
[24] https://www.cbp.gov/
[25] https://www.trade.gov/
[26] http://www.pocib.com/baike/%E9%A6%96%E9%A1%B5.html
[27] https://www.investopedia.com/financial-term-dictionary-4769738